Photographing the American West Aboard the Photon Bus

A Travel Journal and Essays

Black and White Photography Edition

William J Wood Jr

Photographing the American West

COPYRIGHT © 2018

No part of this book may be reproduced in any form, or by any electronic, mechanical, or other means, without the permission in writing from the author or publisher

All photography by William J Wood Jr

Dedicated To

Friends and Hosts

Tom and Jean
Bob
Lori
Rick
Anne Wood
John and Peggy Wood
Jim and Laurie Wood

To Ritchie,
May you rest though you never wanted to.

Photographing the American West

Table of Contents

Introduction	**1**
Chapter 1	**7**
Snaking Through Idaho	
Chapter 2	**20**
Missionaries and Avenging Angels	
Chapter 3	**30**
Into Abbey's Country	
Chapter 4	**43**
Canyonlands and Purple Tatiana	
Chapter 5	**56**
Please Don't Touch the Hoodoos	
Chapter 6	**64**
Zion, a place of refuge?	
Chapter 7	**76**
Where Angels Land	
Chapter 8	**82**
Smokey's Revenge	

Chapter 9	89
Gold Light, Gold Water	
Chapter 10	103
Be	
Chapter 11	113
When You Gotta Go	
Chapter 12	123
Those Who Serve	
Chapter 13	129
Wickenburg	
Chapter 14	137
Phoenix Stories	
Chapter 15	147
Tucson Stories	
Chapter 16	161
No Country for Old or Young Men	
Chapter 17	173
When I Was a Kid, They Called Me Billy	

Chapter 18	**184**
Folk Art and Terrorists	
Chapter 19	**194**
The Curse of the Petrified Forest	
Chapter 20	**205**
The Nicholas Effect	
About the Author	**215**

OTHER BOOKS BY WILLIAM J WOOD JR
216

Introduction

I don't know what this book is about. It could be a travel memoir. The writing and photos describe the route and locations of our meandering RV trip through the Southwest in the winter of 2017-18. Since retirement, my preference is to flee the winter in Oregon where the sun hides behind months of shrouded cloud. Like zombies, we ramble our way south to the desert. *Harvesting Photons* chronicles our first trip south in a comfortable Class A motorhome, my retirement present. In this second narrative I devote less text to pure travel description and expand on ideas that came into my head, springing from photographic-inspired memories of our trip.

Is it about photography? There are photos. The term "harvesting photons" is a lyrical and more accurate term for photography. I christened our 31-foot home-on-the-road, the Photon Bus and considered titling this book "Harvesting More Photons," but then I wondered if people might perceive that the book was about physics. This may explain, in part, the poor sales of *Harvesting Photons*. Or it may not. The Photon Bus, as a title, may be equally confusing. I must hang my hope on an explanatory subtitle.

The American West is a land of inspiring beauty harboring extremes of geologic forms. Photographers, writers and artists strive to project its poetic power and sublime visions. A lifetime of exploration could not harvest all of its treasures. I captured 2,996 images on the first trip. On this trip I took 5,192.

I developed every image in Lightroom, a photography software. I never use an image straight from my camera, a Nikon D-600, full frame. For the interested, I will describe my workflow. I organize each shoot as a collection in Lightroom with a descriptive title. Then I apply one of several development presets I have created and sync the entire collection. The user preset I use most is "sharp, lens, less clar" which refers to sliders in the develop module. This preset increases the contrast by +16, increases shadow exposure by +57, increases clarity by +31, increases vibrance by +28, sets sharpening at 54, noise reduction at 22 and applies profile lens correction. These are changes I was using in almost every image, so I made them a named preset. I fine tune every image beyond the preset changes, often using the brush and gradient tools and Nik plug-ins such as ColorEfex and SilverEfex Pro. Each collection requires many hours of processing. This trip generated 21 collections. The largest was Canyonlands with 612 images taken on one day during our 4-WD exploration of the Island In The Sky.

I find no inspiration to publish a coffee table book of photographs. My sense is people don't look at coffee table books much. There are many coffee table books in the oversize shelves of our library. We rarely look at them. My theory is that the purpose of photography is to re-create the physical and mental experience of the photographer at that instant. The viewer should feel the wonder of being at that location. This requires an effort of imagination from the viewer. A video, with sound and motion, provides more information than a still photo, but I think a photo generates a more intense emotional response. The viewing eyes can roam at will over the details of the image, a captured record of the photon flow at that point in time bounded by the shutter speed.

A year ago, my first impulse was to publish a book of photography. Then I decided a descriptive narrative of our travel and locations would empower the images, similar to music evoking a stronger emotional response when heard in the context of a movie. I used the photographs to jog my memory and inspire my writing. The memories stimulated by the photographs became touchstones for further research. I have traveled this trip twice: the first in real time snatching photos, the second in front of my monitor allowing curiosity to flog Google into disgorging answers to a domino line of questions. The more I learn, the more I like the photographs. Knowledge enhances enjoyment.

Barb and I enjoy the freewheeling style of RV travel. We think our cat, Waffles, enjoys it too. On travel days, Waffles perches in Barb's lap watching the scenery for an hour and then she naps on a foam pad over the engine compartment. We think she enjoys it.

Barb and I have traveled in various styles over our 33-year marriage. Professional guides with safari lines of porters took us on the Inca Trail trek and up Mount Kilimanjaro. On the Noatak River in the Brooks Range of Alaska, our guide, Ramona Finn, showed us grizzlies and howled up a wolf pack. The guides, all excellent, shared their wisdom and knowledge. But I prefer the freedom of an unstructured ramble, never knowing the next destination. We drove around Alaska in a rented station wagon. In Europe we designed our itinerary on the fly, driving the autobahn in a seriously underpowered Ford Fiesta.

Our post-retirement RV trips have been free form. When the map inspires our next destination, I Google the local RV camps, read the reviews, and then call for a reservation. There seems to be no lack of RV camps. There was only one spot on our recent summer trip to South Dakota where I couldn't get a reservation. The camps near the Little Bighorn National Monument were all filled due to the Crowfest, the Crow Nation's annual powwow. The Crows had their reservation, but I couldn't get one.

We targeted a handful of photography shrines: Arches National Monument, Mesa Arch, Zion National Park, Horseshoe Bend and Antelope Canyon. Everyone has seen brilliant professional photographs of these locations. Photographer Peter Lik shot the most expensive photograph in the world at Antelope Canyon. I like the images from these beautiful shrines, but I feel a more intimate joy reviewing scenes from the undiscovered, lightly trod locales. These are quiet and lonely places that radiate their photons with a humble reverence.

Dripping Springs in Las Cruces, new to us, had fields of deep amber, rippling wheatgrass that made a great foreground. The glittering arched shoreline of Bodega Bay evoked time travel to the virginal continent seen by Sir Francis Drake, one of my ancestors. Lake Watson in Prescott painted the exotic charm of a distant planet. The Acker Night Musical Showcase in Prescott was a mirthful fest of music and light. There is a special sweetness in discovering unknown beauty.

I have traveled by backpack and toured on bicycle and motorcycle and auto. They were all great trips. RV travel offers a more immediate access to a comfortable bed, a productive kitchen and a bathroom. Males should not use the bathroom when underway. At age 65, I appreciate comfort on trips of months duration.

The metal beast has limited access to areas like trailheads. For various reasons I decided not to tow a vehicle. Instead, I bought a scooter, a Yamaha Smax, and carried it on a hitch rack. The hitch receiver got an upgrade to a Class IV, which has a 1000 lb. tongue carry capacity and can support the 320-lb. scooter. I have since acquired a Kawasaki Ninja 400, which weighs 366 lb. The hitch rack stayed intact on last summer's trip. The motorcycles allow us to tour towns and ride to trailheads.

Beyond geography, we discovered many friendly and interesting people. Most RV campers are pleasantly sociable and quick to share information and advice. The chatty blond-headed kids I gave scooter rides to at Arches melted my heart. The old Alaskan, who was finally free to travel after caring for his ill wife for thirteen years, was a novel in the making. Unfriendly scrooges, rare in RV parks, seem to hole up in their vehicles.

Since I don't have a literary agent or publisher and I'm too cheap to pay for a copy editor, I sent the first draft of each chapter to an email group of 150 friends. Many comments were about the photos. My close friend, Dr. Pat Fitzgerald, sent back edits on every chapter partly, I think, for the pleasure of making red marks with the stylus of his new iPad. Several medical school friends, who I haven't seen in forty years, returned encouraging comments. Thanks to Jim, Rhonda and Dan. Sean, my cousin, sent many grammar corrections, typical of attorneys. My long-time friend, Bob, an environmental scientist informed me about the Navajo Generating Station. A career Forest Service scientist friend enlightened me about the science of forest fire suppression. Another friend, a biologist with Fish and Game, provided insight on his specialty. A former patient who is an executive with a major power company steered me to information about dam breaching.

A major goal of our winter trips is to spend time with family and lifelong friends in Arizona, my home state. In Phoenix and Tucson our social schedule filled with dinners, parties, card games, theater, golf, hikes, etc. Christmas with family is a cacophony of joy-strained voices.

My brother John and his wife, Peggy, have hosted us many times at their home in Stockton. My close inner-circle friend, Rick, put us up again at his Santa Fe house next to Museum Hill. I think our cat, Waffles, is in love with Rick. Lori, a Tucson friend, invited us to house sit her artist-inspired adobe home that overlooks Sabino Canyon.

I seem to pursue beautiful geography and beautiful people. I like that.

Chapter 1

Snaking Through Idaho

Through fits and starts, we outfitted the Photon Bus, our thirty-one foot Class A Coachman Pursuit, with everything we would need for a two-month voyage through Idaho, Utah, Arizona, New Mexico and California. Preparing for backpacking trips, where forgotten items can have serious repercussions, I learned to make a written list of everything I could think of: laptop computers, golf clubs, cat treats, simvastatin, down parkas, camera gear with extra batteries, tripods, guitar, harmonicas, Oontz speakers, etc. Last summer we forgot Barb's motorcycle helmet on our Canada trip. Or rather I forgot it. Not this time.

Every item got a check mark as it went into the RV. I didn't check "cat." Waffles, our social tabby, was the last item on board since she has a tendency to crouch by the door and make a light-speed dash at first opportunity. I checked off "charger," which made me irritable later in the trip when I discovered I had not brought the charger for my Nikon batteries. My self irritation rose when I discovered I had not brought the quick release plate for my Benro tripod. Thanks to our friend, Bob, we found that item, mid trip, at the best camera store in Phoenix.

Last year's trip was the maiden voyage in the Photon Bus. You may have already purchased the photographic narrative, *Harvesting Photons*, available on Amazon. Glancing over sales reports, I learn the odds of anyone purchasing the book are abysmally low.

The plan last year was to go through Utah en route to southern Arizona and be in my old hometown, Tucson, by Christmas. It had been forty years since I had visited the major Utah parks: Arches, Bryce Canyon and Zion. Last year, the week before our planned departure in mid-December, a massive arctic front iced up I-84 through Idaho, effectively closing any route into Utah. We had no option but to drive through California on I-5 to get south. I've never been a fan of I-5, in case anyone is making a favorites list of interstate highways. Last year, we tried to enter Utah from the south in January, but hit snow on Route 89 ten miles north of Flagstaff.

This year, we were leaving before Thanksgiving. The weather was acceptable, wet in Oregon but not freezing. I thought we had a chance. The risk was if Utah got an early snow we could end up trapped with no escape route. I harbor an untested fear of driving a big RV on snow or ice. In Wickenburg, a month later, I would meet an Alaskan man who had driven his Class C a thousand miles through snow.

At first light, we hugged goodbyes with our surprisingly awake son, Joshua, and headed toward I-84 on the back roads through Troutdale to avoid rush hour on I-205, the freeway I had commuted on for thirty years. Since retirement, I genuflect when I hear a traffic report.

Last summer Troutdale was the command center for firefighters fighting the Eagle Creek fire that burned 50,000 acres in the Columbia River Gorge and threatened historic Multnomah Falls Lodge. A 15-year-old boy threw a smoke bomb into the forest. A witness identified the boy and his friends, whom she heard laughing. The fire cost $20 million to fight, ruined the tourist season in the Gorge, and left a charred landscape at risk of massive landslides that could avalanche down the steep slopes. The teen is being charged with reckless burning. His mother commented, "He is mortified," but she said it in Russian and the reporter might not have had the correct translation. The phrase sounds similar to "Get the hell offa my lawn."

Heavy rain stayed with us down the Columbia River Gorge. Orographic lift of moist marine air brings rain to the Willamette Valley in wet western Oregon. East of the mountains the state is dry. But this was a large front that persisted all the way past Boise east to Mountain Home. The rain had stopped when we hooked up at the Mountain Home RV Park. I was tired. Listening to windshield wipers slap for five hundred miles had put me in a fugue state. The park was clean, landscaped with blue lights at each site. My heart brightened when stars blinked into the sky above our camp.

The next morning I noticed a lot of boats in the park. A man walked out of his boat on a ladder. I told him he had an interesting RV. He said, "Why not, it's got all the same things." That is true.

Looking south toward the Kingdom of Deseret, the sky was blue, a great color for a sky. Again we were escaping an Oregon winter. Lewis and Clark complained about their dreary winter at Fort Clatsop near Astoria. Not only did they choose not to leave a tip for their native hosts, they stole canoes for the return trip upriver.

We drove toward Salt Lake, a less tiring three hundred miles. At the town of Bliss, origin of name unknown, there was a sign for the Thousand Springs Scenic Byway. We took it. Soon we peered from an overlook at the Hagerman Fossil Beds, famous for fossils of Pliocene horses, camels, mastodons, sabertooth tigers and bone-crushing canids known as Borophaginae. I saw no obvious fossils but the view over the Snake River was inspiring. We stopped in the town of Hagerman to discover a closed visitor's center. The sign for the city hall had a picture of a trout. Trout farms around Hagerman, fed by cold water gushing out of the Snake River aquifer, produce half of all the farm-raised trout in America.

The 1000 Springs Water Sports Club sat on the banks of the Snake. Across the river, springs erupted out of the basalt cliffs of Ritter Island. There were less than a thousand visible springs. Ritter Island had been a breeding farm for fine Guernsey milk cows. The Nature Conservancy purchased the island and gifted it to the Idaho Department of Parks and Recreation in 2006.

The "Lost Rivers" of Idaho sink into the Snake River Aquifer two hundred miles away and flow under the Craters of the Moon lava fields. These statewide lava fields erupted from the same magma hot spot that forged the Columbia River flood basalts. This magma plume now lies under our first national park, Yellowstone, entertaining millions with its geothermal magic show.

During my residency in Phoenix, I ruptured my medial collateral ligament at a soccer practice. In those pre-arthroscopy days it was repaired with open surgery followed by six weeks in a straight leg cast. My residency gave me four days off for surgery and recovery. I was on rotation for trauma call at Barrow's Neurologic. My leg would swell in the cast during the day, so at night I grabbed a wheel chair and put my cast on the chair's leg rest. I wheeled into the ER to see a head trauma admission. The patient bolted upright, eyes wide, and said, "Gosh Doc, you look worse than me!"

When the cast came off I saw, with horror, a white, withered leg that didn't look like mine. I had a vacation scheduled and figured it was a great time for a motorcycle trip since I could barely walk. It was May and already hot in Phoenix. I rode my BMW R/90 to Yellowstone through a blizzard at Jackson Hole. There were twenty-foot snow piles on the roadside in Yellowstone. I had the Madison Campground all to myself. In the cold morning air steam billowed from hundreds of thermals. I fly fished on the Madison and soaked in a hot spring right off the river. Thank you, Hot Spot.

Between 30,000 and 15,000 years ago, dozens of massive floods from Glacial Lake Missoula and one extra-massive flood from Ancient Lake Bonneville sculpted the paths of the

Snake and Columbia Rivers. Lake Bonneville, where current-day speed records are set on the evaporated salt flats, burst its earthen barrier and sent a 410-foot-high flood crest into Idaho. The peak flow was 33 million cubic feet per second at seventy miles per hour. Imagine a thousand Colorado Rivers sanding the landscape with boulders and gravel. Maybe we could have outrun it in the Photon Bus. All that injected alluvium created permeable paths through the basalt giving the Snake River Plain Aquifer a high hydraulic conductivity.

The Snake River is the largest tributary of the Columbia River. The watershed of the combined rivers covers all of Idaho, most of Washington and Oregon, and big chunks of Montana, Wyoming and British Columbia. The Snake's name comes from the Shoshone hand sign for salmon, which looked like a wiggling snake to early explorers. Sixty dams grace the Snake and Columbia watersheds.

The big dam era peaked in the 1960s. Most Americans saw dams as overwhelmingly beneficial providing hydropower, irrigation, navigation and flood control. A major cause of the slowdown in competitive dam construction by the Bureau of Reclamation and the Army Corps of Engineers was that the prime dam sites were already built. Also, the environmental movement rose like a grizzly coming out of hibernation. Even in the early build up of the dam era in the 1900s, voices spoke out about the harm of dams: silting, displacement of communities (remember *Deliverance*), destruction of fisheries and habitat, ruination of scenic wilderness and loss of important archeological sites.

John Muir's organized protest against damming the Tuolumne River in the Hetch Hetchy Valley, which Muir contended was part of Yosemite, sparked a groundswell of preservation sentiment. Muir and the Sierra Club lost that fight, but gained a wider membership interested in protecting natural areas from the wounds of development and resource extraction. This was a new philosophy compared to the milder "resource management" philosophy of Gifford Pinchot and the Conservation Movement.

Dams have devastated the wild salmon and steelhead fisheries in the Pacific Northwest. Even with fish ladders, dams damage fish in many ways. Reservoirs pond warm water layers with low oxygen, high salinity and concentrated pollutants. Smolt running the Kaplan turbines of Bonneville Dam on the Columbia run into 12-foot diameter, 10-ton blades spinning at seventy-five revolutions per minute. The cavitation force can scour metal off the blades. In 1946, Frank Bell, vice president of the Columbia River Development League, reassured the public that turbine passage only made the juvenile fish "groggy."

In reality, turbine passage kills 10-15% of migrating smolt. Let's do the math, because as I told my son when he groaned about his homework, "Math is life." If juveniles are running to the Pacific from, say, Redfish Lake, Idaho, a nine hundred mile passage, they must pass through eight large dams. If ten percent of the population die at each dam, then only 48% will make it to the ocean. A group migrating through fifteen dams would end up with only 23% surviving. Perhaps Mr. Bell was actually the groggy one.

Floyd Dominy, the powerhouse commissioner of the Bureau of Reclamations during the big dam era, didn't even try to sugar coat the fish issue:

> *Now, I'm sure people can survive without salmon, but I don't think they can survive without beans and potatoes and lettuce...I think the dams were worth it. I think there's substitutions for salmon. You can eat cake.*

No doubt Dominy and Marie Antoinette are paired in the Dancing With the Afterlifers Show. Read more about the big dam era in Marc Reisner's *Cadillac Desert*.

Dam removal, as a concept, has been gathering steam for several decades. It's not a new idea. Over the past hundred years, 1,150 dams, old and no longer useful, have been removed in the U.S. The push for big dam removal in the Northwest spawned from the desire to restore free-flowing rivers and resurrect lost habitat for salmon, steelhead and other native species.

It's already happened on the Elwha River in the Olympic Peninsula of Washington State. Removal of the Elwha Dam and the upriver Glines Canyon Dam, the largest dam removal project in history, took three years ending in 2014. Workers released 34 million cubic yards of sediment from behind the dams in stages to avoid intense turbidity and catastrophic downstream destruction. Biologists celebrate the restoration as a roaring success. Two years after removal, Chinook redds, the gravel nests made by females, appeared 28 miles above the Glines Dam, which had been an impassable barrier. Three thousand Chinook and a thousand steelhead ran up the river in 2016, still below historic runs of four hundred thousand. A new estuary from the transported sediment is growing at the river delta.

Dam removal and restoration of the Elwha cost $351 million. From what I can tell, the federal government, meaning we taxpayers, picked up the entire tab. The previous owner, James River Corporation, sold the dams to we taxpayers in 2000 and flew to the Bahamas to celebrate with boat drinks. My family hiked to the Elwha Dam in 2010 while waiting for our ferry into Canada. It seemed old and tired, saying, "I've been holding this river back for a hundred years. Somebody, please, breach me!"

The four dams on the lower Snake River produce eight percent of Washington State's energy. They also move barges to international ports and provide irrigation for dry-land farming. The proposal to remove these dams is generating vigorous debate. Grain farmers are against it. Energy providers argue it will raise rates due to more expensive replacement energy sources and undermine the ability to support wind energy, which is as erratic as the wind itself.

Proponents of removal say improved energy efficiency and more carbon-free wind farms can replace the lost energy with a little natural gas thrown in. The sizable funds spent on salmon recovery will diminish as the post-breach runs increase thanks to better access to the Idaho watershed, the most pristine salmon habitat in the lower 48. The Washington State Governor's Salmon Recovery Office calculates the cost of regional salmon habitat recovery at $5.5 billion over nine years from 2010 to 2019.

The story of the proposed Klamath River dam removals is different. If you had approached the Lower Klamath River in September 2002, you would have noticed the stench before you reached the river. Over the bank you would have seen the rotting carcasses of 32,000 dead Chinook. The fish kill may have been closer to 70,000. These fall-run spawners asphyxiated from necrosis of their gills caused by infection from ichthyopthirius, a protozoan, and columnaris, a bacterium. Investigation by the California Department of Fish and Game concluded the die-off was caused by multiple factors: stressful fish passage in low flow sites, shallow depth, a higher density than usual run and warm water temperatures. Crowded runs promoted rapid infectious spread of pathogens. The report states there was enough water behind the Iron Gate Dam to have improved flow in the lower river, had it been released.

Water wars between the salmon-culture Lower Klamath Native tribes and ranchers of the Upper Klamath Basin have raged since construction of the first Klamath dam, the Link River Dam, in 1919. The tribes have senior water rights dating from an 1864 treaty. The rancher's water rights derive from the Bureau of Reclamation's Klamath Project created in 1908. Over time, the effects of damming, water management, logging and settlement reduced the historic salmon population by 90%.

Things came to a head during the drought of 2001. The Bureau of Reclamation controlled water apportionments to irrigators and coordinated dam releases with the owner, PacifiCorp. In 1988, the Lost River and shortnose suckers in the Klamath Basin were listed as endangered under the Endangered Species Act. Biologists listed Basin Coho as threatened in 1997. In 2001 the Bureau of Reclamation generated their required mitigation plan, including recommended minimums for Klamath Lake levels and targets for the mainstream river flows. The U.S. Fish and Wildlife Service and the National Marine Fisheries Service each did their own scientific assessment and recommended a higher lake level and higher minimum flows than those calculated by the Bureau of Reclamation. The 2001 drought hit. The Department of Interior closed the irrigator's gates to maintain the required minimums recommended by the two scientific agencies. Farmers claimed a loss of $250 million for the season, though two academic studies put the loss at $11 million.

After the disastrous 2001 growing season, irrigators called out to a superhero to save their water. Dick Cheney answered the call using his amazing back room powers to stimulate the Department of Interior to order a new study by the Natural Resources Council (NRC). Interior Secretary Gale Norton famously suggested that the irrigators sell their water to the Klamath Tribes, thus allowing the "free market" to solve the issue. Of course, the tribes already owned the water due to senior water rights. The new NRC study disagreed with the higher lake level and river flow minimums recommended by the two federal Services. Irrigators got an increased water allotment during the 2002 drought year and a generation of Chinook salmon died in the Lower Klamath.

Litigation erupted from all sides. State courts upheld the Lower Klamath tribes' historic senior water rights. Government agencies organized stakeholder meetings that included irrigators, Klamath-area Native tribes, commercial fishermen and environmental organizations, everyone but the fish themselves. A delicate agreement, the 2010 Klamath Basin Restoration Agreement, the KBRA, called for breaching four hydroelectric, non-reservoir dams on the Klamath and allowed diversion of a portion of the water to the Upper Basin in drought years. The agreement was scheduled to expire at the end of 2015 if the U.S. Congress had not yet approved it.

Ranchers in the basin formed their own Tea Party chapter and opposed the agreement, as it would threaten not only their water, but also the cheap power from the hydroelectric dams needed for pumping irrigation. Klamath County would lose $530,000 in property tax revenue and Siskiyou County in California would lose $1 million.

Rural Oregonians complain they are forever underrepresented in state government and are at the mercy of the liberal urban centers that know nothing about rural issues. Greg Walden is Oregon's lone Republican congressional representative. His 2nd district covers two-thirds of the state, everything east of the Cascade Range. Walden has been reelected nine times.

Both Oregon senators, Ron Wyden and Jeff Merkley, along with two California senators, placed the Klamath Basin Bill, containing the guts of the KBRA, into the December 2015 senate vote. Just before the deadline, Representative Walden submitted a new draft bill in the House that didn't contain dam removal and proposed to turn over 200,000 acres of federal lands in both Oregon and California that could be logged. In exchange for the land, the Klamath tribes would give up their senior water rights. Walden knew his bill would not pass, but he effectively sabotaged the Senate bill and drew hearty back slaps from every pro-dam rancher in Oregon.

The stakeholders of the KBRA all threatened to withdraw. Time for a Hail Mary. Sally Jewell, Secretary of the Interior during the Obama administration, asked Kimberly Bose, Secretary of the Federal Energy Regulatory Commission (FERC), to approve the dam removals. FERC authorizes dam decommissioning and does not need congressional approval. Bose approved. The Klamath River dam removals plan is back on track for 2020. Funding will come from PacifiCorp consumer rate increases and a California bond, already approved.

Ownership of the dams transferred to a non-profit entity, relieving PacifiCorp of liability. Stakeholders signed an amended agreement. There are still lingering issues such as the replacement of cheap electricity needed by irrigators and how water apportionment will function in drought conditions. Removing dams doesn't put more water in the river. Removing dams decreases the amount of water storage. Years ago, Barb and I had a great raft trip down the Lower Klamath with my brother and his wife. I hope the rapids survive.

We drove away from the enchanting Snake River toward Twin Falls, Idaho, on the way harvesting windshield chip number four. Pulling into the garage of the repair shop we scraped the rear bolt heads off the hitch tightener yoke. Later we found a replacement at Wal-Mart. Such is RV living.

Approaching Salt Lake at rush hour, Siri directed us to re-route on Highway 89 through Ogden. I get nervous when I am close to an IRS stronghold. We tucked into a quiet KOA off North Temple and prepared for our first Mormon Thanksgiving.

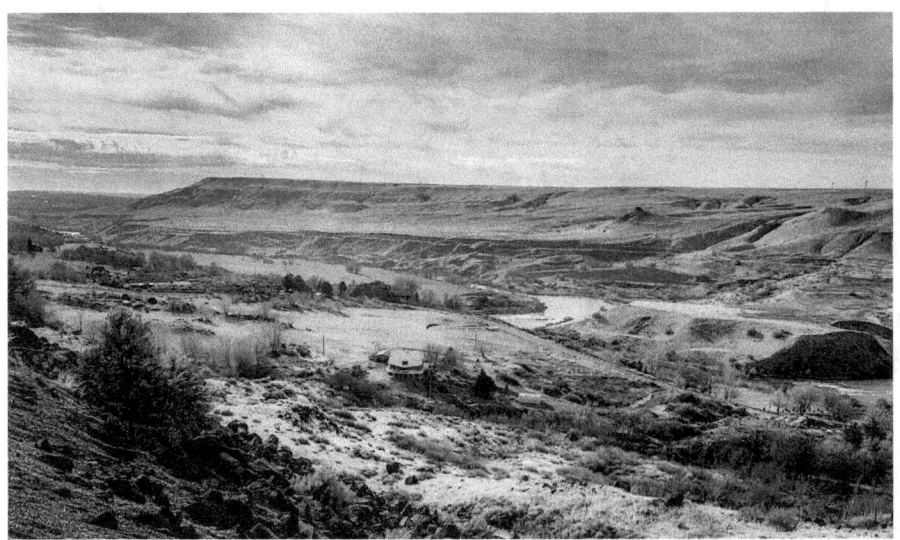

Snake River and Hagerman Fossil Beds

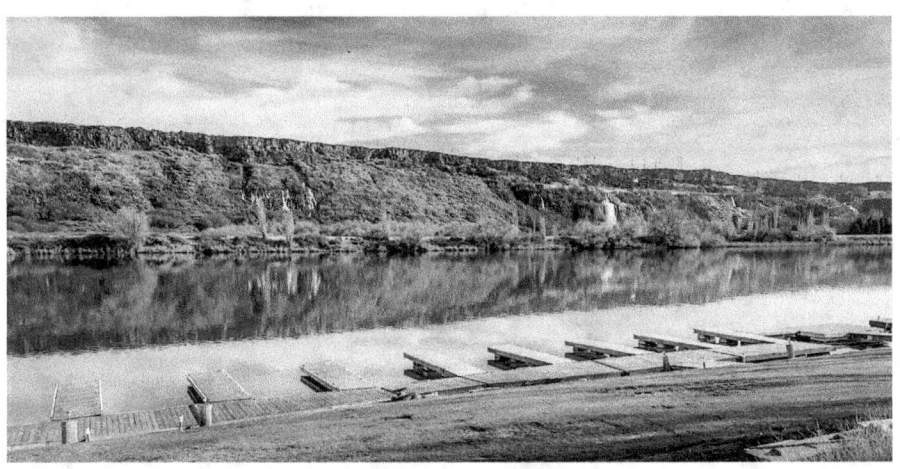

Many springs, if not a thousand

Photographing the American West

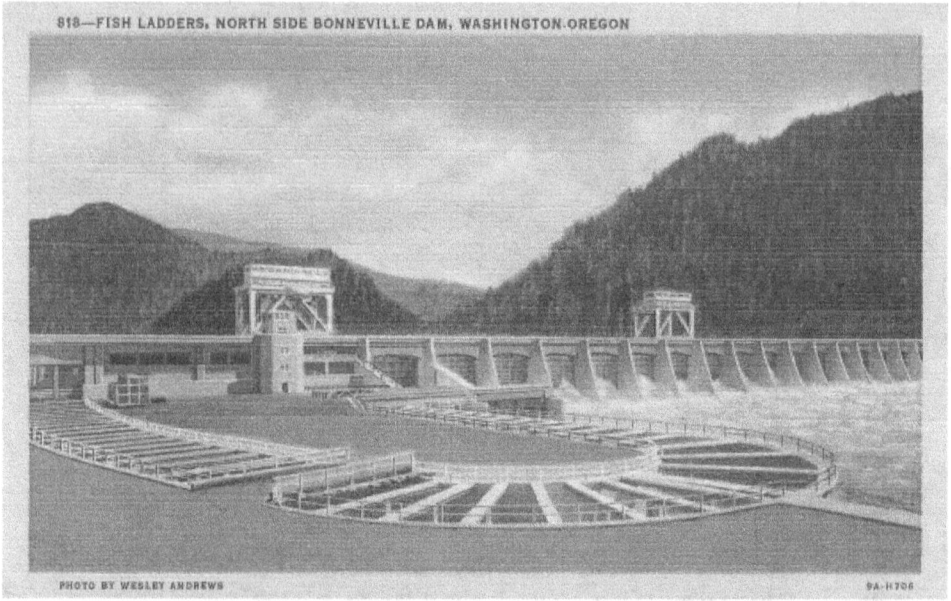

Penny postcard of Bonneville Dam fish ladders

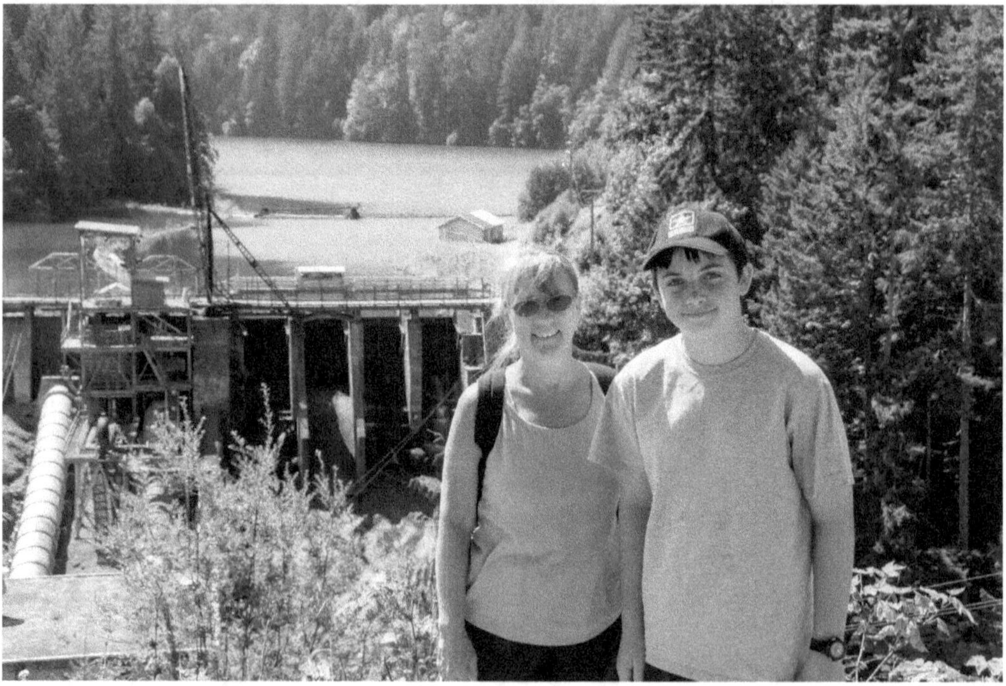

Barb and Joshua at the Elwha Dam before breach

Chapter 2

Missionaries and Avenging Angels

Morning blossomed crisp under a mauve sky at the Salt Lake KOA. Most of the RV slots were empty, quiet ghosts of summer visitors. Accustomed to Thanksgiving in the bosom of my family with the aroma of roasting turkey, it felt pleasantly strange. Before our holiday meal of sliced turkey, we hiked to Temple Square.

The neighborhoods along North Temple Boulevard were rustic. Rustic folk lined up at a building for either food or methadone. I had my Nikon slung over my shoulder. A woman with her back to us staring into a glass window said, "Nice camera, man." Entering downtown, a sign warned we were in a falcon bird watch area.

I had visited Temple Square years ago. Then, an attractive blond woman approached me in the visitor's center and chatted me up. When I told her I was in medical school, she said, "You look too young to be a doctor," which extinguished any thoughts I had of converting to Mormonism.

In 1820, in western New York State, fourteen-year-old Joseph Smith, seeking a path to the ideal religious denomination and inoculated by intense prayer, saw a vision of God and Jesus Christ in the fragrant woods. Their message to the trembling Smith was that all existing religious orders had wandered from the true meaning of Christianity. An angel led Smith to buried golden plates written in an ancient language. He translated the plates. It was a history of an ancient culture, a lost tribe of Israel, the Nephites, who had inhabited the American continent centuries ago. Christ had made a second visitation to the Nephites. The translation was the Book of Mormon.

Spreading across a strange new land, European colonizers of the New World were ripe for new religions during the period known as the Second Great Awakening. People were hungry for a more emotional, energetic church to replace the ponderous, authoritarian mainstream Protestant and Catholic clunkers. The charismatic Smith organized a new church. Since the saints and apostles of this new church appeared after the original apostles he named the church the Latter-day Saints.

The LDS had peculiar beliefs compared to Christian denominations. Mormons believed God had been a flesh-and-bone man and there was a female God, the Heavenly Mother. They called the Trinity, the Godhead. The Mormon afterlife had multiple destinations. At the highest level, exaltation, the deceased transformed into God himself. Revelations came to church leaders through visions and visitations. The most peculiar belief was plural marriage, though polygamy was not practiced until their move to Nauvoo, Illinois in 1840.

The early efforts to establish a new Zion, a place of security for the church, failed. A large Mormon community in Kirtland, Ohio disbanded after a non-licensed banking scheme, the Kirtland Safety Society, collapsed in the Panic of 1837 when almost half of the nation's banks failed. The faithful gathered in Missouri, but tensions rose when Governor Lilburn Boggs declared that Mormons "must be treated as enemies and exterminated or driven from the state."

The Mormons purchased a town in Illinois and renamed it Nauvoo, a Hebrew word meaning beautiful place. Tensions with non-Mormons escalated anew and in 1844 a mob killed Joseph Smith and his brother. Two years later Brigham Young led the first Mormon pioneer wagon train west, believing there was no safe place left in the United States. At that time, the Salt Lake Valley was an uncolonized backwater of Mexico.

With a strong communal organization, Mormons spread from Salt Lake into the Mormon Corridor from Idaho to Mexico. They sent missionaries abroad and recruited seventy thousand converts from England and Scandinavia. Many new converts, lacking funds for oxen and covered wagons, made the trip through the great desert using self-propelled wooden handcarts.

Polygamy is not denied in the Bible. Old Testament patriarchs, including Abraham and David, had multiple wives. King Solomon had a thousand wives, which didn't work out well for him. According to Christians, scriptures show God intended monogamy. The clearest passage is Genesis 2:24: "For this reason a man will leave his father and mother and be united to his wife, and they will become one flesh."

Plural marriage was legal in the United States until the Morrill Anti-Bigamy Act of 1862. In 1878 the Supreme Court ruled that religious duty was not a suitable defense for practicing polygamy. Many Mormons went into hiding until LDS president Wilford Woodruff issued a Manifesto suspending polygamy in 1890.

There are practical advantages to polygamy. Widowed women are taken into a new family and provided for. Population expansion, if that's what you want, is much faster with simultaneous fertilizations. My personal concern would be that all my wives might get mad at me at the same time. I don't think I could take that.

Bowers of autumnal yellow elm trees shaded Temple Square, sparsely peopled on an enchanting Thanksgiving morn. The trees came from the 1893 World's Fair. Two young women doing their missionary year approached us and struck up a conversation. The fair-haired girl from Idaho did all the talking. The black-haired Filipino girl was shy and quiet, but lit up when I said, "Magandang umaga po," which is "Good morning," in Tagalog.

I asked the girls if they knew who Porter Rockwell was. Yes, all Mormons know the story of Porter Rockwell who was a childhood friend of Joseph Smith and was the first baptized Mormon. Devout, quietly fierce, and a crack shot, Rockwell served as Brigham Young's bodyguard and Deputy Marshal of Salt Lake City. He was charged with trying to assassinate Lilburn Boggs, the Missouri governor who signed the Extermination Order. Rockwell beat the charge with the defense that Boggs was still alive. He claimed, "I never shot at anybody. If I shoot, they get shot!" Rockwell, known as the Avenging Angel, killed many. He stated, "I never killed anyone who didn't need killing."

Hoping to impress our young hosts, I let out that I had been in a movie about Porter Rockwell. It was true. In high school, my friend Kim Scott, now Archivist at Montana State University and author of "Yellowstone Denied: The Life of Gustavus Cheyney Doane," (in all the National Park Bookstores), made a movie about Rockwell. We friends were the cast. My bit part was to be one of the mob that killed Joseph Smith.

Ten years ago the Geezers, my group of old friends who liked to backpack, gathered in Bozeman before our Yellowstone pack trip. We located Kim, who dug up the old 8 mm film about Porter Rockwell. That night, drinking fresh applejack, we enjoyed the movie on Kim's porch. For my role I wore a flannel shirt and a droopy hat and carried a double gauge shotgun. Kim drew wild laughs when he commented, "Bill looks like Snuffy Smith." True and funny.

I asked the girls if they knew about the Meadows Massacre. The blond lost her smile and said, "That was horrible. I didn't know about it until I was fourteen." The Massacre is a dark stain in Mormon history, not something for Sunday school.

The Mountain Meadows Massacre occurred during the Utah War in 1857. Utah became part of the United States after the Treaty of Guadalupe Hidalgo. The federal government decided to replace Brigham Young as governor of Utah Territory. Salt Lake City was no longer an isolated island. Waves of fortune seekers, beginning with the Gold Rush 49ers, traveled across the territory. President James Buchanan sent 2,500 troops to back up the new replacement governor. Brigham Young interpreted this as an act of war. The Mormon's armed themselves, set up defensive positions in canyons and abandoned Salt Lake City.

Although the war ended peacefully, fiery speeches from church leadership had tensions high and there was an order to evict or kill all trespassers in the territory. A militia from southern Utah attacked the Baker-Fancher wagon train. This wagon train was from Arkansas, where a prominent Mormon leader, Parley P. Pratt, had been murdered by the estranged husband of his twelfth wife. Rumors circulated that the Baker-Fancher party had poisoned wells and killed cattle.

The Mormon assailants disguised themselves as Paiute Indians. After an initial siege, the militia decided they couldn't leave any witnesses. They massacred 120 men, women and all children above the age of seven. The Civil War delayed investigation. Of several indictments, only John D. Lee, the founder of Lee's Ferry at the entrance to the Grand Canyon, was convicted. He was executed by firing squad at the site of the massacre. The sweet-natured blond missionary paid me a sly compliment, "Are you sure you're not a Mormon?"

I know a few Mormons. Dr. William (Bill) Flake was my mentor during surgery residency at the Phoenix VA Medical Center. Bill told me his great-grandfather and another pioneer, named Snow, founded the town of Snowflake. This means he is related to Arizona Senator Jeff Flake, who grew up in Snowflake. From what I can find by internet, Dr. Bill Flake is still in practice in Arkansas.

We toured the Temple visitor's center with its grand halls full of dramatic paintings and climbed the spiral walk up to the statue of Jesus that simulated the celestial afterlife. The acoustics of the Mormon Tabernacle, famous for its choir, made for an amazing organ recital. Downtown Salt Lake was clean and deserted. We found a trail back to the KOA along the Jordan River. Time for some sliced turkey

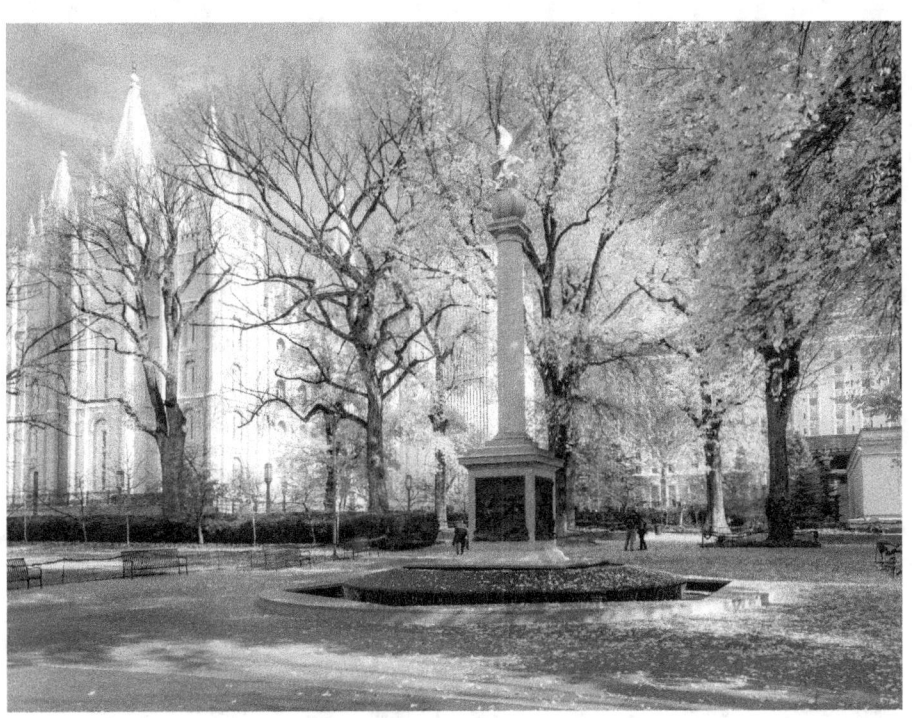

Temple Square

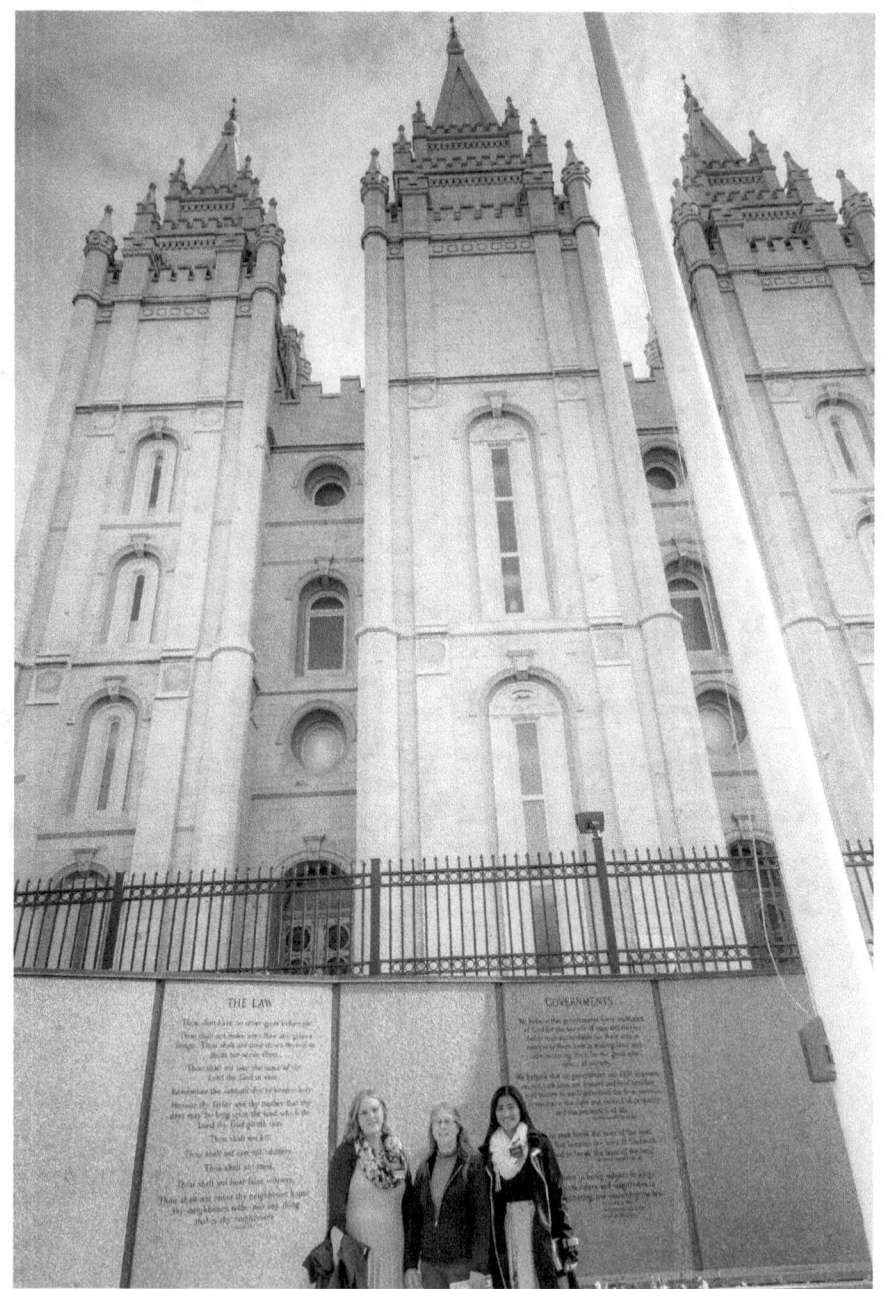

Barb with our missionary friends

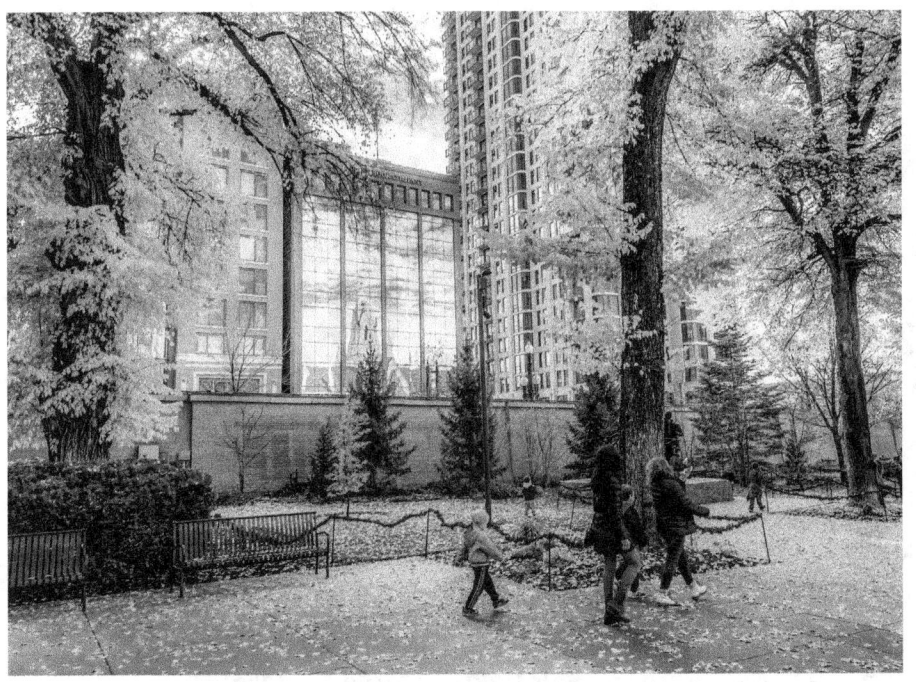

Downtown Salt Lake, reflection

Photographing the American West

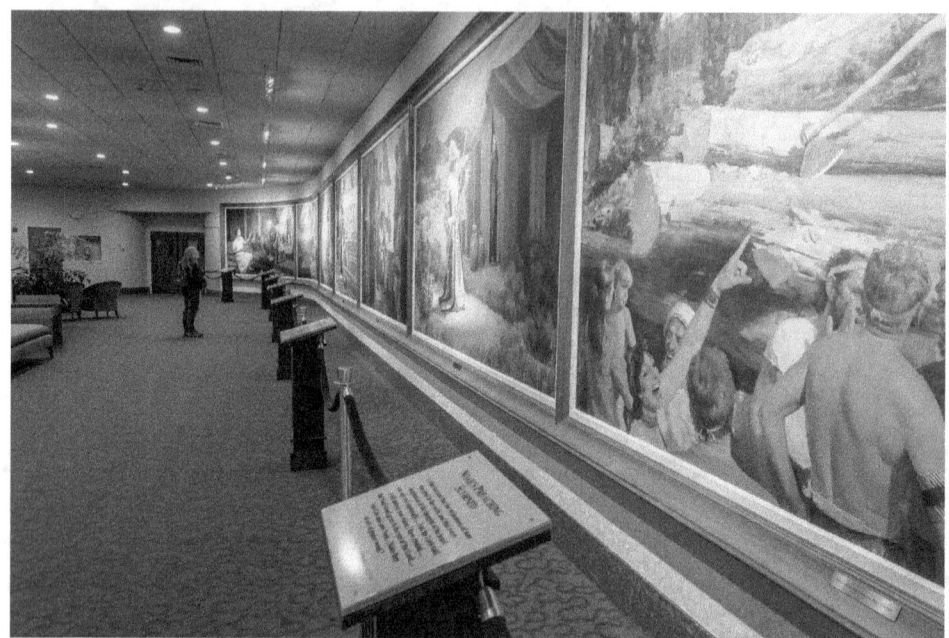

North Visitor's Center at Salt Lake Temple Square

Chapter 3

Into Abbey's Country

Despite its hardy Mormon culture and epiphany-inducing scenery, Utah has faults. The Wasatch Fault, west of the Wasatch Mountains, runs 240 miles through Salt Lake City from Idaho into central Utah and is part of a larger geologic division known as the Wasatch Line that runs from Canada to Mexico. Capable of a magnitude 7.0 earthquake, this fault delineates the Great Basin from the Colorado Plateau. The last big one struck 1,300 years ago, believed to be the average interval, so buckle up. Like Oregonians waiting for a Cascadia Zone earthquake, Salt Lakers have pursued seismic retrofitting. Portland, OR news channels regularly run Sword-of-Damocles stories encouraging citizens to stock flashlight batteries and canned goods. Food storage and self-sufficiency have been part of Mormon culture since before any knowledge of the Wasatch Fault.

Our hydraulic jacks were not working at the Salt Lake KOA. We swung by a Camping World on our way out of town. I tried the jacks in the parking lot and they worked. It's always fun to be level. We continued south on I-15 then turned on Utah 6 toward Moab. In a town named Price, we stopped at a Wal-Mart and stocked our larders. I also bought an HDMI cord so I could plug my laptop into the big screen. Wi-Fi in RV parks is spotty and the cable picture often looks like an old NASA transmission. With good Wi-Fi we could use our Amazon Fire TV. If bad Wi-Fi, the choices were hot spotting through our iPhones if we had cell reception, or streaming through the laptop. Another choice was to read books.

Before Moab, the landscape perked up with the buff-colored Book Cliffs escorting us to an ever-fleeing vanishing point. The ghost town of Woodside, where *Thelma and Louise* blew up the truck of a no-longer-horny driver, blinked by. We crossed the Colorado River in chill darkness. Thanksgiving tourists with mountain bikes were stuffed into every space at the Moab Valley RV Resort. I was thankful I had reserved the last spot.

The next morning, we woke to the sound of an exhaust-perfumed exodus. So long holiday weekend. Our neighbor, before he left, admired my little Smax scooter. He told me they had just finished re-paving the road in Arches. "You'll have fun on that. The road is like glass."

At the Arches' entrance gate I fumbled out my Senior Pass. Great thing that Senior Pass. I didn't know about it until a docent at the Gila Cliff Dwellings eyeballed me and asked my age. She told me to go get a Pass at the ranger station. It cost ten dollars. Barb got one before we left. The price had jumped to eighty dollars.

The Arches entrance stares at the Moab Fault, a 2,400-foot displacement. 295 million-year-old Pennsylvanian rock on the southwest side rests against 150 million-year-old Jurassic rock on the Park side. Hey there, Dino Brother.

We motored up switchbacks into a broad red-orange valley. I was excited to explore Arches. I had visited the park in the early 80s. There was no visitor station then. I drove through the entrance on a dirt road, parked, and hiked to Delicate Arch with my sleeping bag. There was no one around. You can't do that no more.

We pulled into the Courthouse Towers viewpoint. The lot was empty. Thanksgiving marks the end of the tourist season in southern Utah. Imposing stone towers erupted straight out of the rust-red soil. The valley is dense Entrada Sandstone floating atop a giant 300 million-year-old salt dome, an evaporite from the Pennsylvanian period called the Paradox Formation. As the unstable salt dome buckled, it pushed up the overlying layer of sandstone, which cracked, forming slab-like fins. Wind and ice weathered holes in the fins creating arches. Over 2,000 arches grace the Park, the highest concentration anywhere on the planet.

Someone had fun naming the fins and arches. Barb's favorite, visible from the overlook, was the Three Gossips. The Courthouse Towers looked like a courthouse, which made me nervous. Preserve us, the Tower of Babel was nearby. The Organ confused me. Oh, that kind of organ.

I don't know who came up with the fanciful names. It could have been early explorers J. W. "Doc" Williams, the first doctor in Moab, or Loren "Bish" Taylor, editor of the Moab newspaper in 1911. Maybe Doc and Bish enjoyed nicknames and looked at the formations as their friends. Someone else must have named Doc Williams Point. Whoever bestowed the names had a lapse at our next stop.

Balanced Rock is one of the prominent features in Arches. The rock weighs as much as twenty-seven blue whales. What about Many Whales Rock? It used to have a little brother named Chip Off the Old Block that collapsed in 1975. What about Old Block?

We hiked around the Rock. I took lots of photos trying to balance the exposure. I'm not sure where the information came from, but this was the approximate site of Ed Abbey's trailer during his stint as a ranger in 1956 and 1957. *Desert Solitaire*, published in 1968, is Abbey's account of his time in Arches. On the surface, it is a lyrical observation of desert and nature. But it is much more. Abbey comments on the various peoples of the desert: the Ancient Puebloans, the Mormons, the Basques, the miners, the cowboys and their cows, John Wesley Powell, a dead tourist at Grandview Point in Canyonlands. What made the book a bible for the environmental movement was Abbey's intelligent ranting about Industrial Tourism, the mindless, constant thrust of technological culture, ever expanding as it consumes, degrades and destroys.

> *If industrial man continues to multiply his numbers and expand his operations, he will succeed in his apparent intention to seal himself off from the natural and isolate himself within a synthetic prison of his own making.*

Abbey threw darts at his employer, the National Park Service. He railed against building roads into parks, which would cater to lazy and unadventurous tourists. An argument against Abbey's polemic, put forth in Ken Burns' documentary on the National Parks, is that providing access to all people, not just those hardy enough to backpack or horsepack into the wilderness, creates an appreciation and love of the remaining wild areas that will ensure their salvation.

Abbey bristled at being categorized as a "nature writer." He wrote eight fiction novels, fourteen non-fiction books and hundreds of book reviews and letters to the editor. His novel, *The Monkey Wrench Gang*, was a blueprint for eco-sabotage. The fictional Gang fought mining operations in northern Arizona by destroying bulldozers and coal trains. Influenced by the Monkey Wrenchers, Dave Foreman and friends germinated a real-life organization, Earth First, in 1980.

Earth First began as an activist organization supporting research, advocacy, education and minor vandalism, such as unfurling a plastic sign on the side of Glen Canyon Dam that looked like a giant crack in the structure. Over time, Earth First radicalized in the vein of the anarchy movement. Members organized physical actions such as tree sits, tree spiking, roadblocks and arson. Foreman and the original founders disassociated themselves from Earth First after an anarchist-dominated crowd heckled Ed Abbey.

Abbey promoted a public persona of himself known as "Cactus Ed," a taciturn contrarian who loved to scrape knuckles with popular culture. Readers cried racist after he recommended closing the border with Mexico to stop illegal immigration. He might have supported Trump's wall. Feminists labeled Ed a misogynist due to his writings and his many infidelities, though he platonically befriended many women environmental writers. Abbey claimed he had not contributed to overpopulation since he had five children among five wives. Cactus Ed pissed off the ranchers and cowboys with rants about environmental destruction from open range grazing.

The famous author spent his last years in Tucson and became a full professor of creative literature at the University of Arizona. I was long gone from my alma mater or I would have signed up for his class. I saw Abbey speak at the Arlene Schnitzer Hall in downtown Portland in the late 80s, shortly before his death. The packed crowd appeared to be ardent-to-radical environmentalists judged by youth and costume. Ed proceeded to read from his autobiographical novel, *The Fool's Progress*, a chapter about mules on a farm in Appalachia. This was not what the people came for. A low volume murmur rose from the restless crowd. Ed paused, looked at the audience, and said, "What did you think this was going to be about?" Abbey loved playing mind games with his admirers. Once in Montana, he read one of his books in entirety to a dwindling audience into the wee hours.

Ed Abbey's burial site is a legendary mystery. He requested interment under a pile of stones in a lonely patch of wilderness. After he died at home from bleeding esophageal varices, friends and family carried him in his favorite sleeping bag into the Cabeza Prieta Wilderness near the Mexican border. The inscribed stone reads:

EDWARD PAUL ABBEY
1927 - 1989
No Comment

An artfully painted school bus, a skoolie, with a smoke stack coming out of the top, parked near us at the Moab Valley RV. The young couple dressed prairie style. I walked over and complimented their bus. They were workampers, planning to stay an entire year doing maintenance at the camp. I mentioned we had just toured Arches and said, "I wish I knew the exact location of Ed Abbey's trailer."

Their reply was like a punch to the solar plexus. "Who's Ed Abbey?"

I detected the thin whine of my generation slipping into obscurity. I recited a thumbnail of Abbey's history to their quizzical expressions. When I said, "People consider him the founder of the eco-terrorism movement," their eyes widened, "Oh!" I hope they pick up a copy of *Desert Solitaire* at the visitor's center.

Our camp neighbor's claim was true. The shiny black road through the park was glass, like Lebowski's bowling ball rolling between Maude's legs. All apologies to Ed Abbey, but it was nice. We glided to the Delicate Arch Viewpoint and hiked up the trail. From that distance the Arch looked like an ant farm. Tiny bipedal ants scurried about on sandstone. I decided not to hike to the ant farm to preserve my delicate memory of years ago waking up under the Arch, my own private desert solitaire.

The next overlook showcased the Salt Valley and, turning around, a nice shot of the La Sal Mountains. We stopped for a picnic lunch, then rode to the Devil's Garden Trailhead. The lot was full. Don't all these retirees have anything better to do?

The Devil's Garden, a name I will bestow on my garden back home, had the best arches. The first big arch on the trail was Landscape Arch, at 290 feet the fifth largest arch in the world. There are larger arches in China, but thanks to MacDonald's there are more arches in America. In 1991, a large slice of rock calved off the underside of Landscape Arch and almost killed a tourist. Another tourist snapped a picture.

The hard-packed trail ascended in the trough of an enormous fin leading to Navajo Arch and Partition Arch. Juniper trees, also known as Utah cedar, dominated the trail, their tortured trunks struggling into the air from sand and cracked rock. Junipers draw water through 25-foot deep taproots. Four-wing saltbush, rough mule's ears, yucca and Mormon tea made a garden border for the trail. Mormon tea, ephedra viridans, is a source of ephedrine. I took some Mormon tea back to Atlanta when I was in medical school thinking I would use it as a stimulant for studying. One night, I brewed the twigs. It was the worst headache of my life, no doubt caused by a potentially lethal ephedrine overdose.

Partition Arch was my favorite, not to belittle the other arches. You're all wonderful. Peering through the hole of the thick-walled arch was like looking through a portal to an ancient landscape. One expected herds of dinosaurs to be roaming the grasslands. Navajo Arch formed a cave behind its twin windows.

As we headed back up the trail, a pair of sturdy blond-headed fellows passed us speaking German. I spouted all the German I knew in eight seconds. I said, "Gruss Gott," which is what everyone hiking the trails in Switzerland said to us. The lads turned and explained to us that "Gruss Gott" was a trail greeting in Bavaria only. In northern Germany, where they were from, there was a different greeting, "Moin," short for "Guten Morgen," Good Morning. When I told them my son's middle name was Morgan, they brightened like I was the King of Oktoberfest.

The lads joined us in lively conversation for the hike back. They were fresh out of college, traveling the world before deciding what to do with the rest of their lives. Next month they would travel to Australia. I have worked with many German doctors and scientists. I think the education system for doctors in Germany is superior to the overly long American system. In Germany, students begin the study of medicine after graduating Gymnasium, the German high school. The young Germans told me most Americans they met had little knowledge of German society. "So you know what Gymnasium is!"

During my surgical oncology fellowship, a fourth-year German medical student, Fritz von Weizsacker, rotated on my team. I became friends with Fritz. I asked him what his father did in Germany, but he declined to tell me anything for security reasons. On his birthday, I invited him to my house for dinner. Relaxing with wine, I pressed him about his father. He swore me to secrecy. Fritz' father was the President of Germany. Ronald Reagan had stayed at their house. Fritz is now chief physician at the Schlosspark-Klinik in Berlin.

Richard von Weizsacker, who died in 2015, was a popular German President and former Mayor of Berlin, who presided over the Reunification with East Germany. During World War II, von Weizsacker, scion of a Prussian family, served as a captain in the Reichsarbeitsdienst. He took part in two plots to assassinate Hitler, including the famous 20 July plot. von Weizsacker gave a famous speech on the 40th anniversary of the end of World War II. To the disgruntlement of the old guard politicians, he argued that for Germany to move forward it had to take responsibility for the "unspeakable truth of the Holocaust."

After that story, our new friends treated me like a Teutonic rock star. They were reluctant to walk away in the parking lot. We made vague plans to join them for dinner if we bumped into them in Moab.

The eighteen-mile ride back through the park was out of a dream. A brilliant yellow and orange sunset reflected off clouds to the west while stars winked into a blueing sky to the east. Smax purred with joy, floating over smooth undulations through the growing shadows of stone gods. Sometimes, our world takes us out of itself.

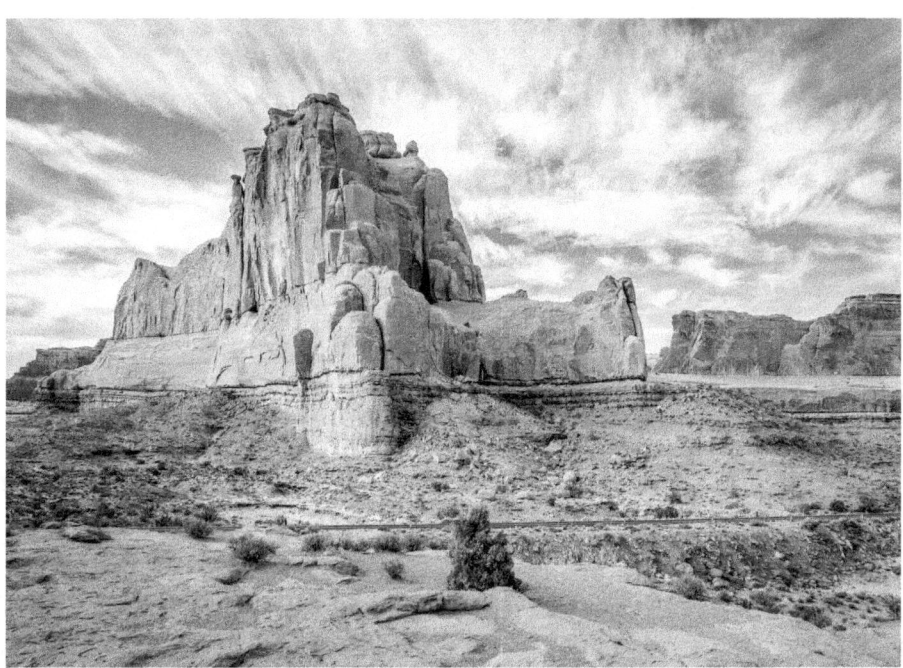

Courthouse Tower. I am innocent!

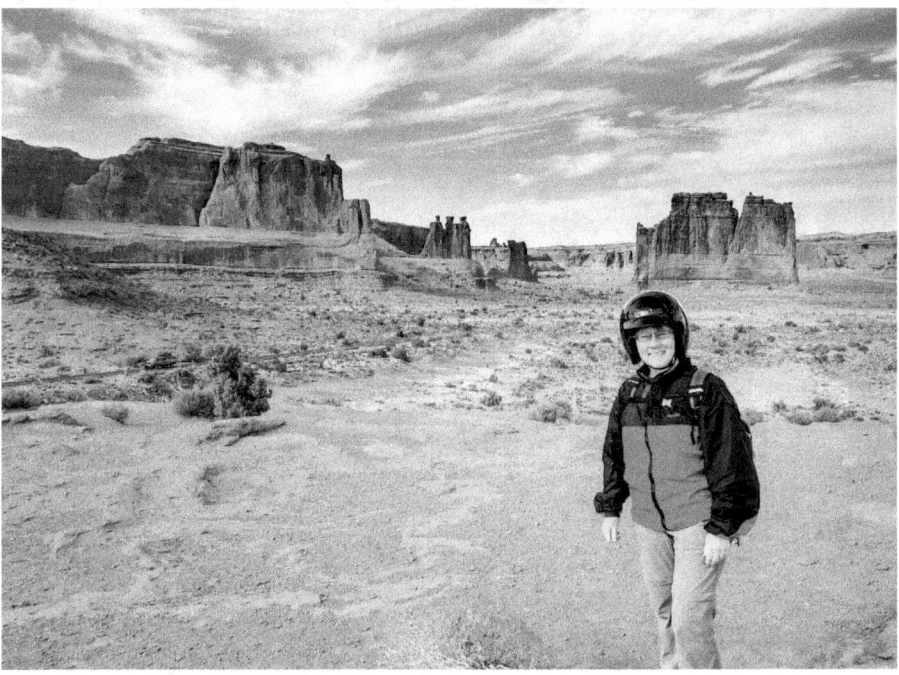

The Three Gossips talk to Barb

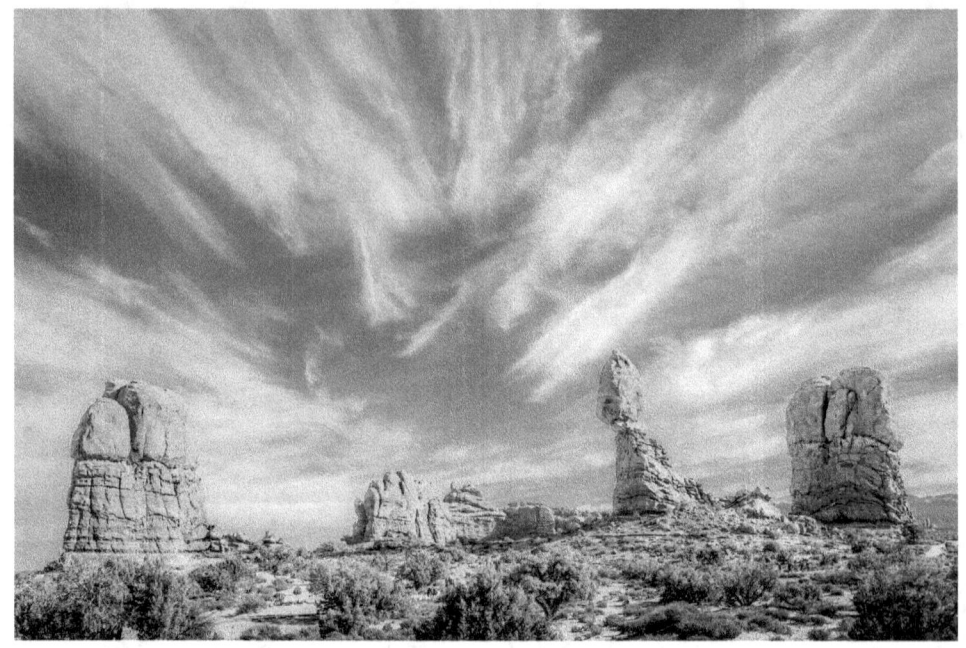

Balanced Rock, site of Ed Abbey's trailer

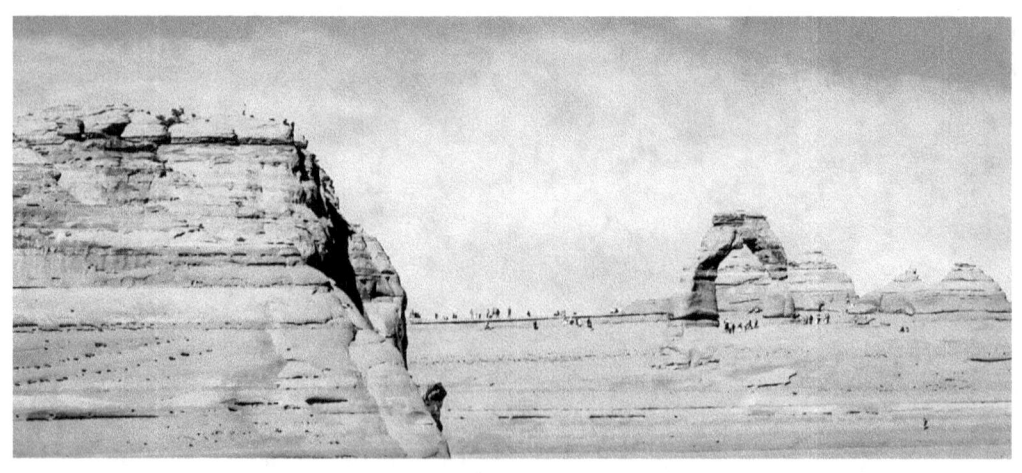

Marching ants at Delicate Arch

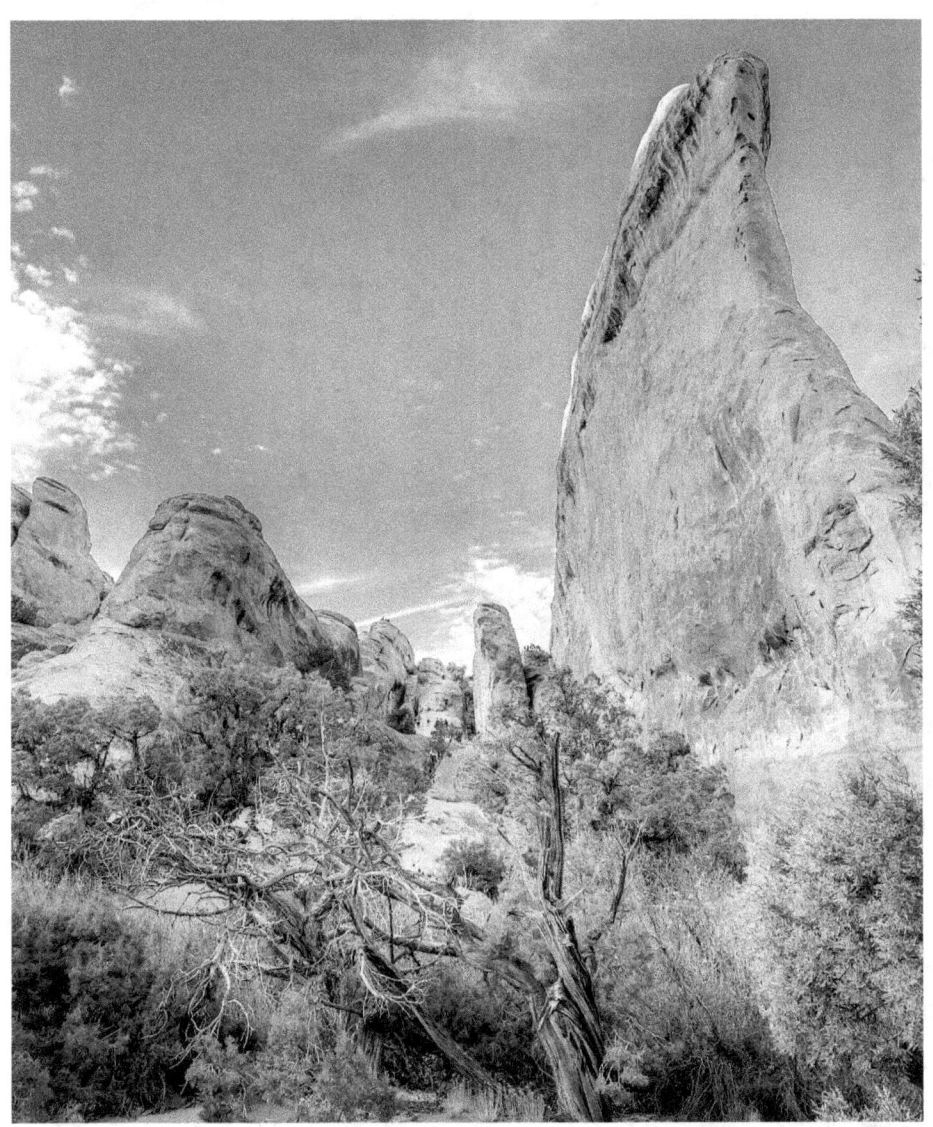

Big fin

Photographing the American West

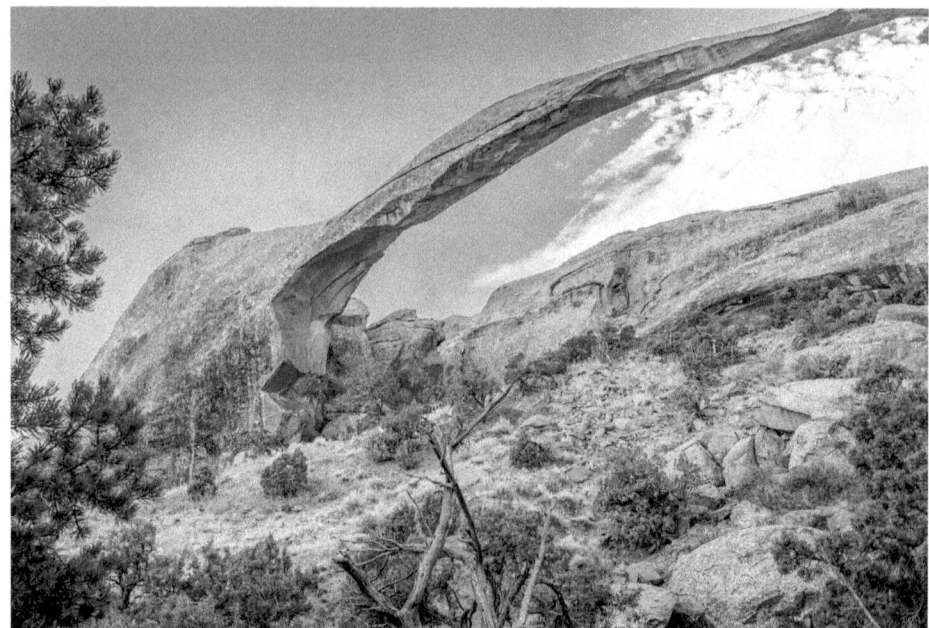
Landscape Arch

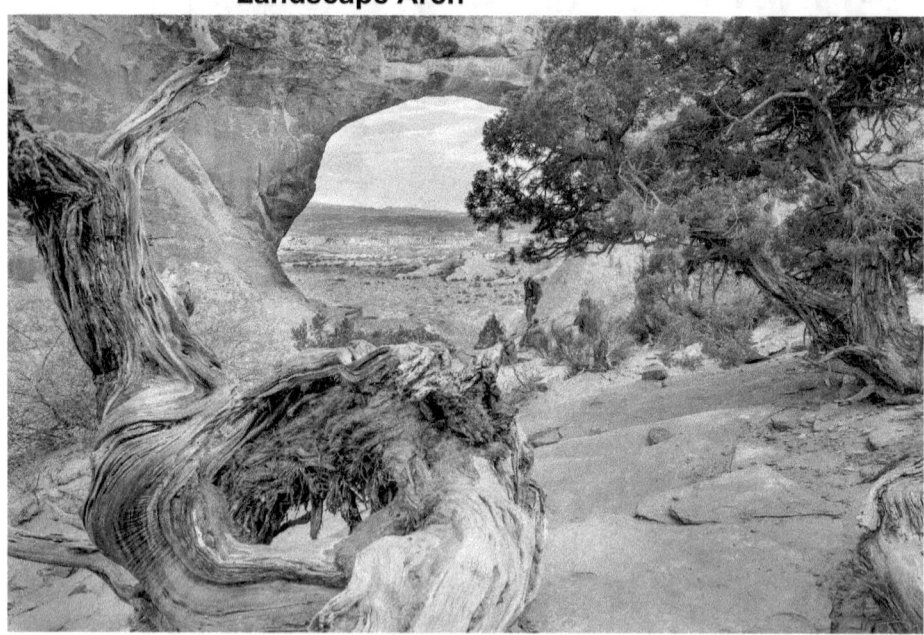
Juniper at Partition Arch

William J Wood Jr

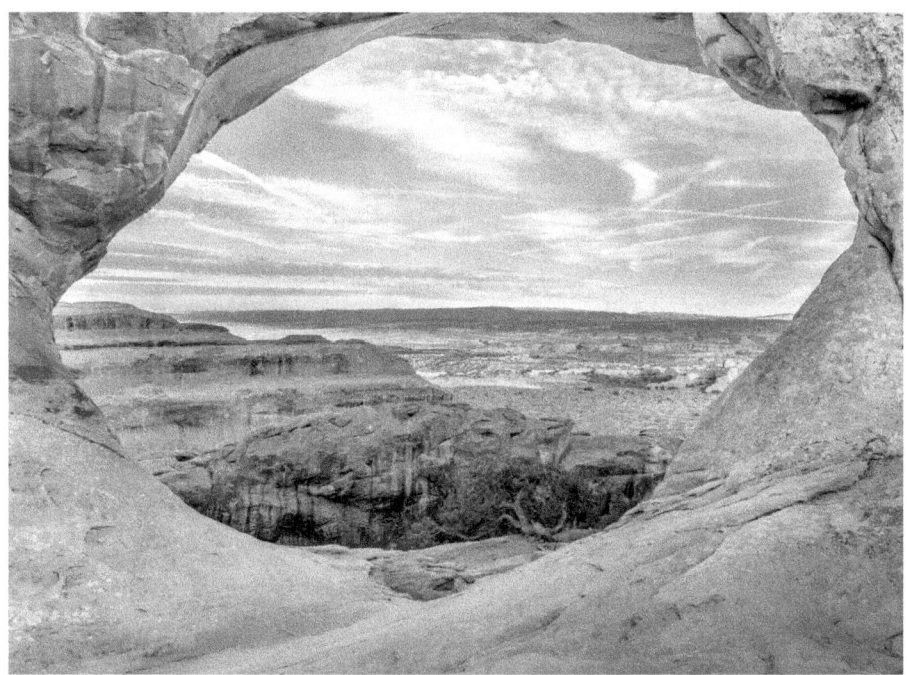

Through the Time Portal

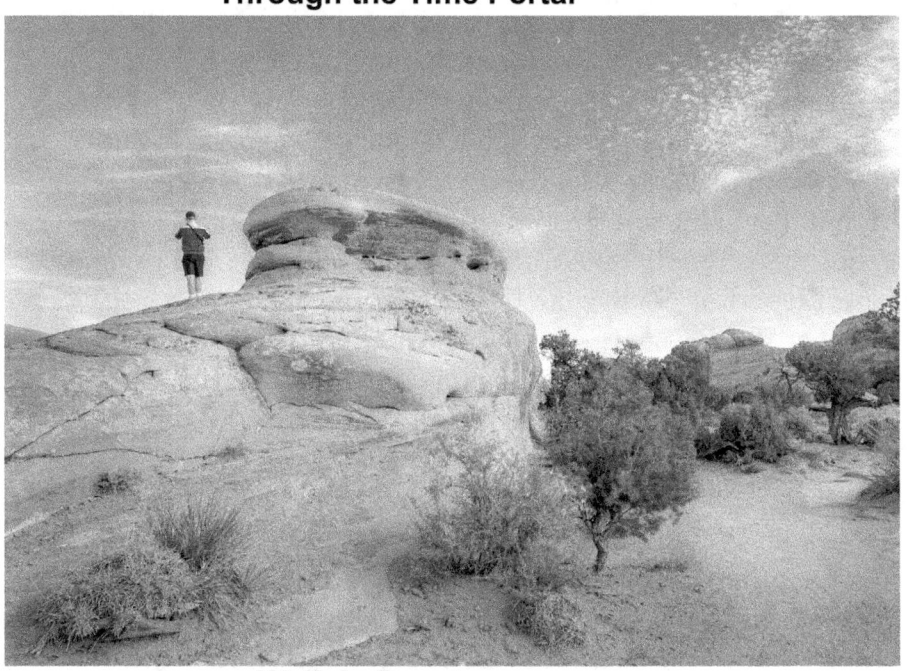

Walk in Beauty

Chapter 4

Canyonlands and Purple Tatiana

The next morning I reported to Barlow Adventures on Main Street, Moab at 8:00 am. We had reserved a 4-wheel-drive Rubicon to explore Canyonlands. The amiable owner asked me if I had proof of my auto insurance, not my RV insurance. I didn't. My insurance agent didn't answer my call on a weekend. After some humming and hawing, I asked him if this was a deal breaker. No, it wasn't. I tried to reassure him by testifying I had experience off-roading in my old Toyota FJ40, an outstanding backcountry vehicle. I asked for the purple two-door Wrangler Rubicon. Her name was Tatiana. I liked that. Russians are strong.

The owner, perhaps named Barlow, showed me how to use the Electronic Sway Bar Disconnect and the Axle Lock. Disconnecting the sway bar allows increased wheel travel. The axle lock increased traction in 4WD low gear. "You should not need first gear on this trail," he assured.

We reviewed a detailed off-road map for our route up the Shafer Trail, which would take us to the "Island In The Sky" district. We would return on the Gemini Bridges Road. If we encountered another vehicle on the narrow road, the uphill had right-of-way. Barlow was weary of the tourist season in Moab. He wanted to close shop and head to Mexico, but people like me kept showing up.

We loaded Tatiana with a day's worth of food and water and camera gear. A half mile up the highway we took a left on Potash Road. I couldn't resist the photo opportunity at the intense blue evaporation ponds of Intrepid Potash, the largest producer of potassium chloride in the United States. No need for bananas out here. In the 60s, there was a hard rock mine that collapsed and killed 18 miners. Now brine evaporation harvests this mineral gift from the Paradox Basin. The blue dye in the ponds speeds up evaporation.

We stopped for shots of the Colorado River at the Gooseneck Overlook. Soon we reached the junction of the Shafer Trail and the White Rim Road, named for the White Rim Sandstone formation. The Atomic Energy Commission dozed a 71-mile road circling the Island in the Sky for the uranium mining craze in the 1950s. The ore proved to be low grade.

Just before we hit the switchbacks, an old truck with a camper shell came lumbering down the heavily rutted road. The unsteady metal beast looked to be on the verge of tipping over with every uneven rut. An elderly man with wild, white hair was driving beside a similar woman. He asked me, in a singsong accent, if there was camping ahead. I said there was a camp about seven miles back. He looked horrified. "Oh noooo, not so far!" My guess was Dutch, as no German would exude such nervous emotion.

Mesas, burnt orange and streaked with black desert varnish, lorded over the approach to the famed switchbacks. At the base of the almost-vertical cliff I engaged the 4-wheel drive, disconnected the sway bar, and shifted into low. This was our personal, and rented, Rubicon. Lay thee still in thy grave, Caesar. Feathering the gas pedal, the die was cast. At a steady crawl up the thin strip of rock, Tatiana sang the Russian national anthem, using the post-Stalin lyrics of Mikhalkov. *Predkami dannaya mudrost narodnaya. Popular wisdom given by our fore-bearers.* A pair of bighorn sheep nodded horns.

Seeing the pitch of the switchbacks from the top, I was glad we had gone up instead of down. We looked at maps at the visitor's center and planned our day on the Island In the Sky. First stop was the end of the road, Grand View Point, where Ed Abbey and his ranger crew had located a tourist, dead from dehydration, under a lone juniper with a beautiful view. Ed's thought was, "Not a bad way to go."

Grand View Point Overlook offered a grand view of Gooseberry Canyon, Monument Basin and the Loop of the Colorado River. Across the basin, rugose red pinnacles punctuated the Needles Section. This was the second goose-related landform of the day. Somehow, this desiccated, rusted, magnificent landscape didn't seem like prime goose habitat, not like my pond back home which is invaded by bomber squadrons of Canadian geese.

Along the slickrock trail of Grand View Point, the hundred-mile view south joined an equal to the west where the Green River joins with the Colorado. I felt a tickle of anxiety on the mellow trail looking at the rounded cliff shoulder that, somewhere, reached perpendicular for 1,200 feet. Signs warned to keep children away from the edge. What about adults? I activated sweat glands perseverating about how close I could walk to the edge to get an award-winning photooooooooo.

We lunched at Buck Canyon Overlook, then drove eleven miles to Upheaval Dome. A 2008 geological study supported impact as the cause of the three-mile diameter crater, displacing the salt-dome theory. The sides of the crater revealed ascending formation strata: the Moenkopi, the Chinle, the Wingate Sandstone, the Kayenta and the ubiquitous Navajo Sandstone. You can remember these layers with the mnemonic: Make Cuts With Knives Nimbly. Just in case.

There are certain locations around our verdant and non-verdant world that attract photographers. I could say, "like flies to honey," but I'd rather not since I'm a photography enthusiast. I'm a Mac-head, but I used Windows PCs for my office. Our next vista had branded into my cortex thanks to the screen-saver for Windows 7.

Every morning, a crowd of five-legged (two human plus three tripod) nature paparazzi shoulder into a photonic feeding trough in front of Mesa Arch. The money shot, diluted to pennies now, is a fiery dawn sun reflecting off the bottom of the arch. As a rule, I cultivate a self-inflating, anti-social smugness toward these digital altars. Like waterfalls, they pop up on every photography website. OK, let's go see Mesa Arch. Oh darn, it's not sunrise. Grab shots. Let's go. Didn't Jesus say at the Sermon on the Mount that we could all keep a few character flaws?

The day was fading. We didn't have time to go to Dead Horse Point. I followed the directions to the Gemini Bridges Road. As instructed by Barlow Adventures, I did not turn on the Metal Masher trail, though I guess I could have since I'd pressured Barlow into renting without my insurance information. A web of mountain bike trails, the Magnificent Seven, 7-Up, the Getaway and others branched off the Gemini Road. I saw no trail named Spoke Smasher.

Jim Stiles is the publisher and owner of *The Canyon Country Zephyr, Planet Earth Edition*, an online bimonthly alt-newspaper that broadcasts "All the News that Causes Fits since 1989." He had a prior motto: "Hopelessly clinging to the past since 1989." Stiles, a former ranger at Arches National Park, was a friend of Ed Abbey's in his Moab days. The Zephyr publishes Stiles' editorial pieces that carry on with Abbey's message about the value of wilderness, as envisioned by Stiles. A favorite topic of the Zephyr is the ruination of wilderness and its border towns by the amenities economy. Stiles labels the promotion of tourism by the big money outdoor industry as "The New West."

> *Even grassroots groups, who once worked for the protection of the land and the satisfaction that they were honest participants in "the good fight," now parse their battle cries and make $100K a year. Their boards of directors are filled with wealthy fat cat industrialists that would have*

> had Abbey deported if they could have found a way. Together, they support a massive recreation/amenities economy that brings millions of tourists to the once remote rural West and with it, untold quantities of money and environmental devastation. Adrenaline junkies from the far corners of the planet descend on canyon country to string slacklines and rock climb and ride bikes off cliffs and BASE jump and "do" the river…

Jim Styles watched his adopted paradise of 70s era Moab, a collection of miners, ranchers and hippies, mutate into a recreation hub for canyon country. The humble local shops and homes fell to bulldozers, replaced by billionaire getaway mansions, restaurants, pubs, art galleries, clothing stores and adventure tourism services. The price of an ad in the Zephyr bought you a flattering personal caricature by the artistic Stiles. His fluently vociferous diatribes against industrial tourism didn't sit well with potential advertisers who depended on tourist dollars. After the demise of the Zephyr's print version, Stiles decamped from Moab and moved fifty miles to Monticello, a less developed town. The Zephyr has taken on both proponents AND opponents of the new Bear's Ears National Monument.

Similar to other presidents who wanted to sweep a final few crumbs of legacy legislation at the end of their terms, President Obama proclaimed the Bear's Ears National Monument on December 28, 2016 under the powers of the Antiquities Act of 1906. President Teddy Roosevelt established the Act to protect Native American artifacts from pothunters. The language of the Act also includes protection of "other objects of scientific or historic interest," and states that the size of a monument "shall be confined to the smallest area compatible with the proper care and management of the objects to be protected." The U.S. Supreme Court ruled in 1920 that large areas, such as the Grand Canyon, could be defined as areas of interest.

The peninsula of the northern end of Bear's Ears' original Obama-defined territory brushed up against our thrilling Shafer Trail switchbacks. To the south, the monument widens to include the land between the Colorado River and the San Juan River, 1.35 million acres. The Monument showcases glorious western scenes such as the Valley of the Gods, Grand Gulch and the Dark Canyon Wilderness. In the lightly trod red rock canyons and pine forests slumber thousands of archaeological remains including Ancestral Pueblo and ancient Clovis sites.

President Trump ordered Secretary of Interior Ryan Zinke to review twenty-seven different monuments and recommend size changes. Trump invoked the Antiquities Act to shrink Bear's Ears by 85% and shrink nearby Grand Staircase-Escalante by 45%. Several groups, including Patagonia and Utah Dine Bikeyah, filed federal lawsuits stating that the Antiquities Act does not allow a sitting president to shrink previously proclaimed monuments. A coalition of five Native American Tribes, many environmental organizations, and retailers such as Yvonne Chouinard's Patagonia and REI strongly support the original Monument size. The support of the recreation industry may not be completely altruistic. Opponents are the extraction industries, most Utah politicians, and local ranchers, all of whom categorize any increase in federal land protection as a "land grab."

Stiles' take on the issue is that monument status does not provide much legal protection anyway. He argues that the Archaeological Resource Protection Act of 1979, ARPA, a stronger and more specific law than the Antiquities Act, already provides legal protection of archaeological resources, though with essentially no funds for enforcement. Stiles wants an ARPA Enforcement Unit. To protect the mesas, Stiles calls for withdrawal of all oil and gas leases below canyon rims. Commenters in the Zephyr argue these measures are unlikely to happen in the current political climate.

I think Moab would be a great spot for retirement. I could spend the last of my mobile time on earth exploring the far reaches of canyon country in exquisite solitude, harvesting only my beloved photons. My only request is that once I'm established, please slam the gates shut to any more people.

A rock-strewn road descended into the lower canyon toward the Gemini Bridges. We spent an hour on foot looking for the Bridges before we noticed faded blue lines on the rock. The lines led us to the Bridges, thick arches over a deep canyon. Barb would not allow me to walk across the top of the arch. A chromatic sunset reflected on clouds over the La Sal Mountains. Someone was flying a drone. Drones are illegal inside national parks.

It was dark when we encountered the High Shelf Road. Beyond the knife-edge of the road's border visible matter eclipsed into an inky void. Big boulders and deep potholes streamed into our headlights. At times, one tire was on a boulder and the other was playing with the last few inches of road next to the black death plunge. Barb doesn't like these kinds of roads. She commented, "Why would anyone want to do this? Why would anyone want to drive on this kind of road?"

I could only think of one answer while playing steering wheel cha-cha: "Because it's fun."

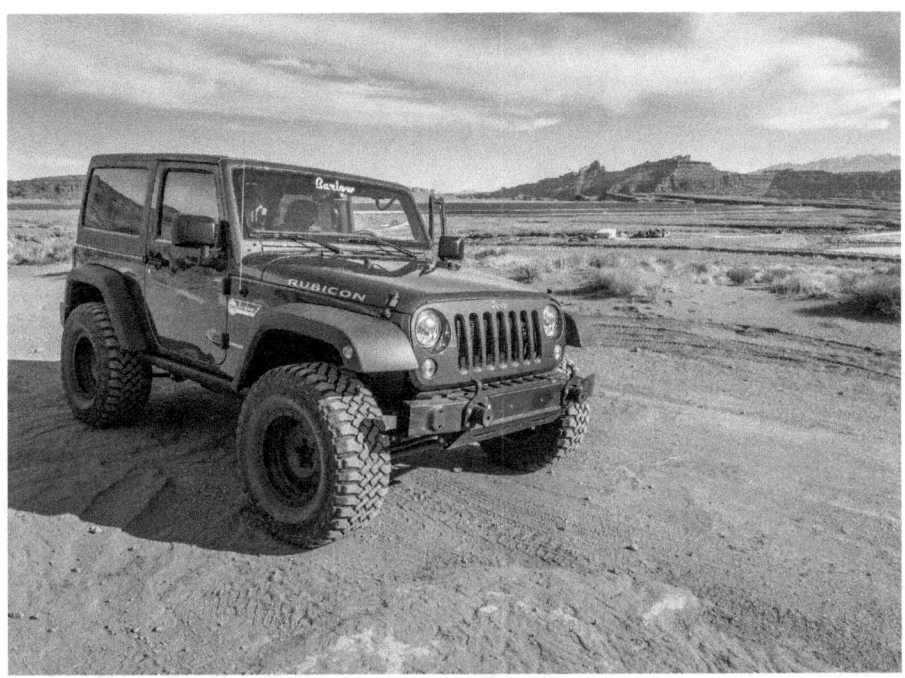
Tatiana took care of us. Brine ponds at Potash.

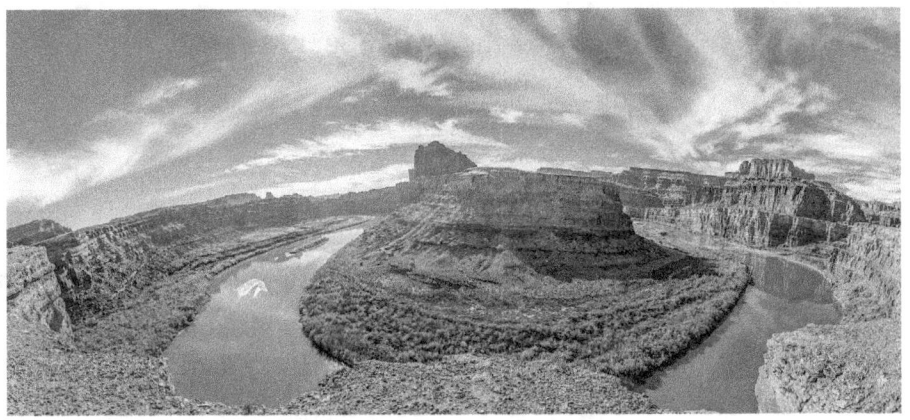
The Gooseneck, Colorado River

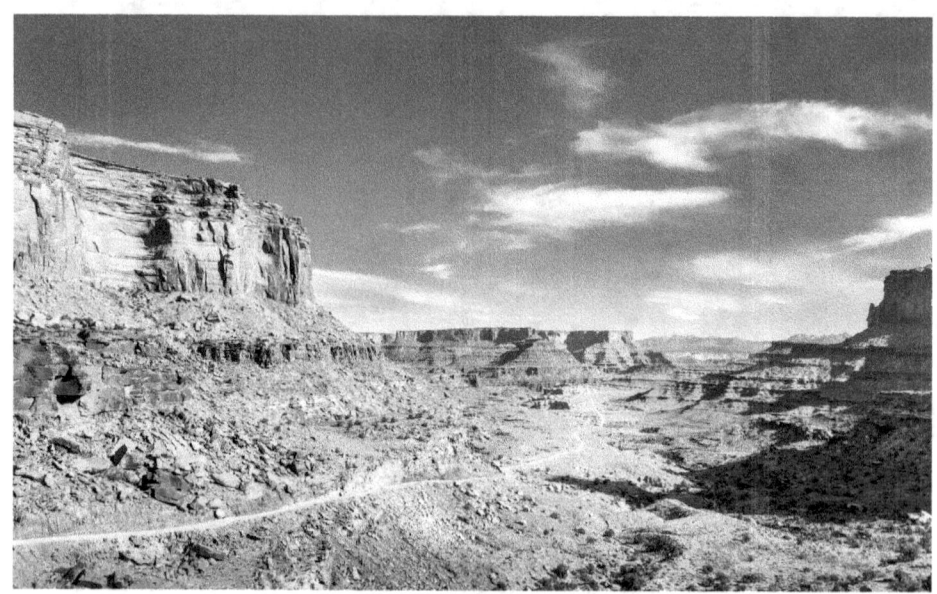

The Shafer Trail approaches the switchbacks

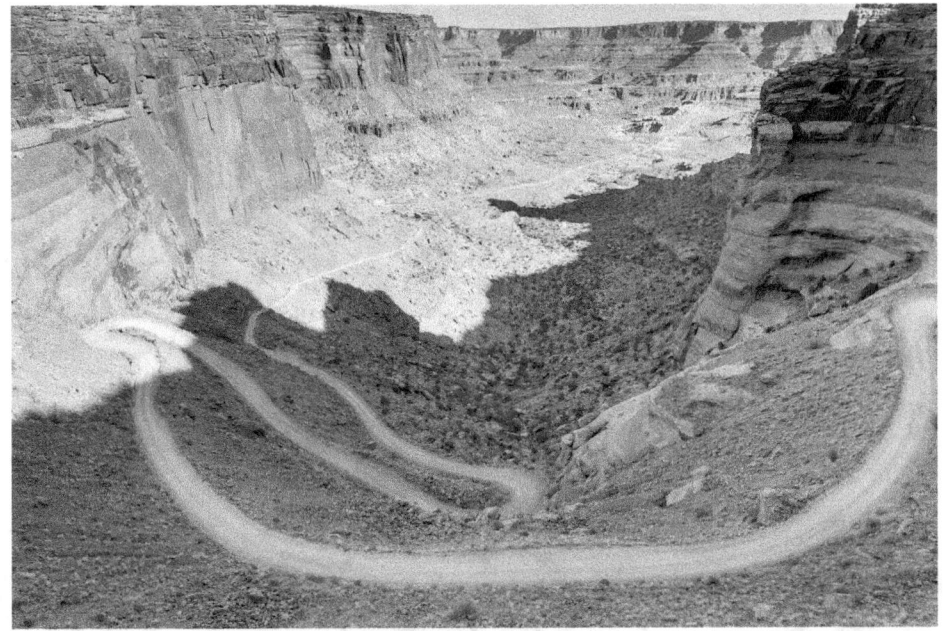

Hairpins for Tatiana

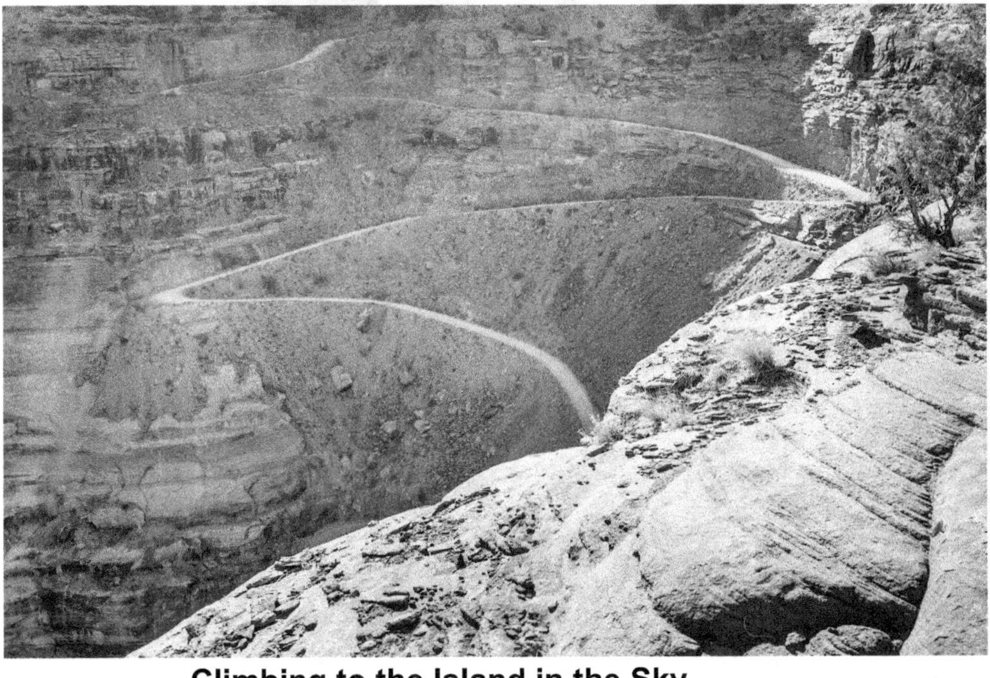

Climbing to the Island in the Sky

Photographing the American West

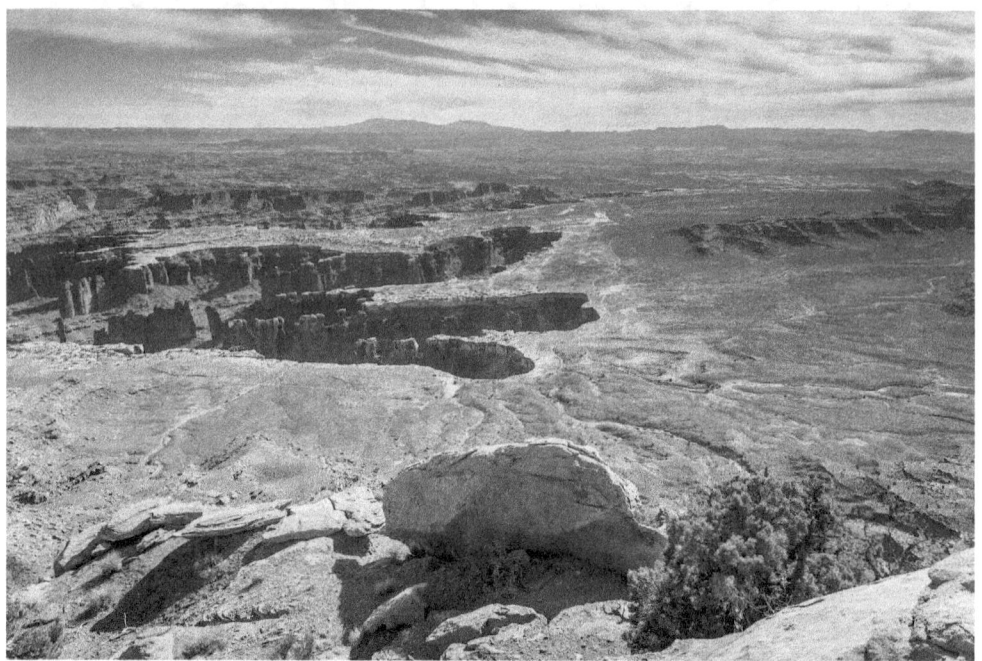
Gooseberry Canyon

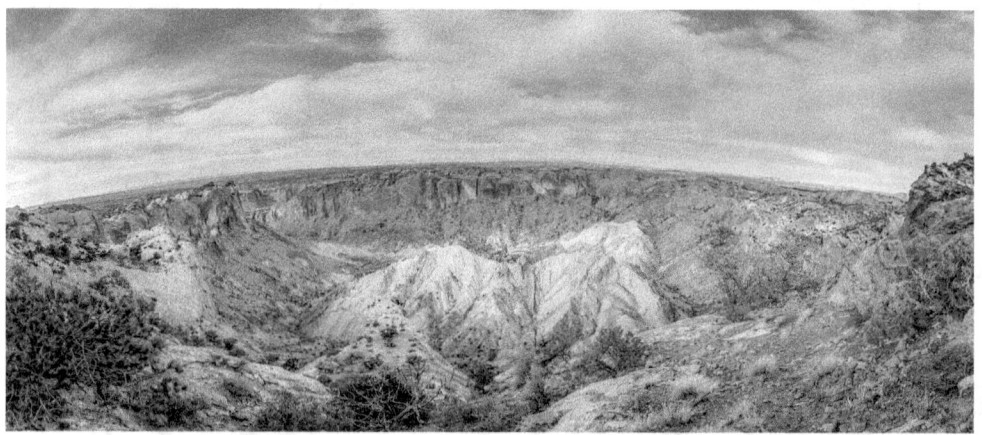
Upheaval Dome

William J Wood Jr

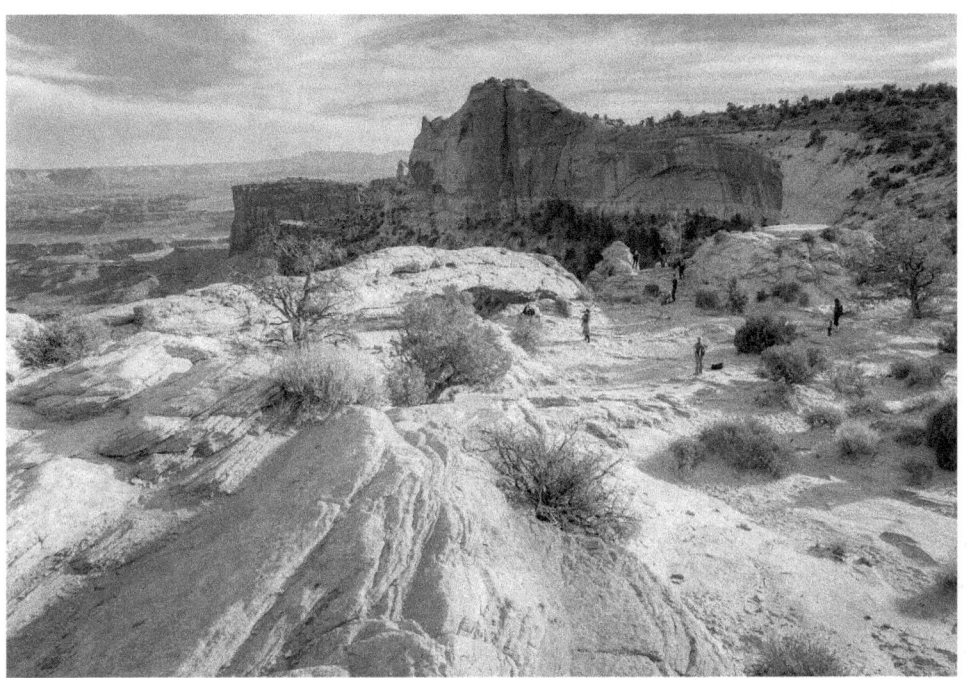

Mesa Arch not at sunrise

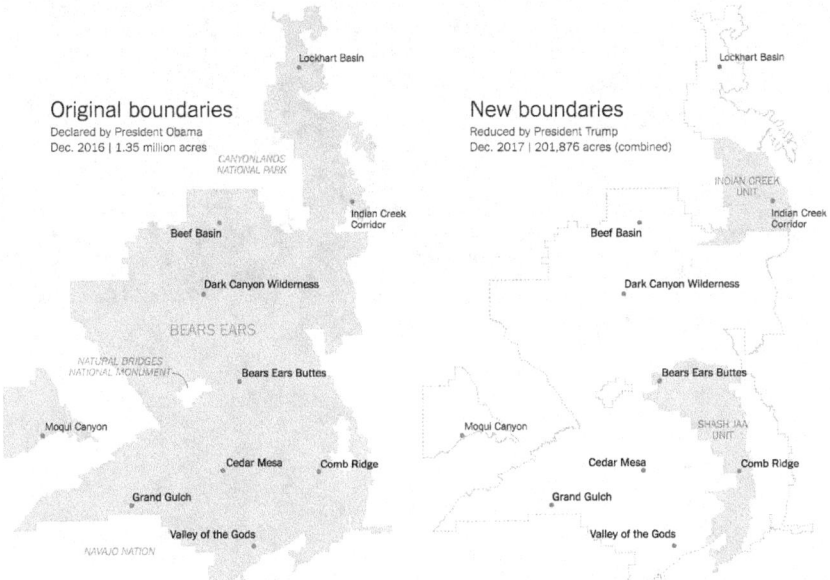

Shrinking Bear's Ears National Monument

Photographing the American West

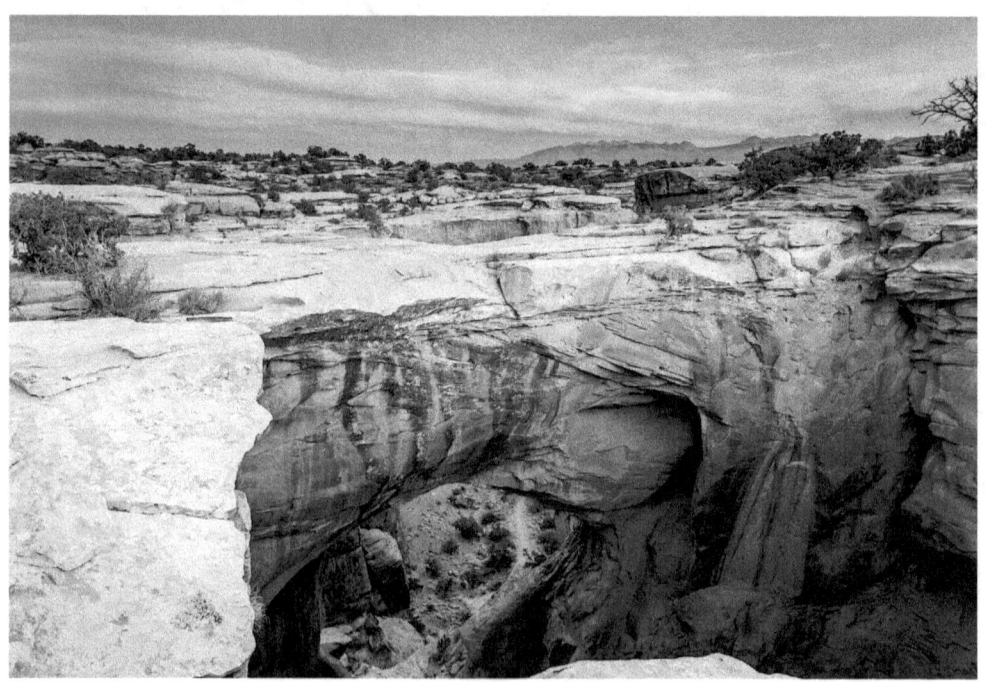

Sunset over Gemini Bridge

Chapter 5

Please Don't Touch the Hoodoos!

After breakfast, I placed an Order of Lenin medal on Tatiana's engine block and delivered her back to Barlow, who still had a faraway Mexico look in his eyes. The day before, I had spied a small boy climbing on our scooter. I told the boy, gently, if he would promise not to climb on the scooter, I would give him a ride on it. His father, tall and athletic, came dashing over. His accent was Kiwi. He was a professional crewman on an America's Cup yacht. The family lived in Vail. They were touring in their new trailer.

    I went over to inspect their trailer. I asked if they knew my old friend, Bob Chadwick, Chad, who lived in Vail. The wife thought the name was familiar. Before starting medical school, in 1976, my friend, Jay, and I drove cross-country to Maine in my VW beetle. Our friend, Sharon, was staying with her boyfriend, Chad, in an abandoned barn at the Hinckley Yacht shipbuilding yards in Southwest Harbor. Jay and I moved in for a few weeks. We explored a good part of Maine, climbing Mount Katahdin and canoeing the Penobscot River.

    The rental barn had no facilities. The procedure was to hang one's posterior out the back window. Right after he had assumed the position, Jay saw me grab my camera and run out the door. He was cursing like a constipated sailor as I rounded the corner. I captured a classic image of white ass-cheeks on a window sill. After I left for Atlanta to start medical school, Jay worked the ski season in Maine at Sugarloaf Ski Resort. Sharon decided she was in love with Jay and road her bike across the state to visit. I never knew where Chad had gone until he popped up on Facebook a few years ago. He was in Vail. He posted lots of pictures of mountain biking, river rafting and moose.

When I pulled up on the scooter after returning Tatiana, the Kiwi father came over and asked if I was serious about giving his kids a ride. Sure! I took the cute blond-headed brother and sister on rides around the camp. The sister chattered away the whole time. "I've ridden on a motorcycle before. It was my Dad's." Oh my!

Barb and I discussed a hike, but I started working on my Arches photos and, before I knew it, it was 5:00 pm. Barb worked on her Boy Scout database.

The next day we headed to Bryce Canyon National Park. We listened to old Christmas songs on Pandora. It put us in a holiday mood. I-70 bisects the San Rafael Reef, a tilted sandstone formation on the side of the San Rafael Swell. The Swell is an anticline (think "hill") that rose during the Laramide Orogeny, 60 million years ago. Erosion exposed 270-million year old Permian rock.

Back in the day, that being the 70s for me, I went to Bryce Canyon with my friend Rick, Tucson Rick not Santa Fe Rick, who went by the name "Rococo" when we were all doing nicknames. We drove from Tucson and rolled up to the canyon rim at midnight. Rick loves to entertain anyone who will listen recounting that I pushed a boulder off the canyon rim. I don't remember doing that. At least, I think I don't.

In full moonlight, Rococo and I crunched down the trail into a purple underworld. Dawn revealed a colorful panorama of red-and-white spires staring mutely at our insignificance. The Paiute name for Bryce is *Unka-timpe-wa-wince-pock-ich*, which means "red rocks standing like men." Natives believe the hoodoos are the Legend People, turned to stone by the trickster Coyote.

Bryce Canyon is on the edge of the Paunsaugunt Plateau, in the High Plateau Section of the Colorado Plateau. Paunsaugunt (say it) means "home of the beaver." I may borrow this name for my home pond. Beaver invaded our pond years ago. We fought them to keep the drainpipe open, but gave up. They were too wary to trap. Finally, I realized they would maintain the earth dam for free so they stay, chewing down trees and slapping their tails in the middle of the night.

The Colorado Plateau is 140,000 square miles of thick earth crust between the Rocky Mountains to the east and the Great Basin to the west. The Laramide Orogeny lightly wrinkled it. A more recent uplift five million years ago raised the plateau to its average 5,200-foot height and also tilted it giving velocity to canyon-cutting rivers, the Colorado, the Green, the San Juan and the Little Colorado.

Other than the tourists pleased by the variety of landforms, the non-tourists of our species treasure the Plateau. Geologists swarm the area. The Grand Staircase is a series of formation stratigraphies that step northward from the Grand Canyon as long benches and cliffs. The color-coded layers read like a planetary Old Testament. The oldest step is the Precambrian Vishnu schist at the bottom of the Grand Canyon and the youngest is the Tertiary-period, red-and-white mudstone of the Claron Formation in Bryce Canyon.

Paleontologists are unearthing tenure-stoking new species from all eras of earth's existence in the Plateau. One of my favorite college courses was Comparative Anatomy at Northern Arizona University, taught by an inspiring paleontology professor, Dr. Ted Goslow. I just learned that Dr. Goslow went on to Brown University and moved to Oregon after retiring in 2004. I would enjoy seeing him again. We'll see if LinkedIn can find him.

Past the town of Panguitch on Utah 12, we stopped at Red Canyon, a charming teaser of red-rock hoodoos. Late afternoon shadows stippled the road as we turned into Ruby's Inn RV Park and Campground, the main hostelry near Bryce. The campground gate had a sign, "Closed for the Season." We drove back to the hotel where a pair of cute Filipino girls explained that the campground had closed for the season. RVs went into an overflow lot behind the hotel. This was fine. I don't like crowds. The Ponderosa pines and the fragrant high-country air put me in mind of the NAU campus in Flagstaff. A gentle peace of memories passed through me.

The next morning our water had frozen. We zipped into warm layers and rode Smax through biting air to Rainbow Point, 9,115 feet, the highest overlook. To the south, Powell Point and the Table Cliff Plateau sculpted the valley over the town of Tropic. Backtracking through warming air, we parked at Sunset Point and spread our maps on a picnic table. Linking several trails made a nice hike through the heart of the amphitheater with an option for a side hike up Peekaboo Trail.

The Navajo Loop Trail switchbacked into a dark slot canyon named Wall Street. It was dry. That's good. A lone Douglas Fir poked out of a bowl of golden light at the narrow end of the slot. The trail followed a wash to a flat bottom park of pine and fir. We went a half-mile up Peekaboo, but we missed our hoodoo friends so we headed back to the Queen's Garden Trail.

In contrast to the grand views from the rim, walking through the Queen's Garden was like morphing into a character in an ancient fantasy in a galaxy far, far away. Tree-sized hoodoos and fins, textured with bands of pink, orange, yellow and white, radiated a mind-altering enchantment. No need for LSD here. The Queen gazed from her high pedestal, a vibratory pink mud replica of Queen Victoria in full regalia on top of a spire. God save us all from runaway hoodoo dreams.

A steep trail brought us to Sunrise Point on the rim. A Limber Pine with exposed roots clung to the eroding cliff face like a Marlon Brando audition. I was thinking it might be better to photograph the sunset from Sunset Point where we had parked. Maybe? After a snack at a picnic table, we tried to wait out the sunset, but it was getting cold. Bryce is one of the best night-viewing sites in the world. You can see 7,500 stars on a moonless night. I decided I would come back at night and shoot the stars.

We returned to our quiet camp at Ruby's Inn and relaxed. Barb made a nice dinner. I stretched out in front of Netflix. After dark, I put on my riding gear and stepped out the door into a butt-cold wind. A full moon illuminated the landscape. With relief, I decided that the godawful moon would ruin the star viewing. I retreated to my warm cave. For a laugh, I texted to Ricky Rococo that I had seen a sign at Bryce Canyon with my picture on it.

Have you seen this man? Contact park authorities immediately.

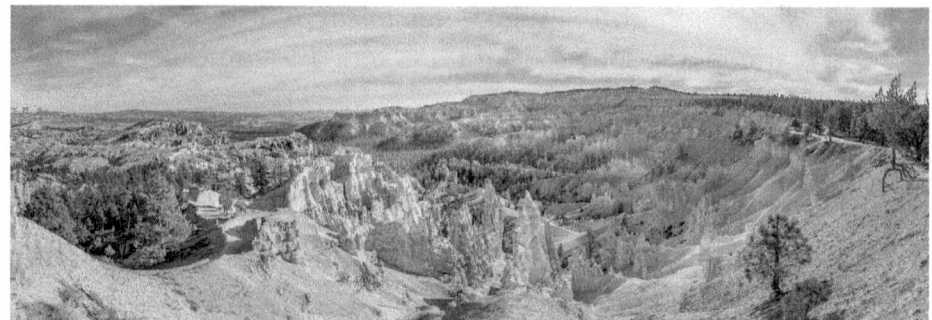
Bruce Canyon amphitheater

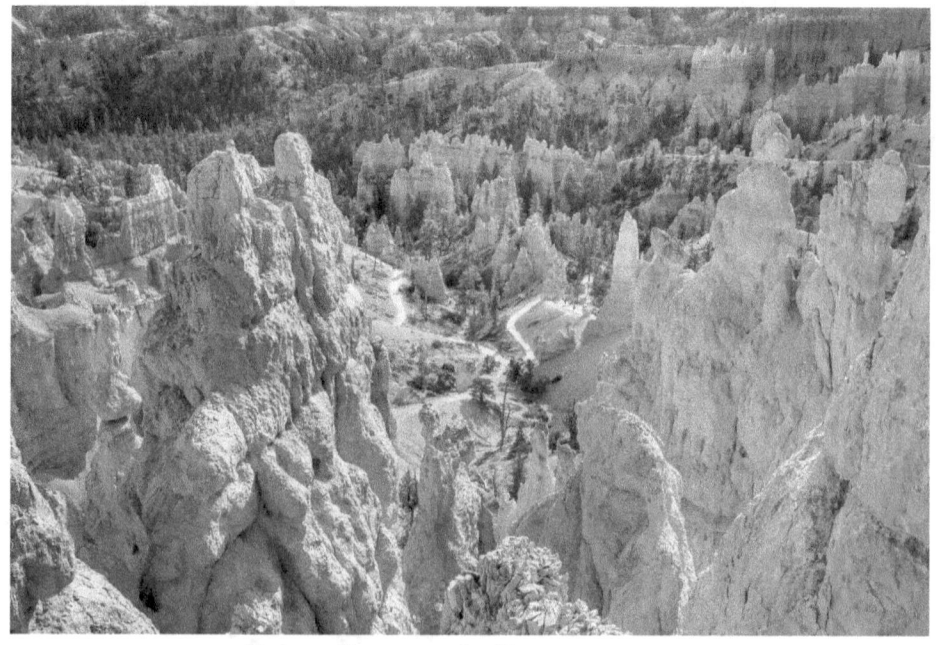
Bryce Canyon, trail

William J Wood Jr

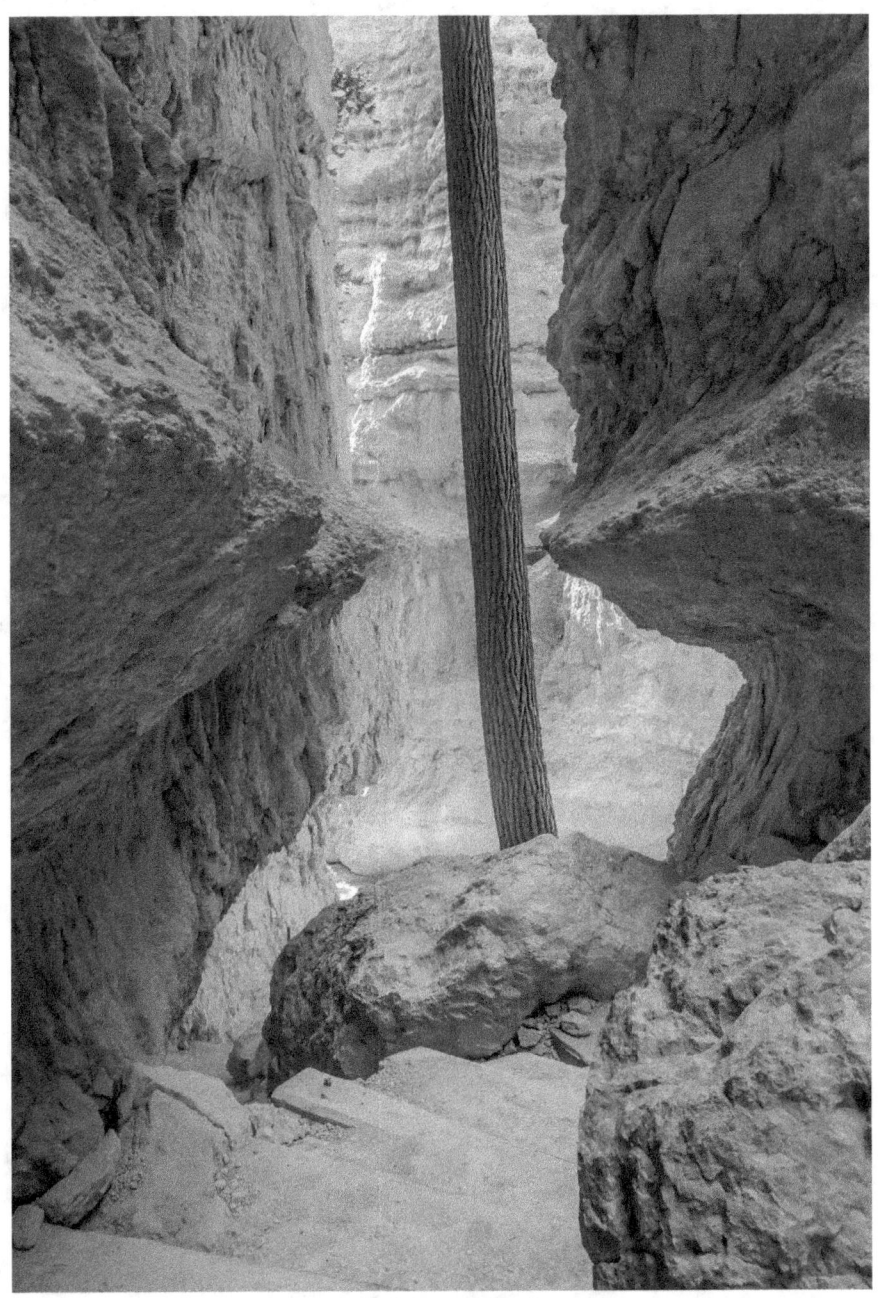

In a golden bowl

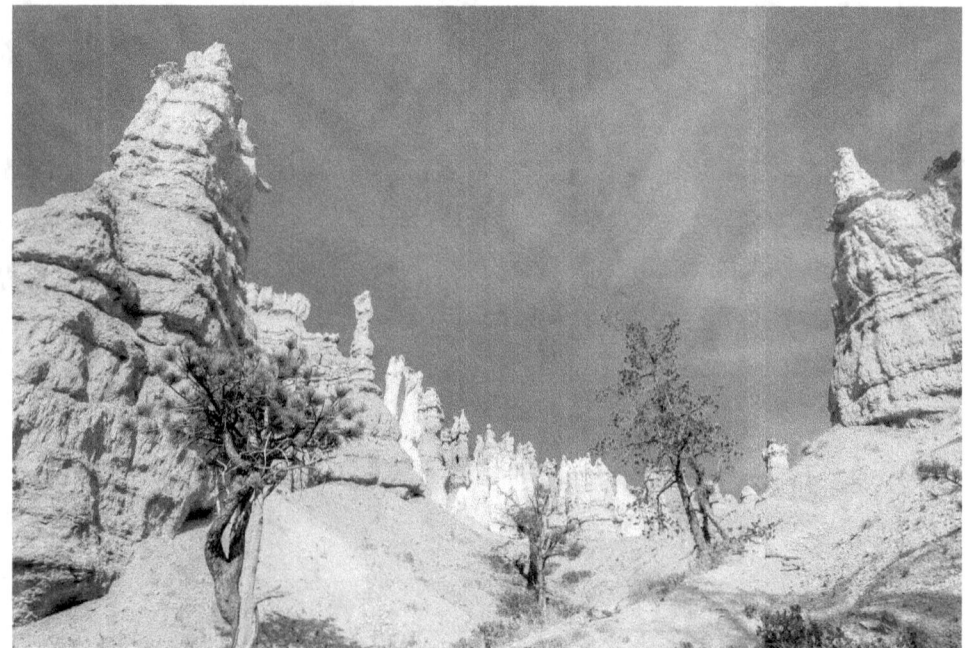

The Queen's Garden. Her majesty on right

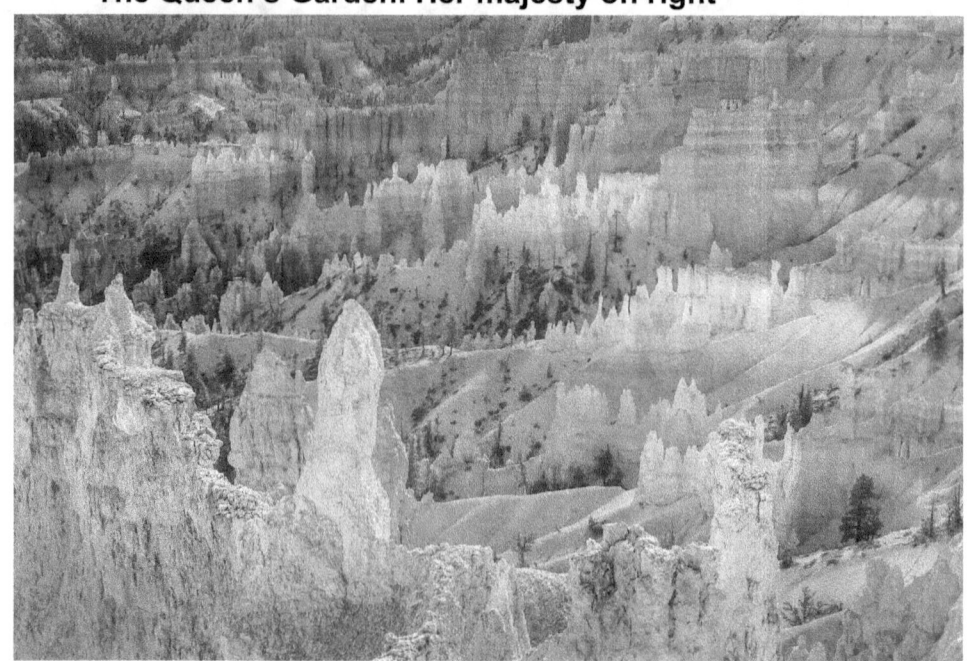

The Claron Formation

Chapter 6

Zion, a place of refuge?

During my morning caffeine infusion, I researched RV camps around Zion National Park. The Zion River Resort was 14 miles west of the Park entrance, near the town of Virgin. Day temperatures were in the 70s. Bryce had been the coldest camp yet. We would lose 4,000 feet of altitude dropping from Bryce's 8,000-foot rim.

Bryce is the pinnacle of the Grand Staircase geologic sequence. The Grand Staircase-Escalante National Monument, reduced by Trump to one million acres, spreads out east and south of Bryce Canyon. After the inaugural Yellowstone camp in 2007, the second gathering of the Geezer group was a trip into the Escalante. The redoubtable Canoe, again, organized the trip with her intense attention to detail, going as far as interviewing a fellow Bozeman resident who published detailed journals of his trips into slot canyons. The original plan was to hike a slot, either Wolverine or Little Death Hollow.

A serious consideration of slot canyons is that they can kill you with a flash flood. Hikers may be under a bright sunny sky, but rain forty miles away can flood downstream canyons. The first warning for hikers is a growing train-like roar that precedes a house-size wall of thick chocolate debris laced with tree trunks and boulders.

On September 14, 2015, at 3:30 pm, a group of seven experienced hikers rappelled the 70-foot drop into Zion's Keyhole Canyon, a short slot canyon with chest-deep wades. That morning they had taken the Zion Adventure Company's canyoneering course. At 2:49 pm Zion rangers texted a flash flood warning for all slot canyons in the park. It's likely the group was out of cell range. In one hour, 0.63 inches of rain fell into Zion Canyon and the flow of the North Fork of the Virgin River rose from 55 cubic feet per second to 2,630 cfs. In the shear-sided narrow canyon, the group never had a chance.

At the Geezer's Calf Creek camp near the town of Escalante, Jay, not a high risk taker, orated upon the risks of slot canyon backpacking. A group paranoia germinated. We discussed alternatives. Canoe was livid. She had worked months organizing the trip. She stood, hands on hips, and let loose at the group, "I didn't think I was hiking with a bunch of pussy-men!" Santa Fe Rick was not on the trip, but after he heard about Canoe's oration, he created a fake newspaper page with the headline, *Pussymen Spotted in Utah Wilderness*.

Paul, a man of calm wisdom, negotiated a truce by suggesting we drive into Boulder and ask the locals where to go. They directed us to Horse Canyon on a tributary of the Escalante River. We packed in, found a great campsite, and day-hiked up the river into slot canyons, making Canoe happy again. I discovered my Teva sandals were horrible for river hiking. With every step in the river, gravel sucked under my feet. Emptying the torturous stones in mid-river, Jay looked at me with a wry smile and said, "Where's your God now, Flanders."

Barb and I headed down Route 12 out of Bryce to Utah 89 to Route 9 to the east entrance of Zion. The Zion-Mount Carmel Tunnel was bored through 1.1 miles of dense limestone. Upon completion in 1930 it was the longest such tunnel in the world. The architects did not foresee that one day vehicles might be higher than 11 feet, 4 inches. A ranger at the entrance gate took our $15 fee that paid for other rangers to stop traffic so we could drive alone through the middle of the tunnel. Huge arched windows, carved through meters of rock, looked down over cross-bedded sandstone cliffs dropping to the green ribbon of the canyon floor.

We lunched and spent several hours at the Zion Canyon Visitor Center. The outdoor information panels were beautifully designed. In the gift shop I bought a grey hoodie with a Zion logo, which has become as dear to me as the little dog with the wind-up tail I had as a child. The view up the canyon was a golden meditation. Fremont Cottonwoods made a formal avenue of shimmering yellow for the Virgin River.

I am plagued by memories. In the 70s, I pulled into Zion for a break during a cross-country drive. I remember a dead end parking lot with picnic tables. There were few vehicles. Now, heading south from the park entrance through the town of Springdale, we saw a miracle mile of tourist restaurants and Airbnbs. Jim Stiles, the crusading editor of the Canyon Country Zephyr, would never move here.

Our space at the Zion River Resort, 14 miles down the highway, was fifty paces from the Virgin River. The camp was clean and landscaped with sycamores rustling in a warm evening breeze. We laid out our riding gear, knowing it would be a cold ride the next morning in a desert dawn. I studied the hiking guides and planned our attack. The last time I came through Zion I had no time to explore. Now I had time, but technically I was still sleeping in my car.

A Mormon settler, Isaac Behunin, named the canyon "Zion" relating to a Bible quote from 2 Samuel 5:7, "Nevertheless David took the stronghold of Zion, which is now the city of David." This quote refers to a hill near the Temple Mount of Jerusalem. The hill had the only water in the area, a spring named Gihon, which means Virgin's Fount. The word Zion also refers to the Temple Mount itself or to the Jewish people as a whole. Behunin probably felt very secure inside the towering canyon walls. The Paiutes believed strong spirits inhabited Zion and refused to enter it at night.

The Zion Canyon Scenic Drive took us through freezing canyon shadows to a parking lot at the end of the road. Riverside Walk meandered beside the Virgin River under the skyscraper red throne of the Temple of Sinawava. The end of the paved trail was the start of the hike into The Narrows. This explained why groups of hikers were wearing wet suits. A group of fit-looking lads hiked towards us. They were ebullient having just finished 16 miles of slot canyon in chest-high water. They were from Alabama and kept calling me "sir". I liked that, but I had the urge to say, "At ease."

Hanging gardens in swaths of green painted the slick canyon walls. Somewhere I had read about Physa zionis, the Zion snail. To survive flash floods, this species evolved into the size of a fingernail, the smallest snail in the world. The snails cluster in riverbanks across from springs coming out of the hanging gardens. Sure enough, I dug into the sand and found one. The Physa need not fear French chefs.

A short backtrack on the Scenic Drive brought us to the parking lot for the Observation Point trailhead. The lot was under construction. Later, that would prove to be a blessing. Greer Chesher, author of the Zion Adventure Guide, had this to say about the hike we were starting: "strenuous, 8 mile round trip, climbs 2,148 feet." She further informed: "…switchbacks through slickrock with precipitous dropoffs, to a slender peninsula overhanging the canyon floor…people have fallen to their deaths from Observation Point." Good to know.

A sign showed a stick figure that looked like a Mummenschanz performer (a Swiss mask theater from the 70s) falling off a cliff. These warnings made me curious. The impatient trail switchbacked immediately, no quarter for this Alamo. The bulk of our elevation gain ascended through the Navajo Formation. Iron oxides have leached out from the white upper half of the sandstone cliffs and colored the lower half buff red. After a mile and a half of grunt hiking, the trail leveled before Echo Canyon. Welcome to Echo Canyon. Welcome to Echo Canyon. Echo Canyon.

The canyon's antechamber, claw-marked layers of white cross-bedded cliff, rose out of bottomless black depths. The trail snaked through shadowed walls painted with moss and black varnish. Lining the trail, maroon and gold oak leaves, like a Renoir, ushered us into the inner sanctum. Pink rock in the canyon floor glowed in a psychedelica of Jurassic foreplay. This was a place of vespers. Here one absorbed the beauty of God without having to find a parking space and sit on a hard-backed pew. I sensed my old friend, euphoria. Swirling rose-colored sandstone formed a gravid canyon belly. A dark canal pointed to a brilliant light. Hold your breath. Time for birth.

We delivered into a white world. Challenging development resumed. On a metal trail sign someone had etched *.2 MI* beside the up arrow. It was a cruel joke. Unrelenting steep cursed a toxic serpent of a trail. A burlesque of rock wall was painted with rainbows, yellow and red. A down-hiker saw our sweat-grimed faces and took pity. "The last mile is flat." If she was a Jew of Zion, that was a mitzvah.

We foot-slapped through the adolescence of our climb. On wobbling legs, I turned a corner and stared at nature's novel of life and death. The wall of the cliff on one side was life. The two-thousand-foot void on the other side was death. Zion was the hewn rock trail, the path of refuge. Barb crouched, hands on knees, "I don't think I can go on. You go."

I croaked out the old parental plug. "We're almost there. Let's just go a little farther." We did. It was twice as far as I had estimated, which means I spoke a half-truth. Red trail dust foreshadowed the end of the steeps. We had made the plateau. Flat trail rejuvenated us.

Past a grandfather oak, we saw it. Here at the end of things was our reward. From this lofty place we looked down at the long valley of our travel. As my cerebral hypoxia recovered, the rock-and-roll superlatives of my thought train squealed to a halt. I resumed normalcy. Taking in the grand vision, all I could think of was a bourbon on the rocks and a hot meal.

My lungs enjoyed the down hike, but my knees presented me with a no-notice resignation letter. The white cliffs of the Navajo glowed yellow in the sunset. Dimming light in Echo Canyon turned to black by the final switchbacks. Our luck, big mercury lights from the parking lot construction painted the trail with a faint glow. I told the construction crew they were doing a great job.

Our stiff bodies straddled Smax' seat. It seemed amazing we could move over the earth without suffering. Approaching the Photon Bus we heard meowing. Big green eyes gazed out the window. Don't worry, Waffles, we're home. Let there be light.

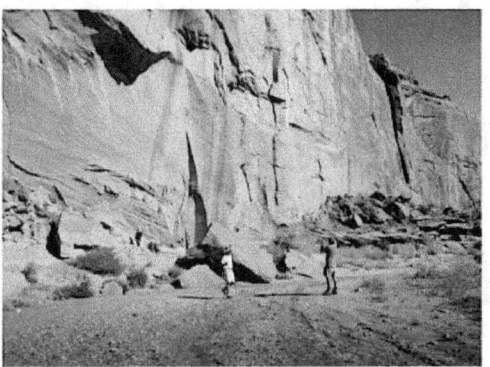

Pussy Men in the Utah Wilds

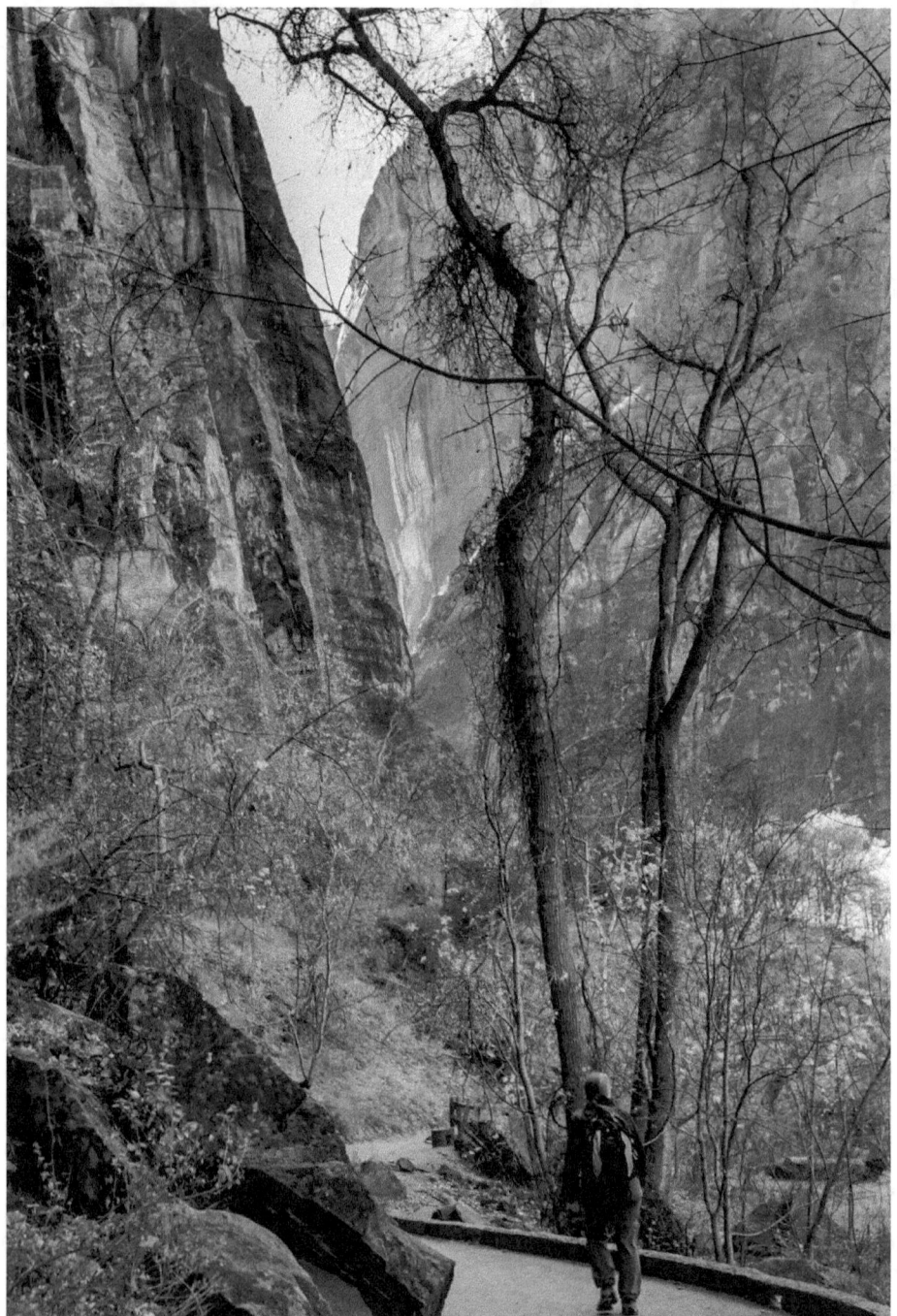

Riverwalk Trail under the Temple of Sinawava

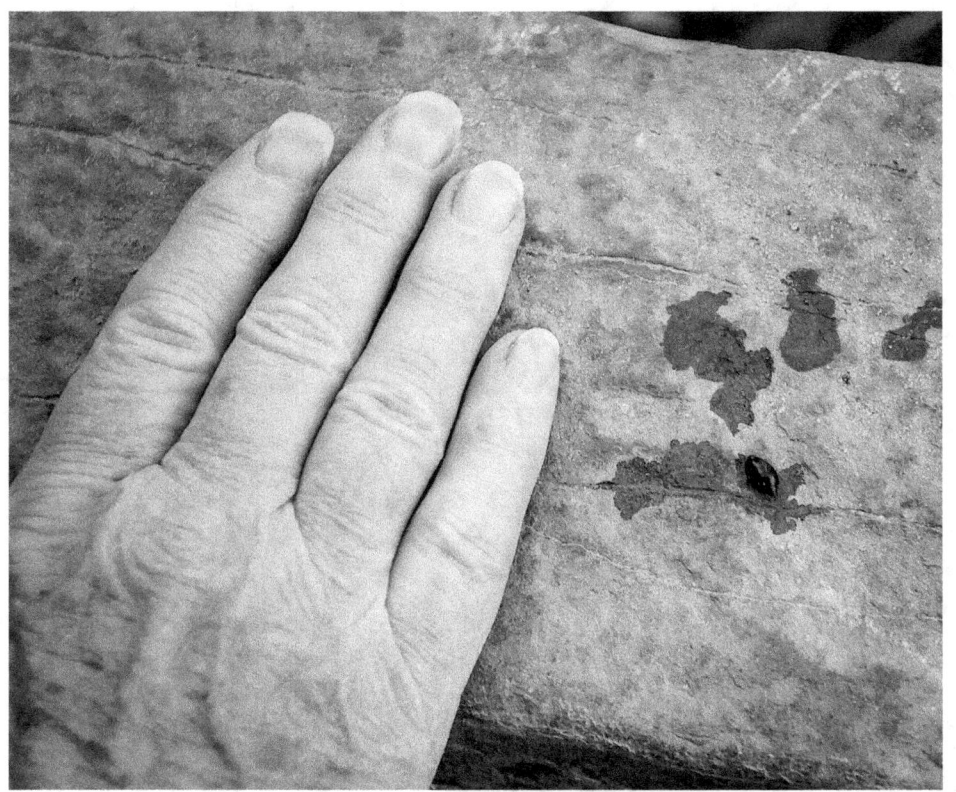

Physa zionis, the world's smallest snail

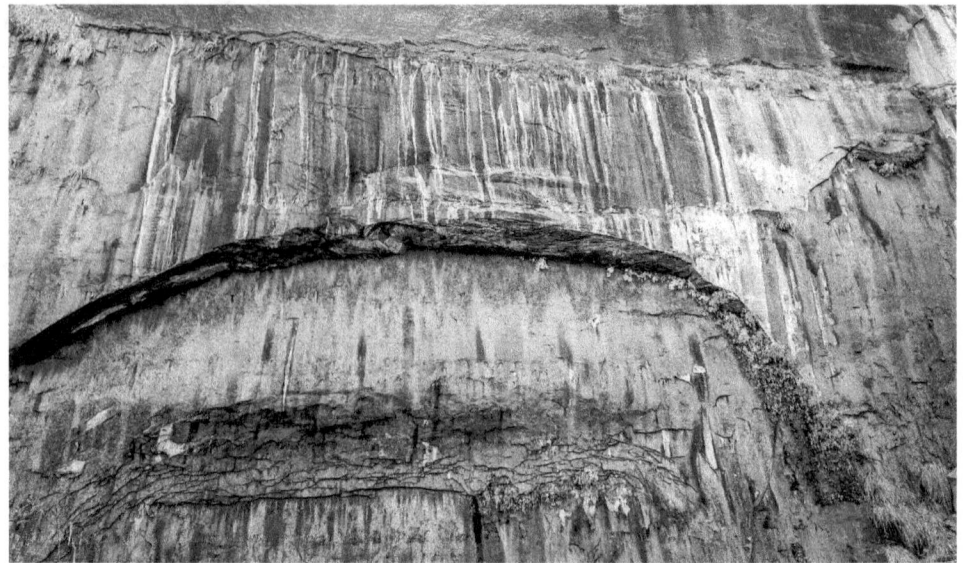
Hanging gardens along the Riverwalk

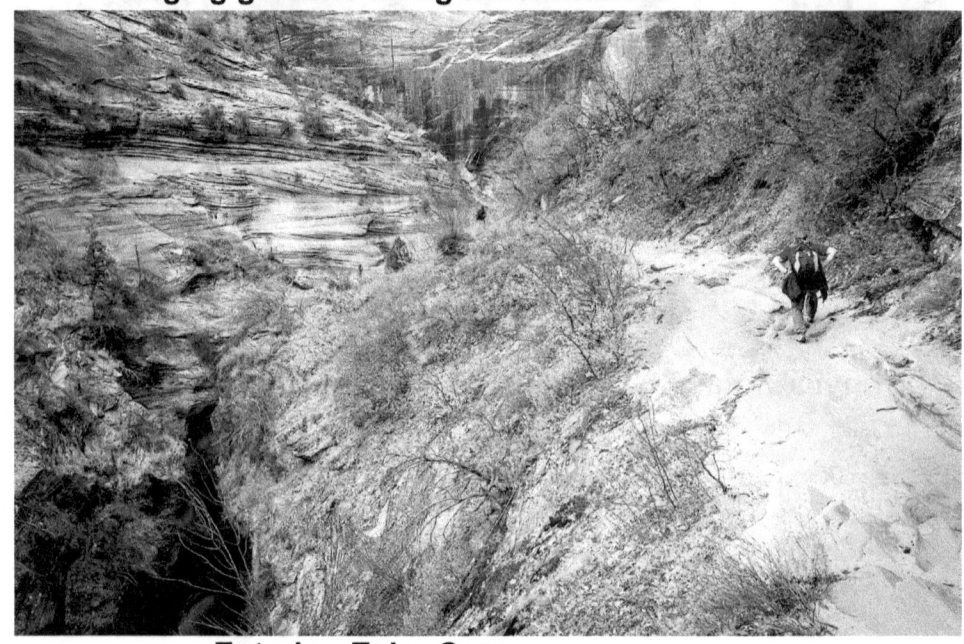
Entering Echo Canyon

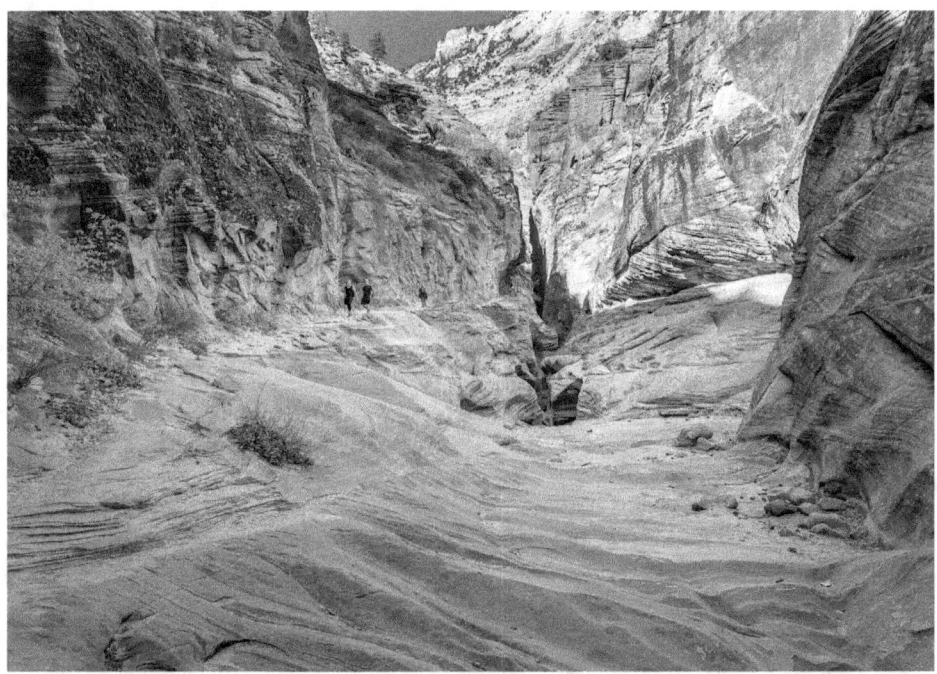

The gravid belly

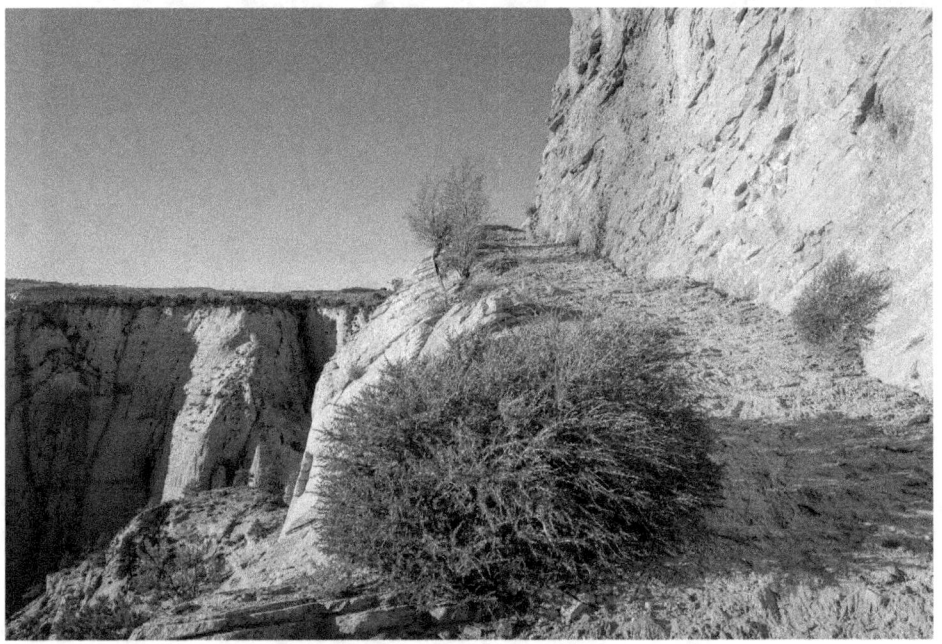

Life and Death. Thy trail be Zion.

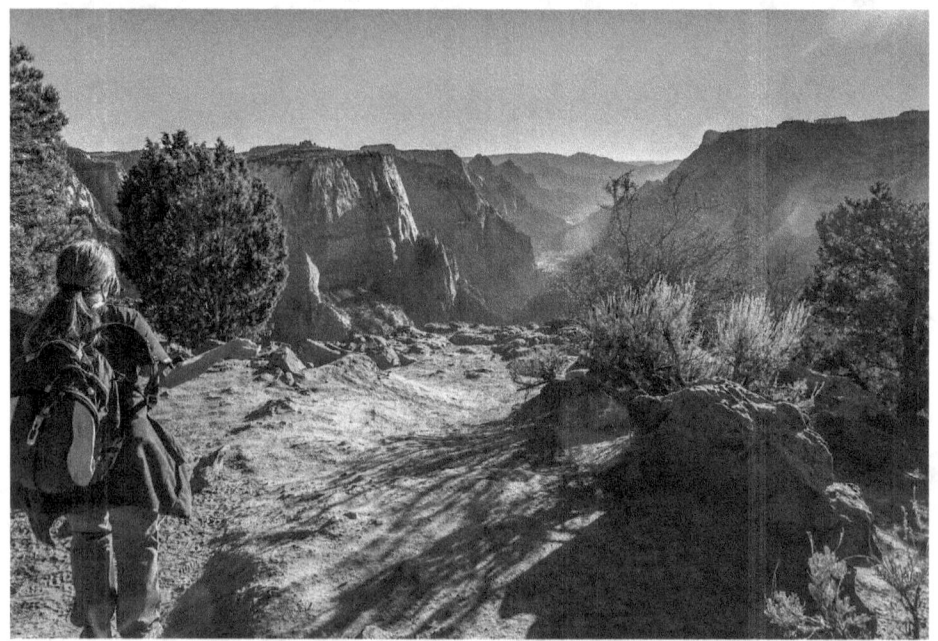

Observation Point. The end of the trail.

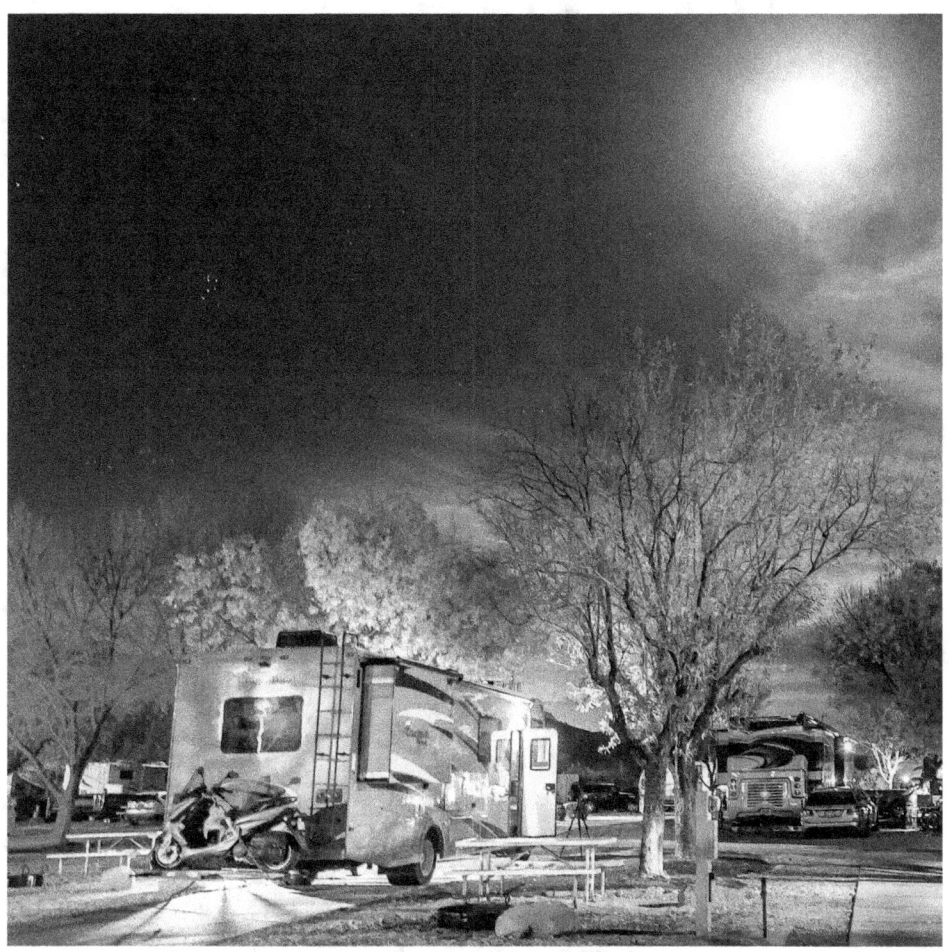

Campsite near the Virgin River

Chapter 7

Where Angel's Land.

Sleep helped. I sensed increased mobility. This day's hiking would avoid the strenuous. After gazing into the void from Observation Point, Barb announced that the Angel's Landing trail was off limits. I didn't argue. I no longer feel at ease on high angle exposures. During my rock climbing days I had become comfortable hanging in the air. Now I'm more comfortable with a 6-iron, or not even that, maybe a sand wedge. On the map, the Emerald Pools hike looked comfortable and we could loop back on the Grotto trail.

Angel's Landing, the most popular hike in Zion, is a rite of passage for all wannabe daredevils. The top of the ascent narrows to a knife edge with a 1,000-foot drop on either side. There is a hand-held safety chain running through steel posts. You must hope the person ahead of you is not sweating hard.

At least seven people have died falling off Angel's Landing since the park opened. In Alex Teufel's article, *5 Most Dangerous Places to Take a Selfie in Zion National Park*, he lists both Observation Point and Angel's Landing. Wait. Hold it. Gimme just one second here. OH SHIT! I didn't read far enough! Teufel writes: "These pools may look like a scene out of Fantasia but more deaths have occurred from falls in the Emerald Pools trail area than Angel's Landing. In fact, more deaths have happened here than any other spot in the park."

I shut my MacBook. "Barb, I think this Emerald Pools hike should be pretty easy. Does that sound good to you? OK, let's get going."

Smax made 70 mph on the downhills of Highway 9. The day before I had noticed a road sign in the town of Rockville pointing toward Grafton, a ghost town where they make movies. George Roy Hill shot the bicycle scene from *Butch Cassidy and the Sundance Kid* there. We had time. The road to Grafton became a rough washboard after a mile. At mile six there was a graveyard. I found my headstone, WOOD. Cedar Pete, a Paiute leader, had the best headstone. Cedar had both a brick gravestone and a metal sign with his name in rivets. He must have been a good leader.

At the cemetery, I noticed my gas gauge said almost empty. We had over half a tank when we left camp. Maybe we would do a different hike today? We continued to Grafton and explored. No one was there. I tried to envision the scenes from *Butch Cassidy*, but without Paul Newman's goofy smile it was hard. Getting on the bike, I saw we now had a half-full tank. The rough ride must have splashed fuel on the sensor float. Of course. Crisis denied.

In Zion, we stopped at the Court of the Patriarchs so Barb could grab a picture for her Bible study group. Zion Lodge blended in with the canyon. There was a massive cottonwood in the center of a huge green lawn. Heading up the Emerald Pools trail, I kept a wary eye for potential death spots. No need to disturb Barb. The first pool was a weeping overhang that gave you a little shower as you hiked under. The second pool was higher. It didn't seem precarious. At the third pool, I had seen no dangerous trail sections. I shot a pano.

A man appeared with three, maybe four, cameras hanging from his shoulders. He looked like a pro. He reeled off some of his publications. I told him my theory about lower light sensitivity with higher megapixel sensors. He said, "That's an interesting discussion." I fished for a reaction with the story of my serendipitous UFO shot at Rhyolite. His girlfriend gave me a knowing smile. The UFO subculture is strong in America.

We hiked the Kayenta Trail above the river. A valley of skeletal winter cottonwoods crowded the riverbanks. Construction nixed our planned return on the Grotto Trail. They were laying water pipe from a spring. We walked the road back to Zion Lodge. There were other hikes we could have done, but we didn't. I felt the urge to hit the road. Antelope Canyon, another photographer's shrine, was in Page, a comfortable day's drive south. The weather in Utah had been perfect, but that could change. The best route south after Page went through Flagstaff, elevation 6,910 feet. Often, Flag had snow by late December, but this year it was still dry.

We rode Smax through the south entrance one last time, ran the amenities gauntlet of Springdale, and enjoyed gliding through the curves along the maroon cliffs of the Chinle Beds. At camp, we secured Smax on his ramp with our overdone system of ratchet ties. Tomorrow south. We would pass through Colorado City, home of the Fundamentalist Church of the LDS, former kingdom of polygamist Warren S. Jeffs, now in prison for child sexual assault. I wanted to see the place.

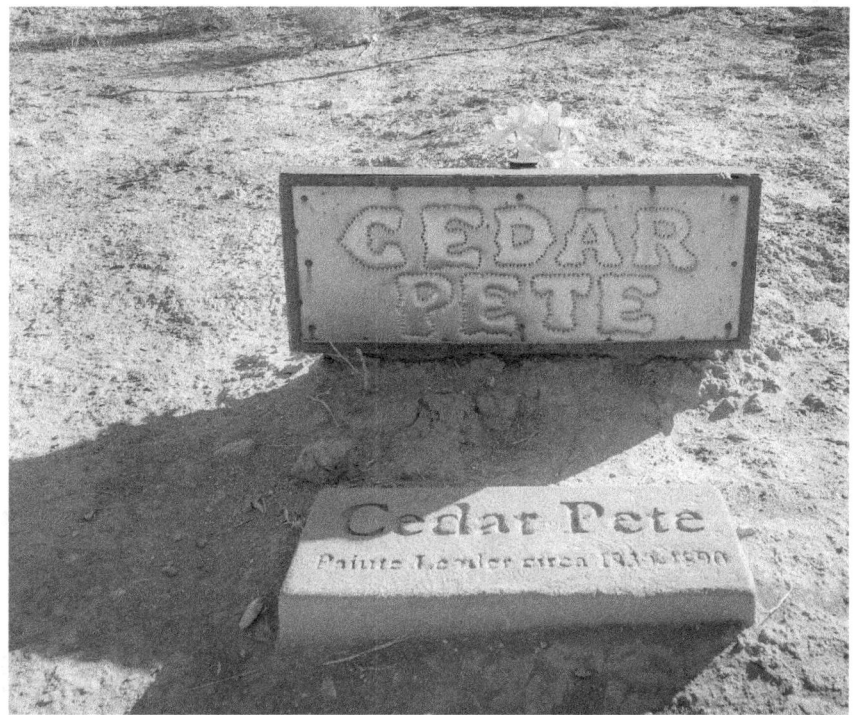
Cedar Pete, Paiute Leader

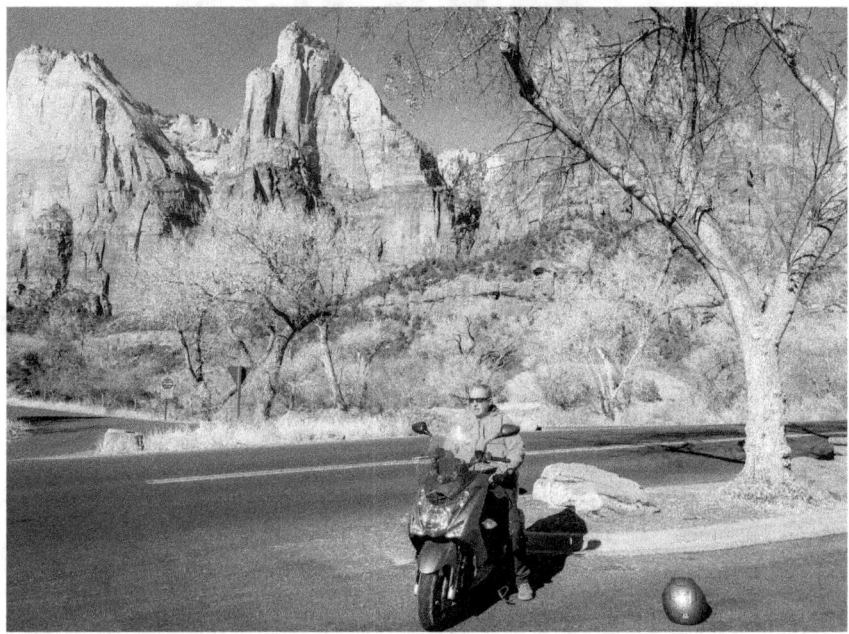
Trusty Smax at the Court of the Patriarchs

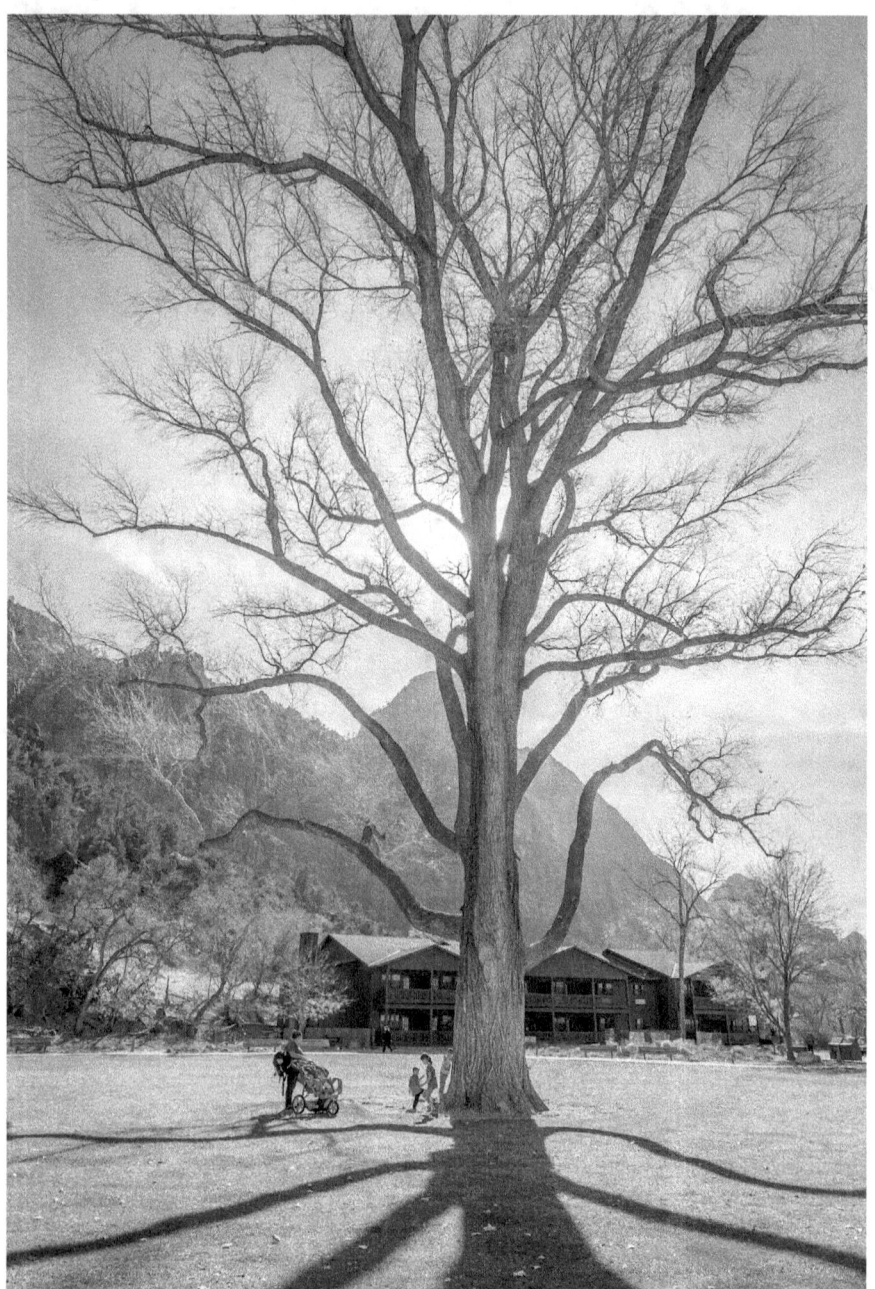

Fremont Cottonwood at Zion Lodge

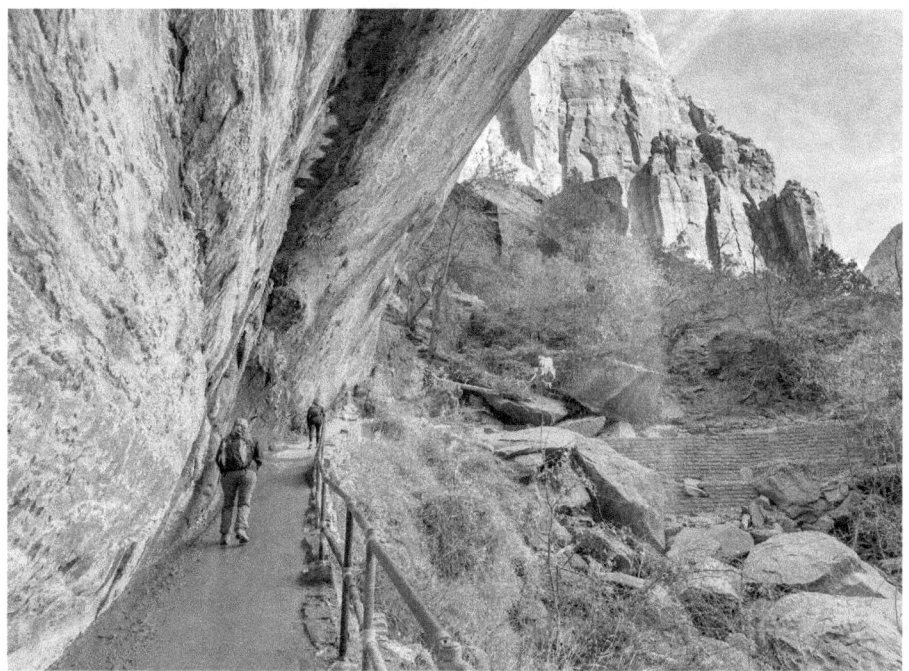

Emerald Pools Trail

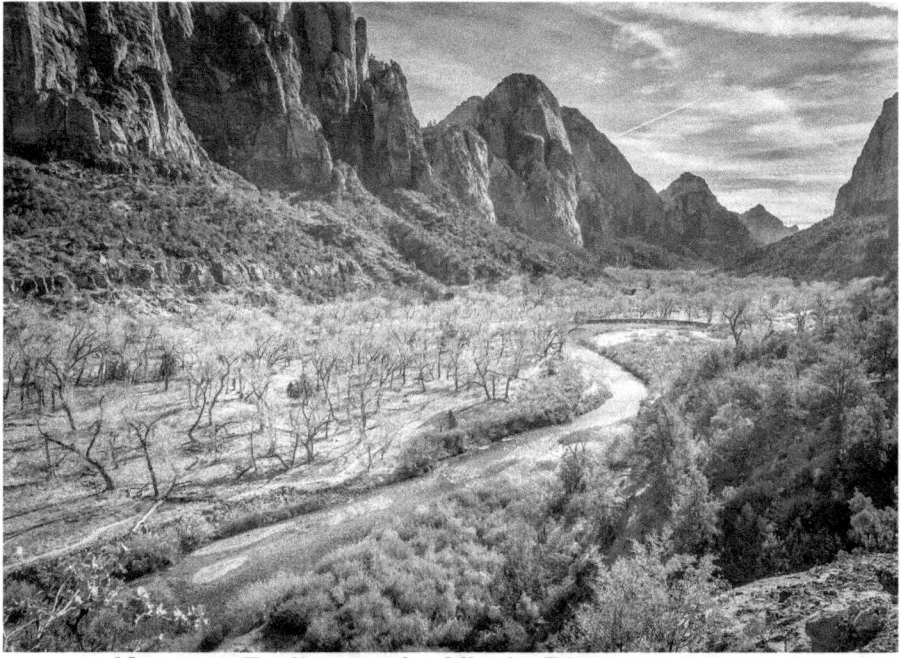

Kayenta Trail over the Virgin River

Chapter 8

Smokey's Revenge

We got an early start and blew through the town of Hurricane, heading south on Utah 59. Just below the Arizona border lay Colorado City, site of Short Creek, the commune of Fundamentalist Church of Jesus Christ Latter-Day Saints' (FLDS) leader Warren Jeffs. The town was quiet. Jeffs is serving a life sentence in Texas for child molestation. He must have ignored those "Don't Mess With Texas" signs.

In 2007, Elissa Wall, the victim of an arranged marriage at age 14, sued the UEP. The United Effort Plan trust holds the land properties of the FLDS, worth $100 million. The court awarded Wall $2.75 million. Another suit brought by boys and men, the "Lost Boys," ousted from the community after displeasing Jeffs, settled for 21.5 acres of property and $250,000 in an educational trust. A woman forced to have ritualistic sex as an 8-year-old filed suit. It looked like such a peaceful town.

We moved on to Fredonia and turned toward Jacob Lake on State Highway 89A. The road climbed out of the basin to the Le Fevre Overlook, elevation 6,700 feet. From the Overlook you can see the entire geologic parfait of the Grand Staircase: Chocolate Cliffs, Vermillion Cliffs, White Cliffs, Grey Cliffs and the Pink Cliffs of Bryce Canyon. Yum.

A few miles later, before Jacob Lake, we hit smoke. We drove through a smoldering pine forest, a prescribed burn. One thing we didn't see was any of those old Smokey-the-Bear signs. "Remember! Only you can prevent forest fires." Smokey might have been a little confused about a prescribed burn. If he had come charging out of the woods with his shovel, workers would have had to run him off or shoot him.

In 1942, Japanese bombers dropped incendiary bombs over southwest Oregon, but failed to start a forest fire. In 1944, they launched 9,000 fire balloons over the U.S. coast, killing a teacher and five school children in Bly, Oregon. During World War II, the U.S. Forest Service had a skeletal staff since most young men were off fighting the war. Before the war, throngs of hard-working men and women had serviced national forests and public lands in the CCC, the WPA and the nascent Forest Service. Artist Albert Staehle created Smokey the Bear in 1944 as an ad campaign to educate the public about preventing forest fires, a strategy designed by the Forest Service since there were few firefighters available.

After saving the world from fascist empires, Americans were tired of fighting and dying and wanted to do other activities. One of those activities increased the population and fertilized the era of the great American suburb. Suburbs need houses. Houses need trees. The timber harvesting industry heard the call and responded with their own call, the ripping squeal of thousands of chainsaws.

In the post-war baby boom years, forest fire prevention was a no-brainer. We needed forests to provide "fiber" for houses and products like paper so our fifth-grade teachers could give us those ridiculous math tests. A new cultural phenomenon, the family vacation, brought people out of the suburbs into areas of natural beauty: the mountains, the beaches, the rivers, the lakes, the deserts. Other than a few sociopaths, no one thought it would be a good idea to burn any of these scenic getaways. If some nutcase ever started a fire, Lassie would smell it and go get Timmy, who's dad happened to be a forest ranger. The motto of the Forest Service was "all fires out by 10:00 am." Fire Lookouts sprang up like spring flowers, staffed by seasonal rangers like Ed Abbey and *Grizzly Years*-author Doug Peacock.

Beyond the economic argument of absolute fire suppression, the horror of uncontrolled historic fires loomed large in the public mind. The deadliest fire in U.S. history, the 1871 Peshtigo Fire in Wisconsin, killed 1,500 people. The Great Montana Fire of 1910 burned three million acres. Yet some in the early years of the Forest Service realized the natural role of fire in forest ecology. Aldo Leopold, who unveiled his Land Ethic in *Sand County Almanac*, championed prescribed burning. Our native forests and rangelands evolved with frequent, low-to-moderate intensity burns, most caused by lightning. Native tribes learned that prairie fires rejuvenated grazing for buffalo. Fire clears out deadfall, the fuel that acts as a ladder for lethal crown fires. Many species need fire for reproduction. Fires help control diseases and, in the right conditions, can ward off invasive exotic species.

The 1964 Wilderness Act allowed fires in designated wilderness to burn as long as structures or people were not at risk. The National Park Service adopted a similar policy. Firefighters fighting the 1988 Yellowstone fire allowed remote areas to burn while protecting towns and structures. Moist fall weather doused the backcountry fires naturally. Forest biologists found multiple benefits from the clearing of overgrown stands of lodgepole pine.

Is it too late? The size of wildfires in acres burned, intensity, cost of suppression and damage-related monetary losses began increasing in the 1980s. Average yearly acres burned rose from 2 million in 1986 to 8 million in 2015. The cost of suppression (firefighting) was $203 million in 1986, tenfold lower than the $2.1 billion spent in 2015. Last year, 2017, fire-battling costs set a record of almost $3 billion. The causes of the acceleration are multifactorial as the saying goes. Deadfall has accumulated on the forest floors through the years of intense fire suppression. Cut and run forest harvesting practices have increased fire susceptibility. Climate change is warming the atmosphere, which then holds on to water vapor, drying and killing the understory vegetation.

More people live in and around forests, increasing the urban-wildland interface.

In recent years, the Forest Service and the National Park Service have bankrupted their budgets from the expense of firefighting. The 2018 Omnibus Spending Package, signed by President Trump with entertaining derogatory comments, tries to fix the problem. The fire suppression account will have $1.011 billion yearly. Beginning in 2020, the USDA (Agriculture and Forest Service) and the Department of Interior will have a new annual budget authority of $2.25 billion. If spending goes above these levels in fire season, the departments will have to ask Mom and Dad, Congress, for some extra movie money.

The cost of fire suppression is only a minor pie slice of the true cost of wildfires: add in timber and agricultural loss, structure and infrastructure loss, injury and health impacts, deaths, disaster assistance, fuels management, insurance, community economic impact, legal costs, research and development, evacuation costs and psychological impacts. The cost of other fire effects such as loss of biodiversity and degradation of water quality can't easily be estimated. In the state of California, the actual cost of the 2017 fire season was estimated at $180 billion. As a comparison, the cost of the BP Deepwater Horizon spill cleanup was $65 billion. If we could prevent all wildfires in California, we could afford three more major oil spills.

Call me paranoid, I believe I am pursued by fire. Last summer we drove the Photon Bus up to Canada intending to drive all the way to Alaska. We pulled into a camp outside Jasper at the northern end of the Canadian Rockies on a beautiful July day. Through crystal-blue air I could see the Jasper Sky Tram silhouetted above Whistler Mountain. We made plans to ride it.

The next morning, what I thought was early fog turned into obvious smoke. By noon the entire valley was in a thick haze. There were 206 wildfires in British Columbia (BC). The highway south of St. George was closed. We hiked up the Old Fort Loop Trail and enjoyed a shrouded vista of the Athabaska River. By the end of summer, three million acres had burned in BC and 45,000 people were evacuated. We had entered Canada through the Okanagan Valley. Across the valley from our camp in Washington State, we saw the blackened stumps of the 2015 Okanagan Complex Fire, at 302,224 acres the largest in state history.

We changed plans in Jasper and travelled south through Alberta, Montana and Idaho. When we got back to Portland, the south-drifting smoke from the BC fires welcomed us. Portland was campfire-scented all summer from fires in central Oregon and the nearby Columbia Gorge fire. We went to a camp outside Madras with Barb's Boy Scout Crew to witness the solar eclipse. Smoke drifted in on alternate days, but stayed out on the morning of the eclipse.

Looking over a random list of sixteen wilderness areas I camped in over recent years, I found seventeen major fires had visited these same areas. I explored Yellowstone for the first time in 1983. The park-wide fires followed in 1988. Mount Lemmon, north of Tucson, lost 84,750 acres to the Aspen Fire in 2003 and, last summer, the Burro Fire burned the east side of the mountain. In 2011, the Geezers had a great camp in the Chiricauhua Mountains of southeastern Arizona. We stayed at the Herb Martyr Campground. A week after we left, the Horseshoe II fire burned that campground plus 222,954 acres. The Frye Fire of 2017 consumed my hundred-mile-view campsite in the Pinaleno Mountains. Our favorite backpack in the old days was the Gila Mountains, the first designated wilderness area in America. The 2012 Whitewater Baldy Fire took 297,845 acres surrounding the summit of the Gilas. Last autumn we hiked through burnt stands of the record-breaking Wallow Fire of 2011 in the White Mountains of Arizona.

I can't even escape out of the country. Our family did a month-long tour of Greece in 2006. Huge fires broke out throughout the Peloponnese in 2007, killing 84 people. Olympia, the World Heritage Site of the original Olympics, almost succumbed to a modern Olympic torch. Barb and I would learn more about wildfire in Prescott, AZ.

We pulled over at an overlook overlooking the Vermillion Cliffs. An old Mormon wagon trail route, the Honeymoon Trail, ran below the cliffs. A train-like wind almost blew us off the hill. We crossed Lee's Ferry, the starting point for all Grand Canyon raft trips and former home of executed Meadows Massacre participant, John D. Lee. The highway climbed up the mesa above Marble Canyon. We bought jewelry from an informative Navajo woman at the roadside. Just before Page, we hiked to Horseshoe Bend, another photographer's altar. Some people will slide on their bellies to shoot over the precipitous cliff edge, otherwise you can't get the entire horseshoe of the Colorado River in your lens. I didn't. My old romance with death falls had run its course.

Before checking in at our camp in Page, we drove out to Antelope Canyon. It was too late in the day for a tour. We made plans for the next morning. It had been a pleasant day of travel. Time for a nice meal and a movie.

Photographing the American West

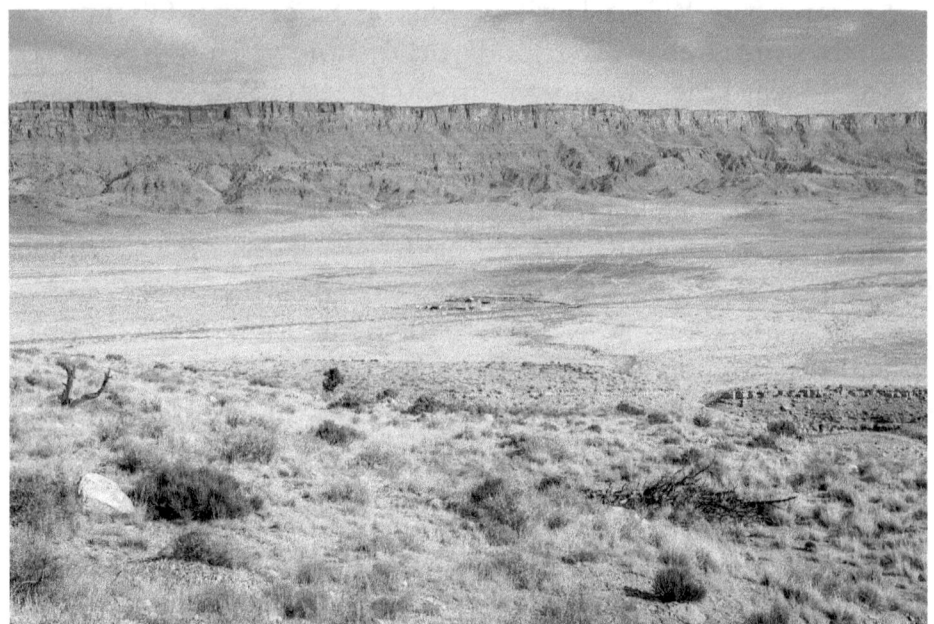
Vermillion Cliffs

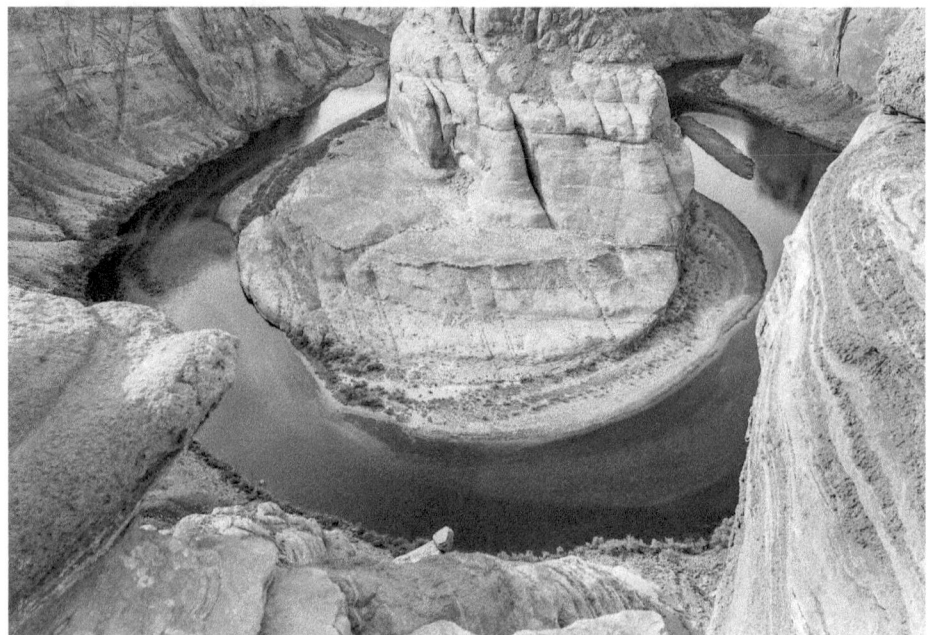
Horseshoe Bend, Colorado River

Chapter 9

Gold Light, Gold Water.

All landscape photography buffs know about Antelope Canyon. If you watch TV or read magazines you have seen the money shot from Antelope: a shaft of sunlight knifing into a narrow pink-orange chamber of chaotic free-form swirls wrought from the wheel of a drunken ceramist. Those sunlight shafts are not just yellow, they are gold. Images of Antelope are not only valuable for the advertising industry, they can be a photonic lottery ticket for commercial photographers. Peter Lik, an Australian fine arts photographer, captured the most expensive photograph in the world in Upper Antelope Canyon. "Phantom," a black-and-white shot of a sunbeam shaft filled with dust that looks like a human form, sold for $6.5 million. The anonymous buyer, a Los Angeles resident, also bought two other Lik photos for $2.4 million and $1.1 million. Who is this guy? I don't mean Lik, I mean the Los Angeles buyer. I've got some photos I'd like to show him or her.

There are three photographer honey traps in the area: Upper Antelope Canyon, *Tse bighanilini*, where sun shafts beam through in the summer months, Lower Antelope Canyon, *Hazdistazi*, and Canyon X. Lower Antelope is more V-shaped with a narrow bottom. The Navajo owners require guides. You can purchase a walking tour or a photographic tour where you can bring a tripod. Trapped in the brain of a cheapskate, I chose the $35 walking tour of Lower Antelope. Instead of a tripod, I cranked my ISO to 400.

We lucked out with our guide. Donny Scott was not only knowledgeable about the Canyon, but was willing to continue a long discussion with us after the tour about Navajo history and issues. Thank you, Donny, and yes, I gave you an outstanding recommendation on the website.

When we met Donny, I cavalierly asked him if his name was Yazzie or Begay, the two most common Navajo family names. He explained that his grandfather had been a WWII code talker. At a field hospital, the nurse could not figure out how to spell the grandfather's Navajo name, so she used hers, Scott, on the admission form. The grandfather kept the name and now there is a large Scott family in the Navajo Nation. John Scott appears on the official list of Navajo Code Talkers.

There are several tribes that acted as code talkers in both WWI and WWII. Neither the Germans nor the Japanese could decipher the strange Athabaskan phonetics. At the time of WWII there were no publications in Navajo and only thirty non-Natives knew the language. It was the perfect, unbreakable code. An original group of twenty-nine Navajo men enlisted in the Marine Corps and developed code words like buzzard, *jeeshoo*, to refer to a bomber, or iron fish, *beesh loo*, for a submarine. Four hundred code talkers fought in the Pacific Theater. They were a key factor in the victory at Iwo Jima.

In 2000, President Clinton honored the original twenty-nine with belated Congressional Gold Medals and gave another three hundred Silver Medals. The last of the twenty-nine, Chester Nez, died in 2014 at age 93. President Trump met with three surviving code talkers in 2017 to pay tribute in the Oval Office. The respected Navajo leader Peter MacDonald was present. Trump took advantage of the photo-op to slur Massachusetts Senator Elizabeth Warren as a "Pocahontas," referring to her claim to have Native bloodlines. The National Congress of American Indians voiced disgust at Trump using the name of a beloved, historical Native

American as a derogatory term. "Too bad Trump put his foot in his mouth. He needs to grow up."

The narrow crack-in-the-earth of Lower Antelope Canyon is invisible until you get within a few yards. In Navajo mythology, the earthbound people, the Dine, ascended through three underground worlds of "holy people" before emerging into the fourth world, the "glittering world." We followed Donny down a steep metal staircase into the dark. Before the installation of fixed metal stairs, eleven tourists died in the depths from a flash flood in 1997.

The Navajo Generating Station looms on the eastern horizon above Lower Antelope like an invasive species. Three tumescent flu stacks stare menacingly at the vulnerable earth gash of the canyon. Donny told me the history of the NGS, including the sad tale of forced displacement of Navajos from their family homes on Black Mesa to make way for the coal mines. The reason the NGS exists requires a look at history.

Water may look like water, but to settlers, farmers, land developers and politicians in the arid west, water looks like gold. The oft-quoted phrase from Marc Reisner's *Cadillac Desert* is, "Water runs uphill toward money." As more citizens moved west in the early 20th century, the four states in the Colorado River Upper Basin and the three states in the Lower Basin all wanted their maximal share of river water. The Colorado River Compact of 1922 allocated 7.5 million acre feet to each of the two basins and flipped Mexico a shoeshine tip of 1.5 million acre feet. Arizona deferred ratification until 1944 because of fear it did not have enough population to use its share of water and would therefore lose "prior use" legal standing to California. California has always treated Arizona like a poor out-of-town relation.

River inflow from snow packs in the Rockies is highly variable from one season to the next. Only dams and reservoirs can modulate water delivery through wet and dry years and control disastrous flooding in the lower river.

Hoover Dam was the first big one. The Bureau of Reclamation, BuRec, next had its eye on Echo Park on the Green River in northern Utah, an area described by Major John Wesley Powell with a burning reverence. This reservoir would have flooded Dinosaur National Monument. David Brower and the Sierra Club, having lost the fight to prevent the Hetch Hetchy dam in Yosemite, invoked the ghost of John Muir to fight for Echo Canyon. BuRec agreed to drop Echo as long as the Sierra Club agreed not to oppose the Glen Canyon site in northern Arizona. Back then, no one seemed to know much about Glen Canyon. After construction of the dam had begun, wilderness devotees and influential nature writers floated through Glen Canyon and sang its praises, causing Brower to become heartsick at his Sophie's choice.

In the meantime, Arizona Senators McFarland and Hayden came up with the Central Arizona Project, CAP, a 336-mile canal that would deliver lower basin water to Phoenix and Tucson. There was not enough power from the Glen Canyon Dam alone to move the water uphill. BuRec proposed two dams inside the Grand Canyon. Brower, still smarting from Glen Canyon, called for an intensive campaign to save the Grand Canyon with full-page ads in the New York Times and a coffee-table book of majestic photography. The American public got on board, forcing BuRec to abandon plans for any in-canyon dams. The Navajo Generating Station was built to replace the power from the lost Grand Canyon dams.

Coal has such a dirty image. It's the Bernie Madoff of minerals. It's a pretty stone, shiny-to-dull jet black into whose luring depths you can see either the future or the past depending on your political persuasion. I found a seam by the Crowsnest River in Alberta when I was fishing and brought a piece to my son. I said, "I got you something, a lump of coal."

He said, "Cool!"

Coal-fired generating plants are on the way out. Gas-fired plants produce cleaner and cheaper energy. One reason gas energy is cheaper is that it doesn't require as expensive cleaning equipment, scrubbers and precipitators, to meet Clean Air Act standards. The NGS has struggled to meet ever more stringent environmental standards.

Bechtel Corporation built the NGS in 1976 at a cost of $650 million. In 1990, amendments to the Clean Air Act for protecting visibility in national parks led to studies such as the Winter Haze Intensive Tracer Experiment, which concluded NGS needed to lower SO_2 emissions by 70%. The scrubbers cost $420 million, requiring three new large-diameter 775-foot flue stacks. In 2005 the electrostatic precipitators were upgraded. In 2007 the plant installed Low NOx burners. The breaking-bad last straw was new Mercury and Air Toxic Standards, MATS, from the EPA that would require Selective Catalytic Reduction equipment at a price tag of $1.1 billion. There is no way the plant can maintain profitability. I'm strongly in favor of greenhouse gas reduction, but I can't help but feel a little sorry for the NGS, which is one of the cleanest of the coal-fired plants in the U.S.

NGS will cease operation in 2019. The Los Angeles Department of Water and Power, a 21% owner, and Nevada Energy, left the project since they can buy cheaper power from gas plants. The biggest loser is the Navajo Nation, who will see 1,600 living-wage jobs disappear from the reservation and will lose substantial lease monies. To quote Donny Scott, "The government always does what it wants."

The hour spent in the exotic underworld of Lower Antelope Canyon was a dream I didn't want to end. Donny, a guide well above federal standards, showed us the high points, the shadow that looked like a cat and the protruding slab that looked like a shark. I had never been in a slot canyon that looked like this. Barb pronounced the tour "excellent."

We drove around Page. Like a Twilight Zone episode, Page sprang from the soil to house workers during the construction of Glen Canyon Dam. Now, it services the houseboat culture on Lake Powell. Back at camp, I was excited to develop my pictures. A cold wind moved in that night. WeatherBug showed Flagstaff to be snow-free. We had an open road to our next destination, Sedona.

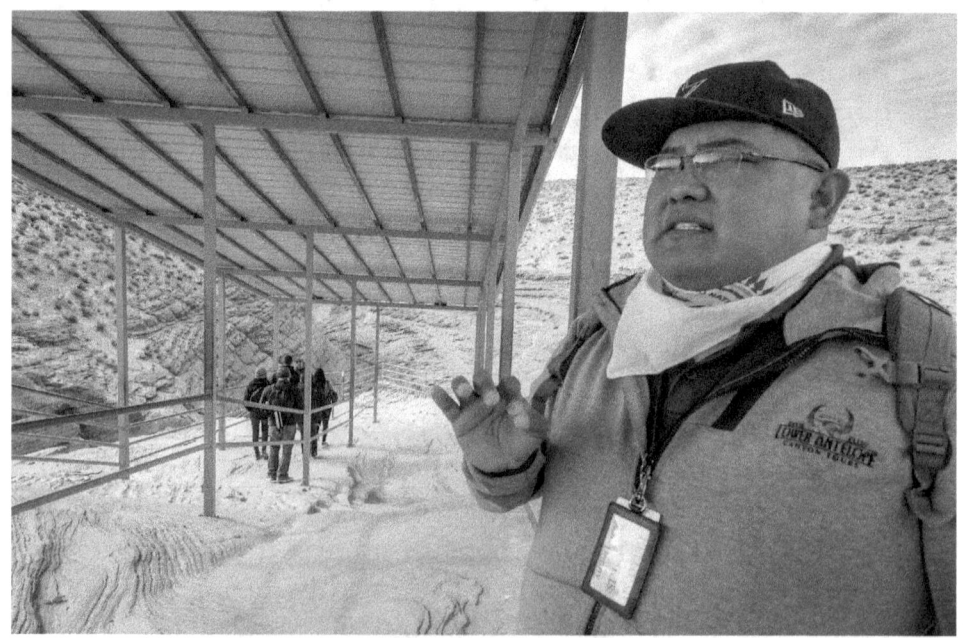

Donny Scott, excellent guide

William J Wood Jr

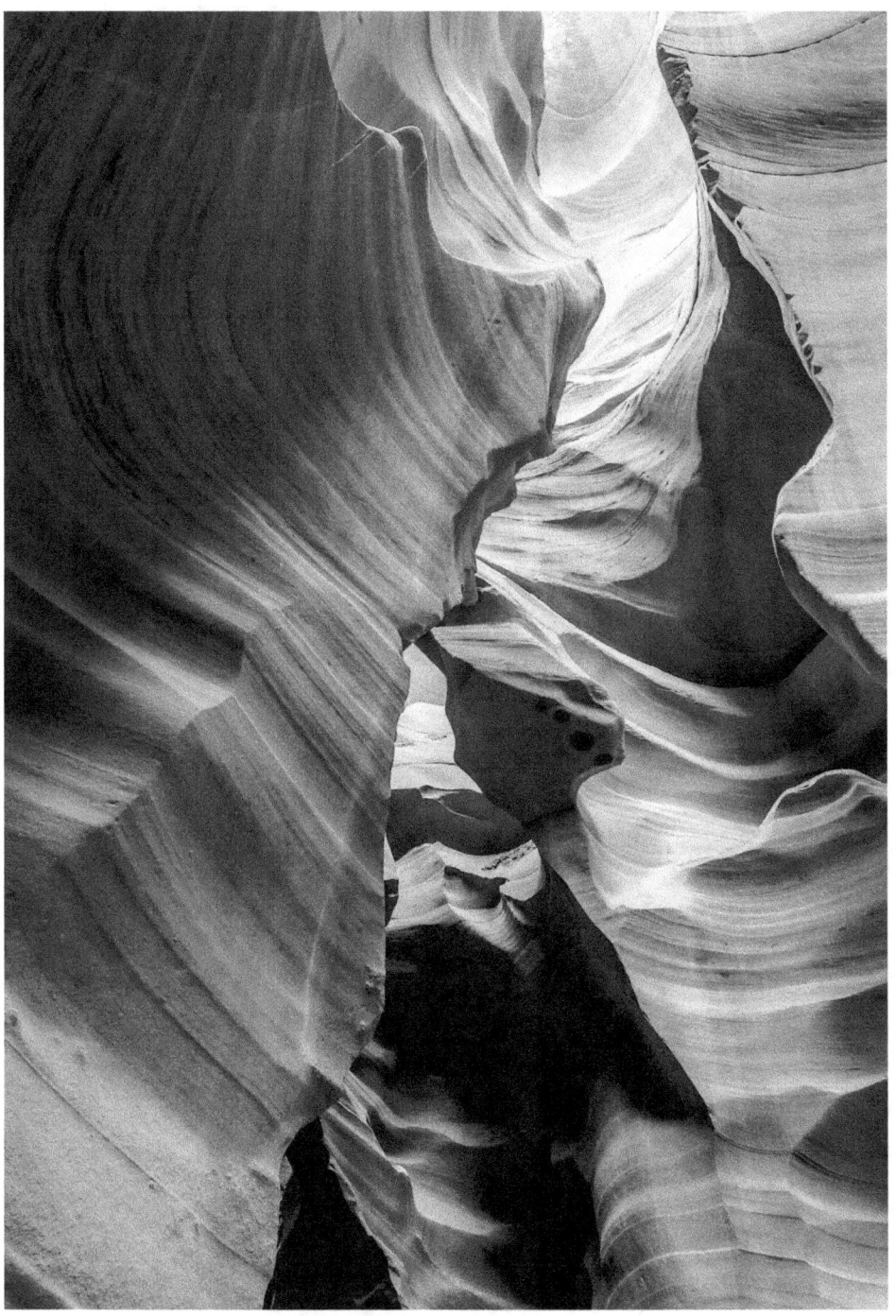

Lower Antelope Canyon

Photographing the American West

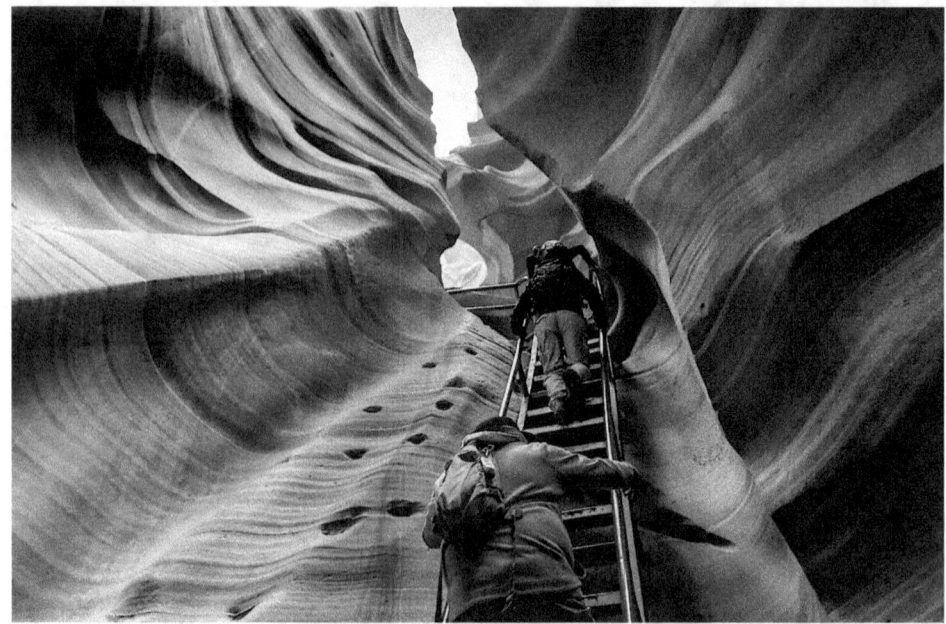
Handy stairway

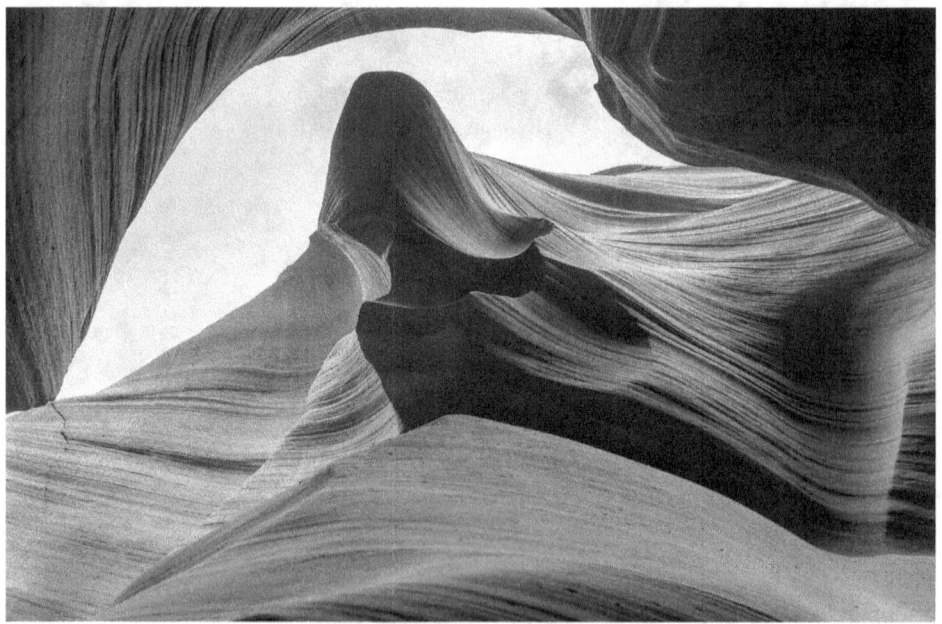
The Shark

William J Wood Jr

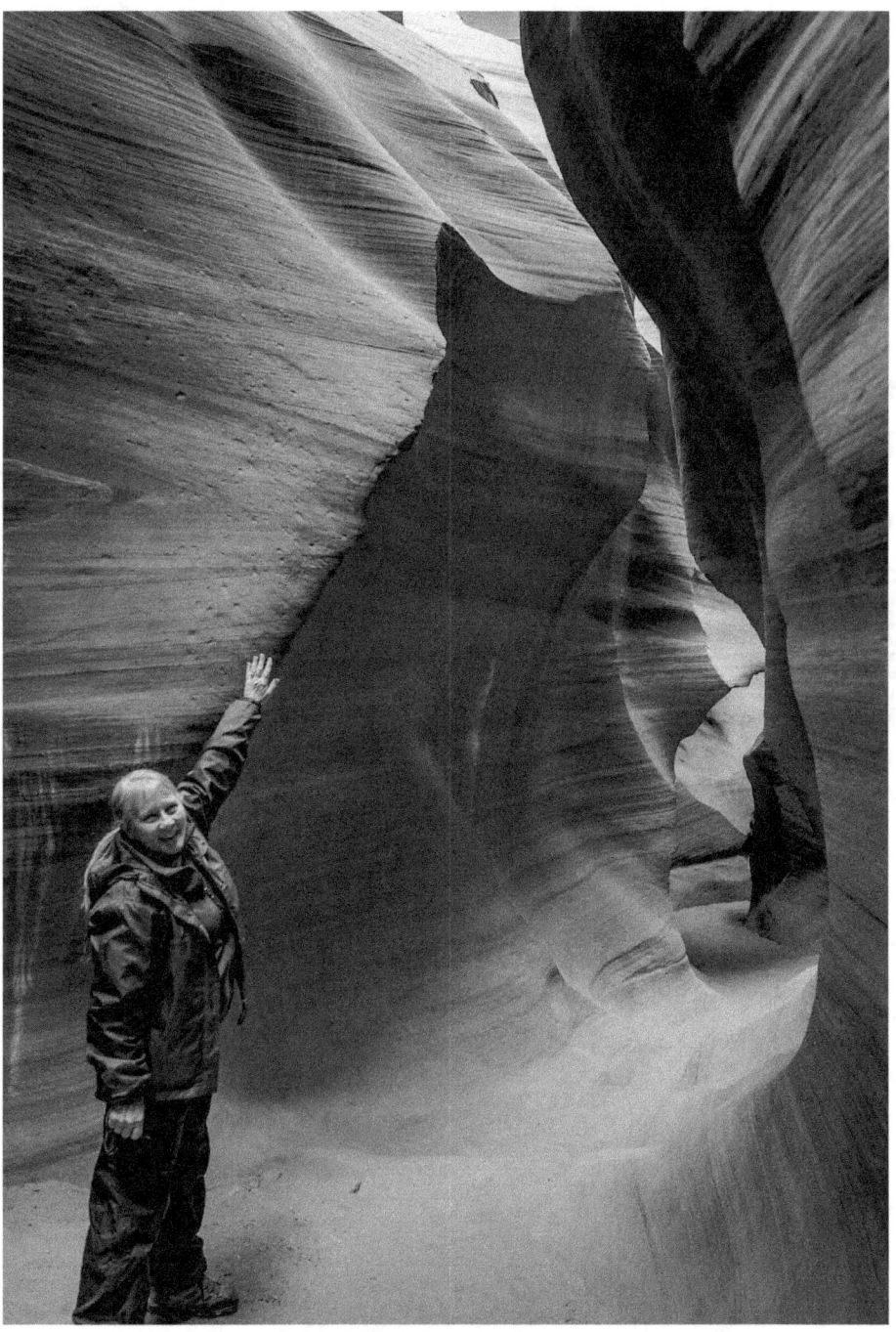

The Cat

Photographing the American West

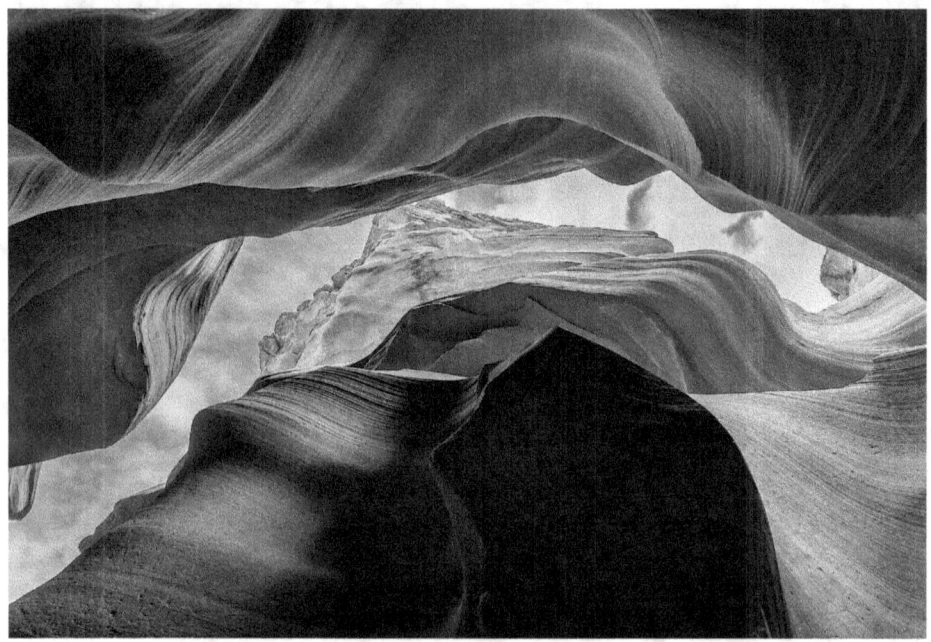

Asking price, $3.2 million

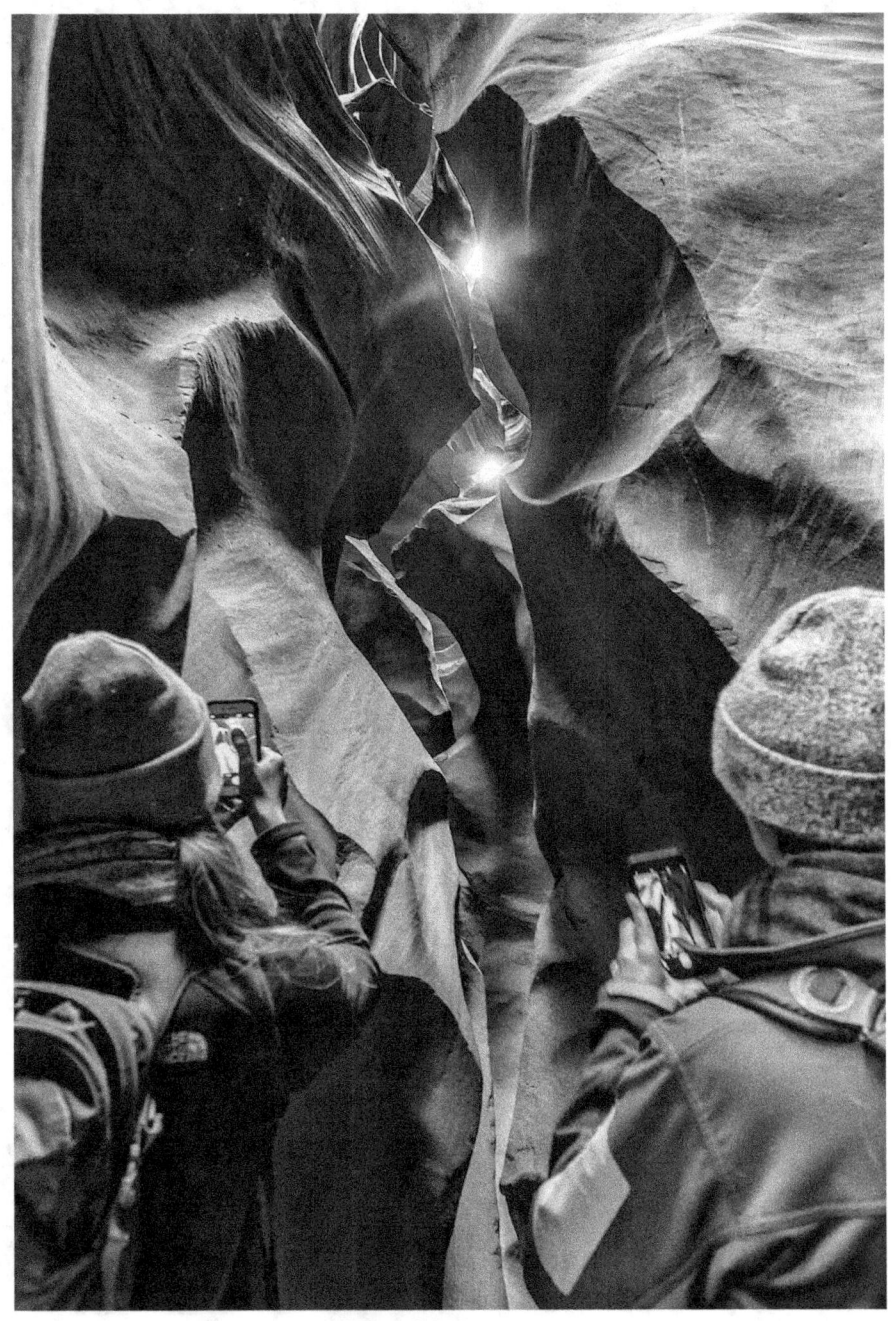

The Light

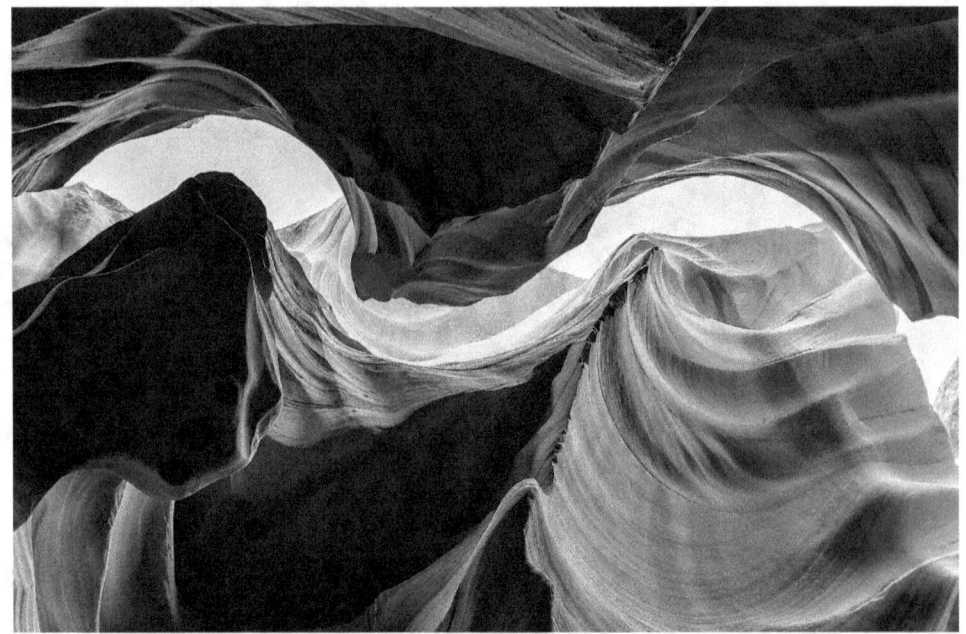

Owl's Eyes?

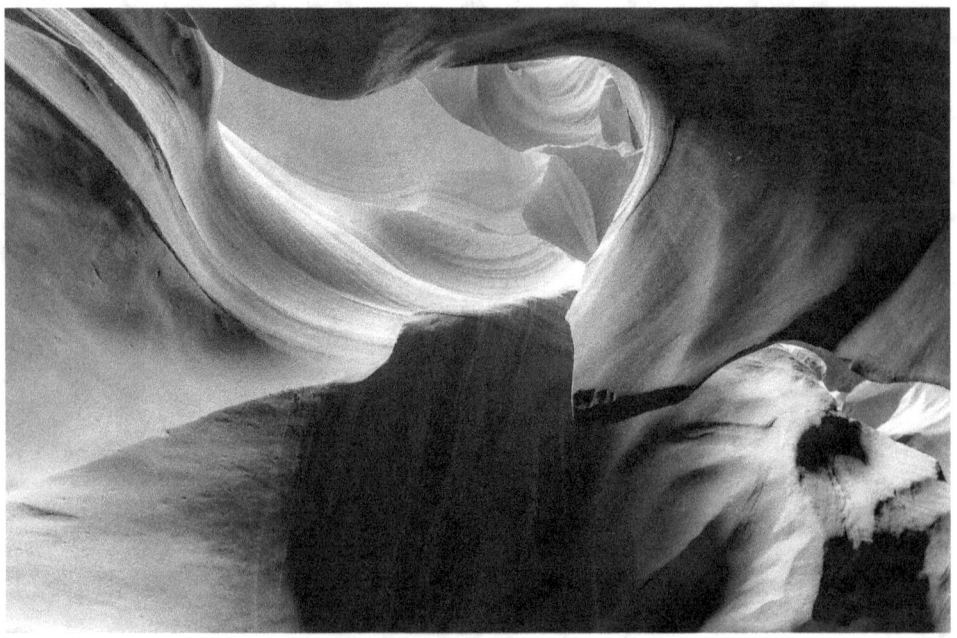

Gold Light

William J Wood Jr

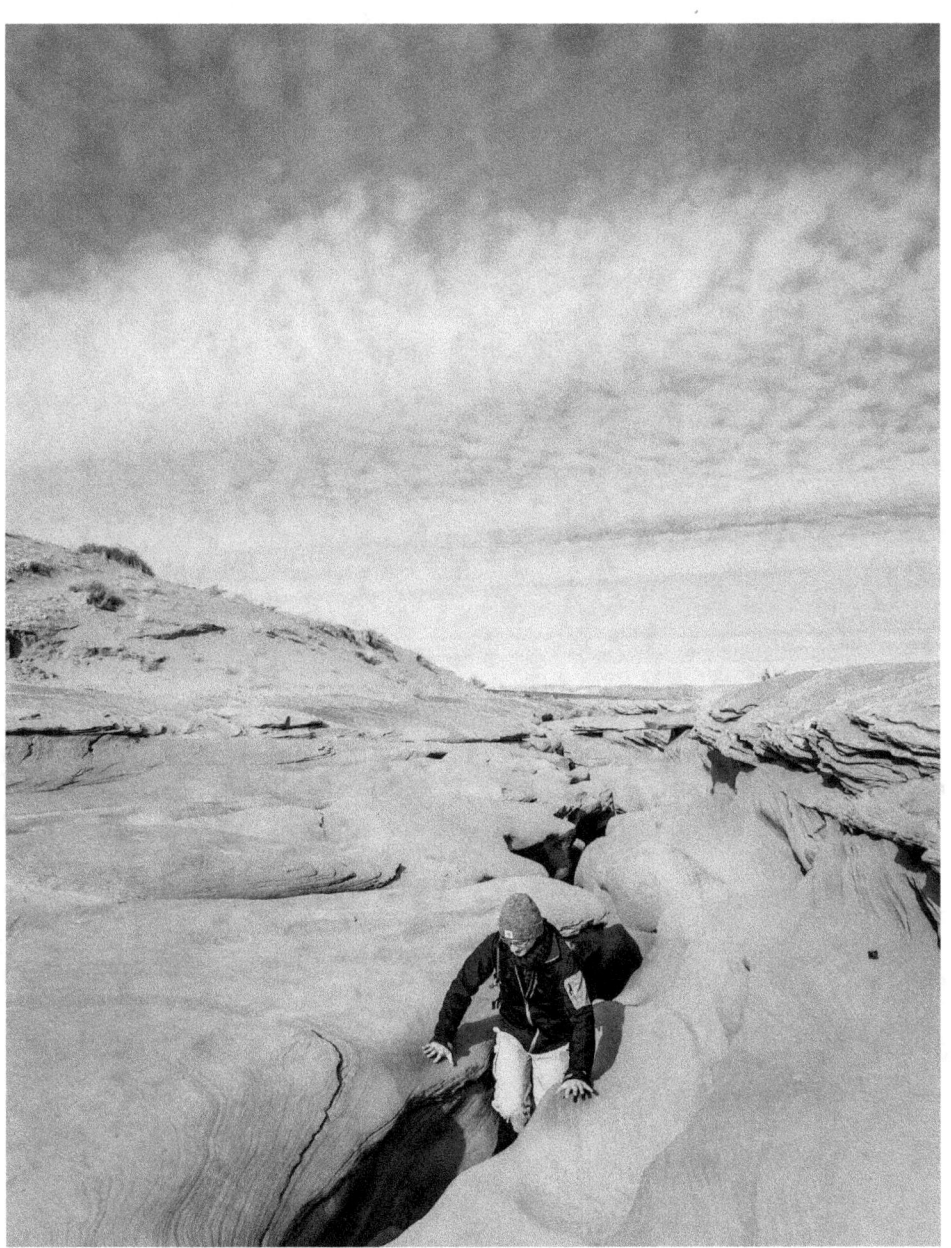

Into the Glittering World

Photographing the American West

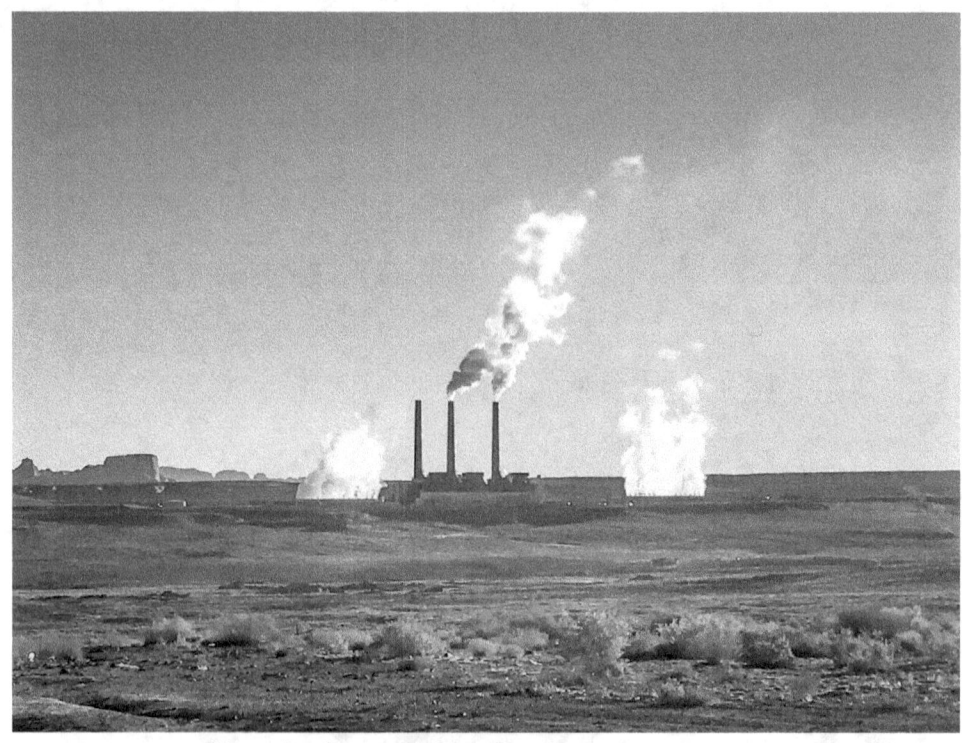

Navajo Generating Station

Chapter 10

Be

The woman on the phone at the Rancho Sedona RV Park told me to not drive on Highway 89A through Oak Creek to get to Sedona. It was not a good road for RVs. I looked at the map. If we took I-17 south from Flagstaff, we would have a long loop back north to get to Sedona. I knew Oak Creek well. When I was a student at NAU, Oak Creek was the place to go in the first sun-drenched days of spring as the snow was melting. I wanted to see its Elysian depths again.

I learned to rock climb in Oak Creek. Friends took me for my first climb on a route called Mint Jam. It was a double crack, rated 5-7. It scared the hell out of me seeing the ground get farther away. At one point, I got sewing-machine leg. A week later, a guy I knew told me he was into rock-climbing and I told him I knew a place. We took his motorcycle out to Mint Jam. He looked at the route and told me he didn't want to lead, so I did. Most climbing novices don't lead on their second climb. I put in way too much protection and the rope friction pulled me backwards. Approaching the crux move near the top, I freaked out. I looked down and there was Ross Hardwick, my friend and climbing mentor, free climbing up a nearby route. Someone back at the dorm had let the word out I was heading out to climb with another newbie. Ross coached me through the crux move. My motorcycle friend climbed up behind me, top roped, and commented, "I can't believe you climbed that."

The highway slid off the plateau of the Mogollon Rim into the basalt trough of Oak Creek. The road was tight hairpins on a shiny new blacktop, a legacy of the 2014 Slide Rock Fire. Steering was a symphony in sinuosity. We cruised by Slide Rock, a natural water slide where NAU students often gathered on warm halcyon spring days. In my day, you parked by the side of the road. Now there was a Slide Rock State Park with a ranger station and a parking lot. Farther down, resorts tucked in under the cliffs. I remembered none of those. Again, old memories were dismembered.

Sedona is a gem of a tourist town surrounded by postcard scenery of redrock spires and towering stone thrones. The red-orange rock is Schnebly Hill Sandstone. Theodore Schnebly was the town's first postmaster. Sedona was his wife's name, made up by her mother.

The time-share darling of Arizona, Sedona is branded as a mecca for New Age tourism. Page Bryant was a professional psychic and first apprentice of the Chippewa medicine man, Sun Bear. In the 1980s she identified six locations, all close to town, where strange energy spiraled out of the earth. She named them vortexes. Like the sirens of Odysseus, the vortexes attracted spiritual seekers.

Bryant, who died in 2017, had a psychic Midas touch. She identified vortexes around Waynesville, NC in the Smokey Mountains, turning that town into another New Age hotspot. She published several books including, *CRYSTALS AND THEIR USE, A study of At-One-Ment with the Mineral Kingdom.*

According to Bryant and the brochures stuffed into an epidemic of visitor information kiosks, vortexes are sites of concentrated spiritual energy. They are not magnetic anomalies. The receptive will feel a tingling of the skin and a sensation across the nape of the neck and shoulder blades. Claimed benefits are clearing emotional blocks, unlocking female energy, release of frustration and anger, joining with your animal totem and leaving your past behind. Vortexes cause juniper trees to have highly twisted branches. I'm not sure I want to go to a vortex, since I feel I have lived much of my life in one already.

The term New Age refers to a hodgepodge of beliefs and spiritual practices that foster the goals of enlightenment, healing, and maximizing human potential. Practitioners choose from a large shopping list: 18th century occultism, Hinduism, Buddhism, Christianity, Taoism, shamanism, Sufism, Native American religions, paganism, UFO religions, spirit channeling, psychology, yoga, alternative medicine and almost any belief system not already claimed by organized religions. Early roots sprouted in the United Kingdom with the Aetherius Society and in New Zealand with the Heralds of the New Age in the 1950s.

In America, the cultic milieu germinated after the crash of the countercultural wave of the 60s. New Age culture attracted the disenchanted and disenfranchised and those longing for a way of life not dominated by political wars or nuclear annihilation. True believers swam out of the turbulence of the receding hippie wave and continued a more private quest. The conspicuous age of the movement peaked in the 80s and 90s, but myriad evolutions still hum along in places like Sedona and health spas and rehab centers and Portland, Oregon. Today seekers, shamans and meditators eschew the tag of New Age, which detractors use as a pejorative.

Devout Christians condemned New Age beliefs since Jesus was not the sole focus and source of redemption and the afterlife was not a big deal. Macho culture mocked the feminist agenda of New Age, whose adherents were two-thirds women. Native Americans accused New Agers of stealing intellectual property and described Natives who ran sweat lodge ceremonies for white seekers as "plastic shamans." Working joes, like me, were miffed that, between work, family duties and a little exercise, we didn't have a lot of free time to meditate, get massages, go to sweat lodges, have extended tantric sex or do any channeling except on a TV. At least that's my theory.

The New Age social phenomenon is now retro enough that academics analyze it and write books about it. Corporate America incorporated New Age practices and terminologies to prove it is hip and with it. My former health care mega-corporation offered mindfulness lessons and yoga. Don't worry about your shrinking pension, do some yoga, relax.

New Age marrow gels in a multitude of consumer products: organic foods, alternative medicines, recyclables, the scent industry, fad diets, music festivals, video games and the *Lord of the Rings* movies. You can now enjoy these hip products without being ridiculed as New Age. (Am I the only one who has noticed the *Lord of the Rings* is a giant metaphor for WWII? When things get bad, the eagles always come to the rescue!)

On August 16, 1987, the sun, the moon and six of the planets of our solar system aligned into a "grand trine" formation. According to Tony Shearer, author of *Lord of the Dawn*, the astrological alignment landed on a significant date in the Mayan Calendar, the end of the nine "Cycles of Hell" that began the day Hernan Cortes landed in Mexico in 1519. Jose Arguelles, founder of the first Whole Earth Festival, spearheaded the Harmonic Convergence, a global meditation event. Arguelles called for meditators to travel to a "place of power" to receive the gift of the Convergence. Five thousand seekers came to Sedona. Experiences differed.

A woman, who later became a spiritual teacher of transformation, wrote:

> *My soul responded immediately to the place. It held a perfect vibration for me. My crown chakra turned into a spiraling vortex and began to ascend way, way up into the lighted heavens. It slowly spun my awareness up and up and into Infinity, and there was a kind of subtle sound*

that accompanied the spiraling energy, cosmic chords of a faintly tinkling, electronic nature.

A Sedona local described his experience at the Bell Rock vortex during the Harmonic Convergence:

We decided the only way to get a grasp on this thing was to go up the mountain with the thousands of whack jobs that had shown up in our town. This was the perfect opportunity to wear our Welcome to Sedona, Now go home *T-shirts. An Indian woman told us, "There will be an event like never before. Mother Earth will be destroyed and all will die!" Well, I was stoned at the time but I had enough wits about me to state back to her, "Well here is how I see it lady. If we are all going to die tonight you won't need any money! You can have the fucking place."*

It's all in one's perspective.

The Rancho Sedona RV Park was right off Schnebly Hill. It was spacious, park-like and dappled by an umbrella of Arizona Ash with shimmering gold leaves. I've noticed at many of the better RV parks the receptionist will recite a long list of rules as they check you in, as if campers miss their nanny-like neighborhood associations. "Don't put recycling in the cans on Thursday." The parks always ask if travelers have dogs. Some will not allow certain breeds such as Pit Bulls or Dobermans. One time, the camp host asked if we had any dogs and I said, "No, we have a cat."

She then asked, "What breed?"

I was stunned. "You only let in certain breeds of cats?"

She apologized. She had mis-heard me.

We rode Smax to the Jim Thompson trailhead at the edge of town. Our plan was to hike the Brin's Mesa Trail and link up with the Soldier Pass Trail, a popular hike. The trail started on an open flat of pine, juniper and manzanita along Mormon Canyon. None of the juniper had excessively twisted branches. After a mile we climbed to Brin's Mesa, where our view opened to a grand circle of ancient earth. Cream-colored Coconino Sandstone, deposited during the Permian in the Pedregosa Sea, layered the top half of the formations above the red Schnebly Hill Sandstone. I could not see any remnant of the 2006 Mesa Fire that had blackened 4,400 acres.

We turned left on an unsigned trail we hoped was Soldier Pass. Through a gap in the towering redrock lay Sedona camouflaged in its green valley. Passing a stretch of cool shaded forest the long views returned at the Apache's Seven Sacred Pools, a series of tinajas holding water in sandstone bowls. The friendly British couple we had met on Brin's Mesa going the opposite direction smiled as they passed. Coffeepot Rock perked across the valley. A side hike led to Devil's Kitchen, a sinkhole. Every kitchen needs a coffee pot.

We chose the Cibola Pass fork for the return. The trail climbed to nice views of stately red thrones. We wound through agave gardens before emerging into the parking lot. It was a comfortable trail through brilliant scenery. If I lived in this fair red refuge, I would come back to this trail often at dawn or sunset.

But, I didn't live in Sedona and we were leaving the next day. We would visit friends in Prescott, Tom and Jean, who had moved to an intentional community in the cool mountain air after retiring from careers in the baking oven of Phoenix, the real Devil's Kitchen. Tom, also known as Tomas, is my long-time friend and honorary Geezer. Tomas turned me on to the wonders of the Superstition Mountains, which he knows well in both normal and altered states, but that's a chapter in another book. Tom was excited we would be there for the Acker Night Musical Showcase. I didn't know what that was, but we would find out and it would be the highlight of our trip.

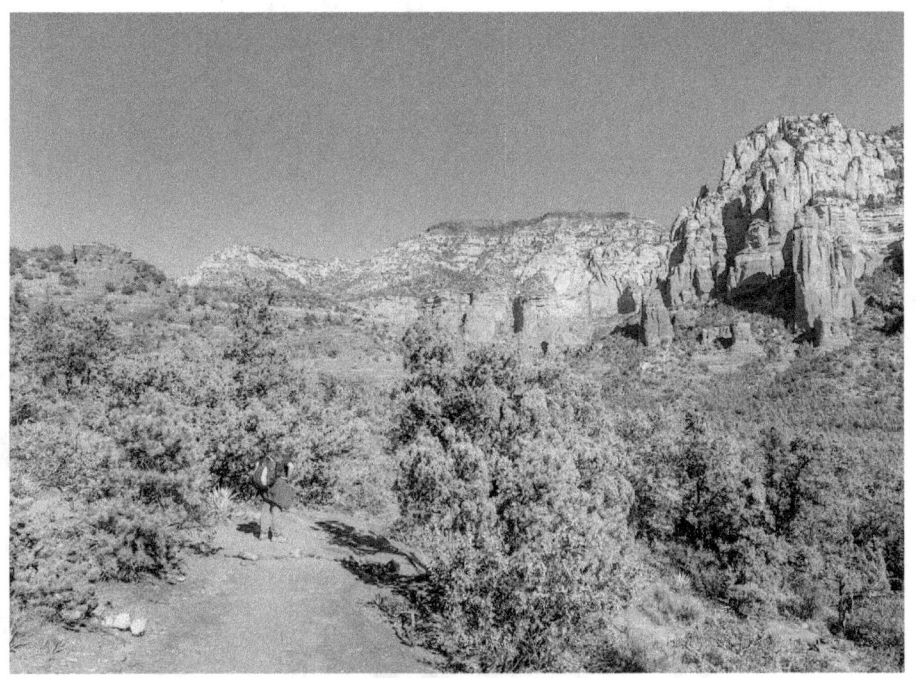

Sedona. Schnebly Hill Sandstone.

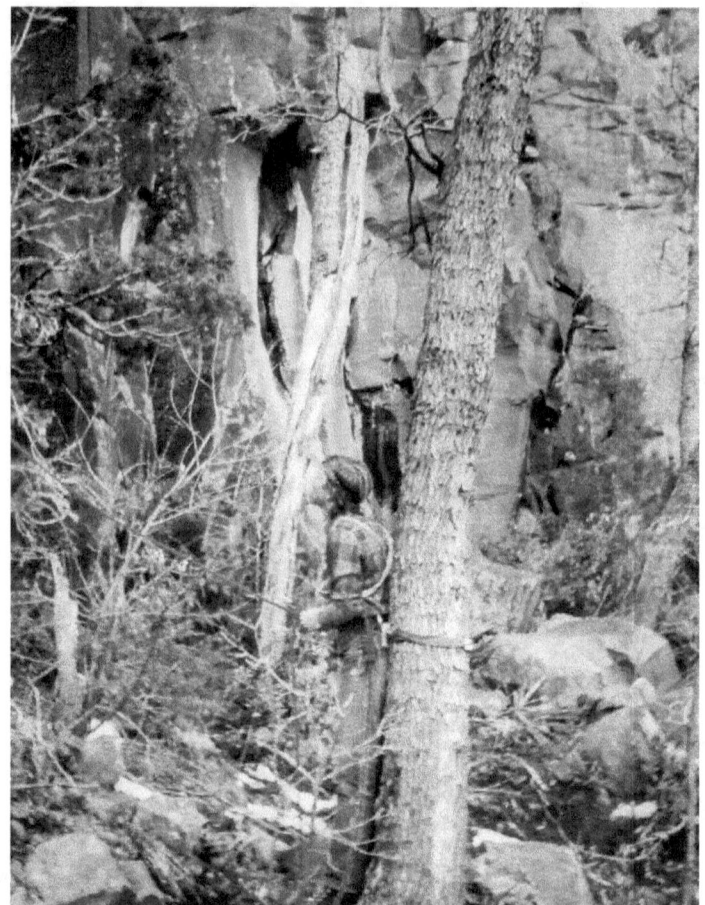

Me, belaying on Mint Jam

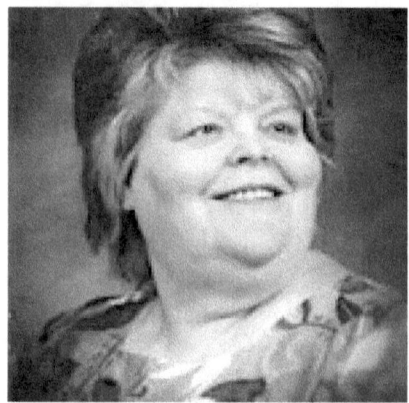

Page Bryant, founding psychic of Sedona

William J Wood Jr

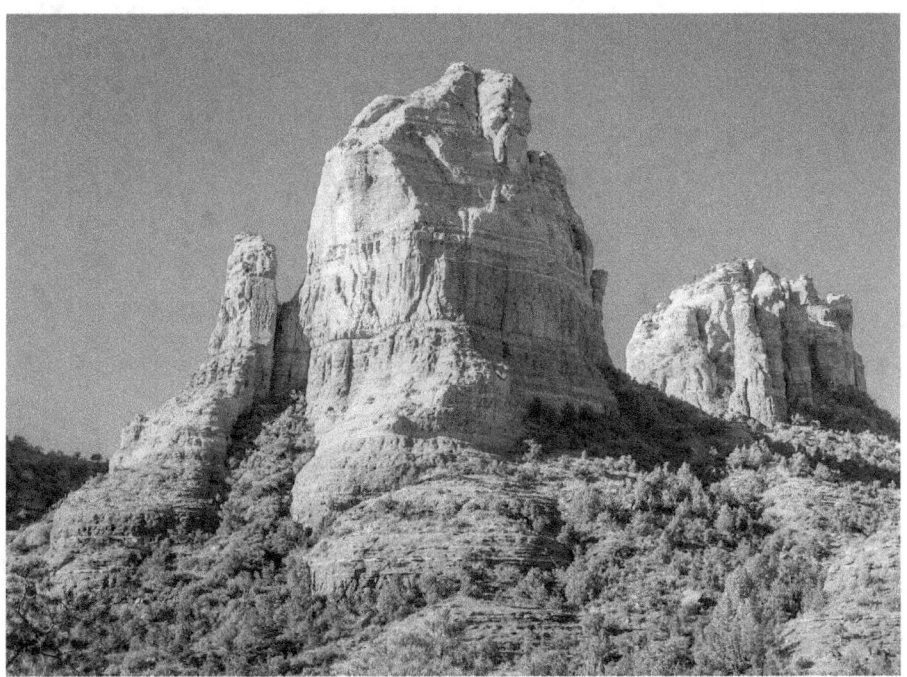

Thrones of gods

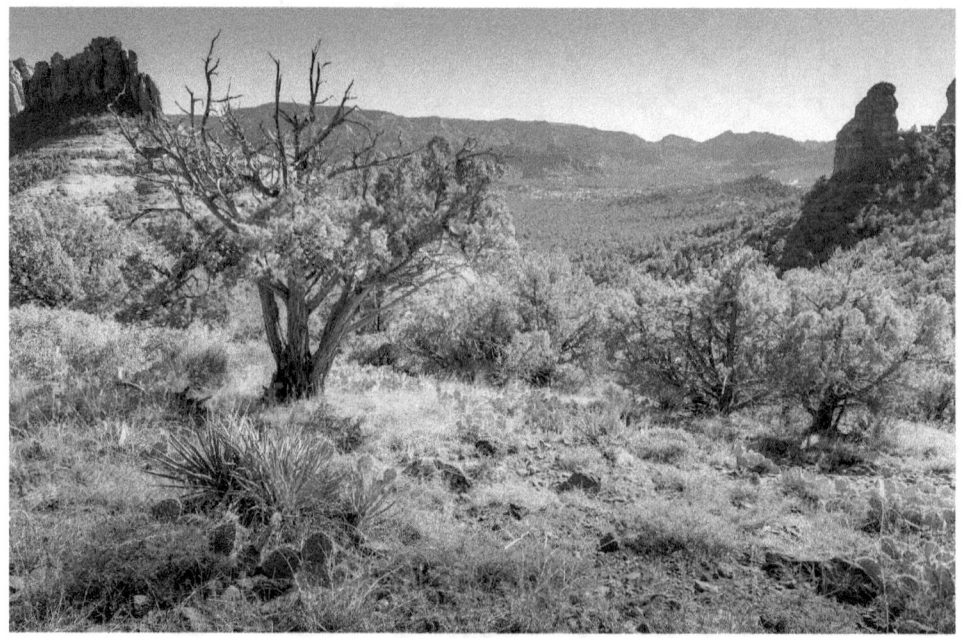
Sedona's valley

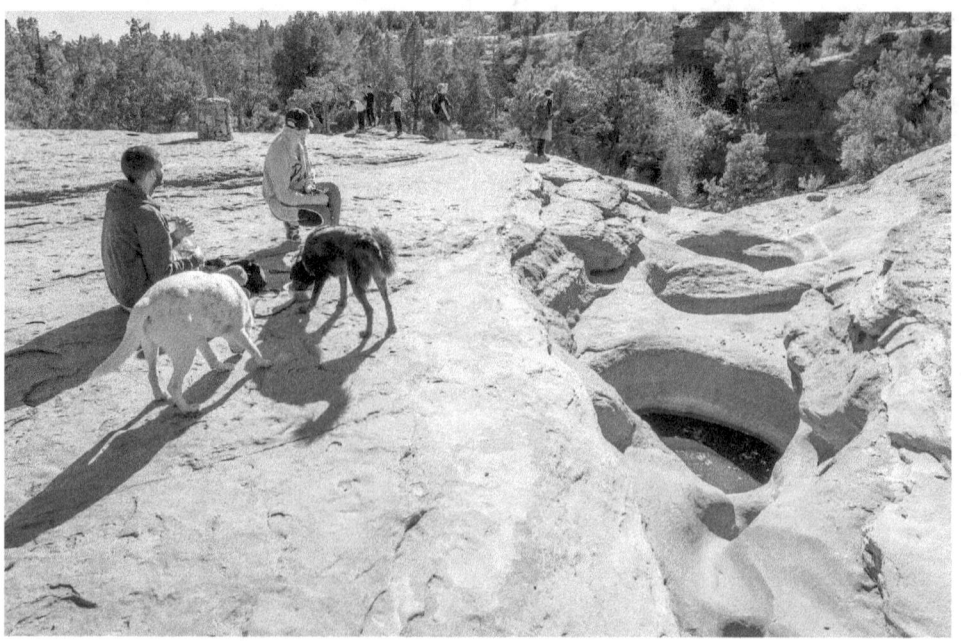
Apache's Seven Sacred Pools

Chapter 11

When you gotta go.

We headed south out of Sedona, then west, crossing the Verde River before entering the pleasant town of Cottonwood, another retirement mecca, cheaper than Sedona. In adjacent Clarkdale, we took a break and toured the Arizona Copper Art Museum. Arizona is a major copper producing state. Named for mine-owner William A. Clark, Clarkdale housed the smelter for the United Verde Mine, one of the richest copper deposits ever found, producing 33 million tons.

The museum's building didn't seem that big from the outside, but there was an impressive tonnage of copper inside. Anything you could think of made from or related to copper was on display: cookware, intricate WWI trench art made from shell casings, winemaking equipment, sculpture, copper plate paintings, candelabras and minerals. I asked the curator if the mining industry supported the museum. He shot me a laser stare. "We don't want anything from the mines. We don't want them telling us what to do." I could understand. If they took mining money, the museum would have to display an exhibit showing how open pit mines were good for the environment. OK. Somehow I lost all my photos of the place.

We goaded the Photon Bus up steep switchbacks to Jerome, a gentrified mining town in the sky, now a major tourist stop. On a clear day, the view from town stretches across the Verde Valley all the way to the tips of the San Francisco Peaks north of Flagstaff. Ten thousand miners inhabited this mile-high worker's town in the 1920s. Now, four hundred locals service the brisk tourist trade. Galleries and brewpubs occupy historic brick buildings that no longer sink into the ground during mine explosions. The former House of Joy is a Brothel Boutique. The pleasure is in the purchase.

Historian Thomas E. Sheridan (*Arizona: A History*), sums up Arizona's colorful past as the three C's: copper, cotton and cattle. A century ago, Jerome's miners were a palette of diversity: Irish, Chinese, Italian, Slavic and Mexican. Labor unions across southern Arizona went on strike to get their fair share of the profits pouring out of the ground. Mine owners responded by hiring armed vigilantes to round up agitators and ship them out in railroad cars. In 1917, sixty strikers, IWW Wobblies, were shipped out of Jerome. They were lucky. They ended up in Kingman, 160 miles north.

Victims of the Bisbee Deportation were not as lucky. As Sheridan describes, Phelps Dodge, the most powerful mining company in Arizona, herded 1,186 striking miners into railcars in 103°F heat. The train hauled the strikers into the middle of the New Mexico desert and abandoned them without food or water. Orders from President Woodrow Wilson saved the day. Federal troops arrived from El Paso with rations and set up a camp. The State of Arizona failed to convict even one of the two hundred vigilantes indicted for kidnapping.

The streets of Jerome were the perfect width for a Model T. I drove with gritted nuance. West of town, State Route 89A became a scenic drive through a fragrant pine forest up 7,818-foot Mingus Mountain. Near the summit, a woman coming down the mountain blinked her lights at us. Around the corner we braked in front of a curious scene. A pickup truck with four flat tires sat horizontal across our lane, its back end halfway into the opposing downhill lane. Two young men, one with blood on his shirt, guided us through the narrow space. I had a half-inch clearance from the guard rail. Later I discovered I had scraped my wheel well. Barb called 911 when our cell signal kicked in on the far side of the mountain. They said they would send help.

We called Tom when we hit the flats of Chino Valley. Tom and I have been friends since my residency days in Phoenix. We met through his sister, Christine, who moved to Sweden after college. Christine bought a house in Cottonwood, near Jerome, planning to escape the cold Nordic winters. She discovered her Swedish national healthcare would not cover her in the states, and for the outrageous price of U.S. medical insurance she could afford a house in Spain. She bemoans that we Geezers have stayed in her Cottonwood house more than she has. Her other brother, Ray, now owns the Cottonwood house.

Tom grew up in Mesa, Arizona. He learned the surveying business from his father, Alex, who piloted fifty-one B-24 bomber missions out of Italy in WWII. Tom worked as an industrial construction planner for many years. He met Jean, a Beatles fan from Nottingham, when she worked at Honeywell in Phoenix. After retirement, they moved out of the desert heat to the cool high country of Prescott. Tom and I share an exploratory mindset. We like ruins, wilderness, live music and the thin edge of total consciousness.

I was glad I had reserved a site at the Point of Rocks RV Park. The Park was full thanks to the Acker Night Music Showcase. The host gave us a list. There were 137 live music acts scheduled to play in all the shops and bars and restaurants around Courthouse Plaza, famous for its Christmas light display. I couldn't believe it. Tom's cousin, George, was playing a venue. I dropped a bowling ball on my foot and asked Tom if he would ask George if I could play a song or two. I had little hope. I've learned my lesson. If an amateur musician ever shares the stage with a friend, it will mean the rapture has arrived.

James Samuel Acker left his home in Alabama for California in order to "see the country." He wandered around the West arriving in Prescott in 1902 where he found success in real estate. Acker left all his money to the city of Prescott "to be used for parks and for promotion of music, particularly for children." He died in 1955. The Showcase raises money for scholarships through voluntary donations.

With Tom and Jean we hiked a short trail from our camp to Watson Lake. The lake sits on a formation known as the Granite Dells, exposed 1.4-billion-year-old bedrock that looks like a giant's child tried to make a sandcastle. The busy jumble of rusted granodiorite radiates an extraterrestrial ambience, like Mars with water. I showed a photograph of Watson Lake at a Portland Photographic Society showcase. Everyone wanted to know where it was. Somewhere, I heard they filmed *Planet of the Apes* at the lake, but I can't find any confirmation. To quote Charlton Heston, "Behold the Lord's mighty hand."

A night of urban partying was just what I needed. All this hiking through gorgeous scenery was wearing me down. Our first stop was a hipster second-hand store where cousin George was playing. He had an interesting setup. In addition to the usual amps and stomp boxes, he had a CD player. He ordered custom CDs with hit songs that had vocal and guitar tracks erased. Like me, George is a retired MD who never gave up on the adolescent power fantasy of being a guitar god. Unlike me, he can nail the leads flawlessly. I didn't know if Tom had talked to him. George waved me up to sing back up on Mustang Sally. But that was it. He never took a break for the next three hours. His solo performance sounded like a full band. Hearing all that sound come out of a lone performer induced a karaoke effect.

I was excited to see George's brother, Jim, who had gone to Honduras with us years ago. Jim pulled me into the alley. I wondered if he wanted to sell me something. No, he wanted to talk about book publishing. He had read some of my *Harvesting Photons* chapters. Jim had four hundred journal pages of his travels around South America. As far as I know, he coined the term "chicken-bus." I told him how I published my book on Amazon. The formatting was a pain-in-the-ass but it was free.

Tom, Barb and I hit the streets. One act down, 136 to go. It was like live Pandora, any genre you wanted: rock, country, folk, jazz, grunge, Christmas choirs, classical. My favorite was a traditional bagpipe band in full kilts. An Elvis impersonator was spot on. Two venues had belly dancers. A family of ten-year-olds played perfect swing on trumpet, trombone and cello on the sidewalk. You could throw a Christmas tree and hit a Santa.

Molecular joy, the natural kind, infused my élan. The buoyancy never let up. Gauzy colored lights in the huge American elms of Courthouse Plaza made a perfect yuletide backdrop. These elms survive here because they are outside the range of Dutch Elm disease. It was an enchanting evening until I felt the cramp of a precipitous bowel movement.

Tom led me through a bar to the restrooms. As we approached Tom dashed ahead of me and said, "I gotta go real quick. I'll be right out." He locked the door. I was sweating. I couldn't wait. I peeked into the women's restroom. The stalls were empty. I went for it. No choice! People entered, certainly women, while I was doing my business. When I came out of my stall, a woman gave me an ice-cold stare. I smiled, "Sorry, Ma'am, it was an emergency," and fled before she could call a bouncer. Goodness returned. We partied on. George was still playing when we returned to his gig. The guy was a machine.

My head was swirling from all the positive energy when Tom dropped us off at the Point of Rocks. We made plans for a hike up Granite Mountain. I made plans for some sweet dreams.

Photographing the American West

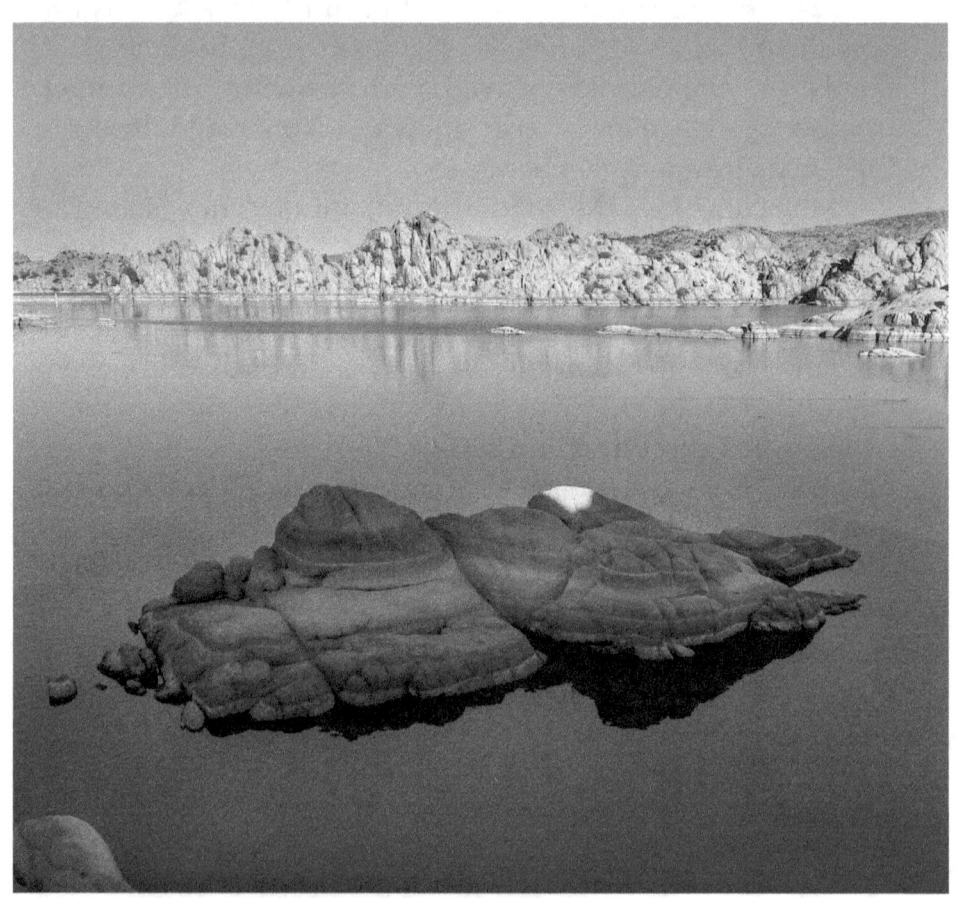
Watson Lake. Like Mars with water.

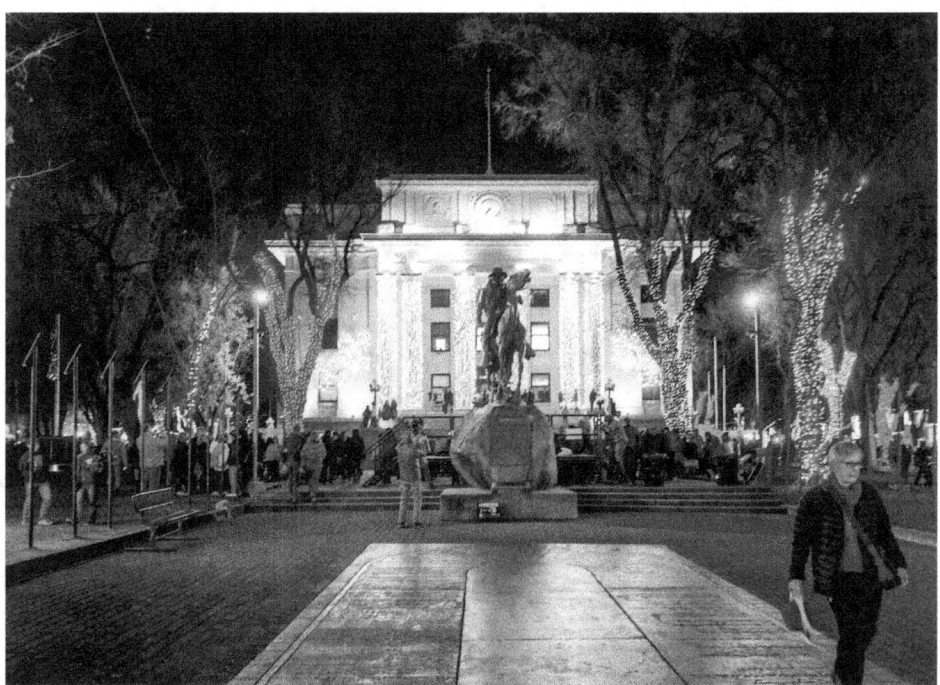

Prescott Courthouse Square

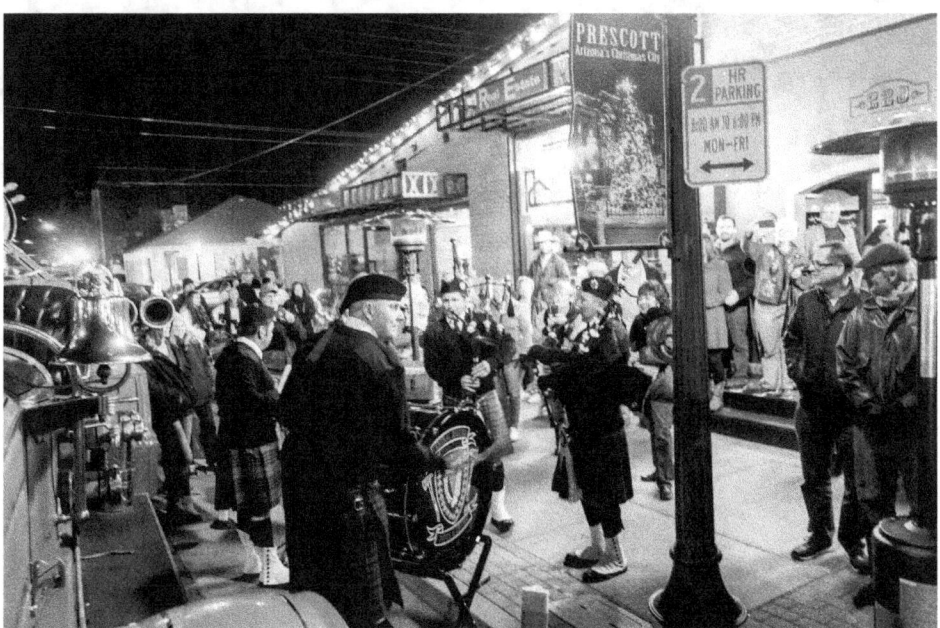

Bagpipes at the Acker Night Music Festival

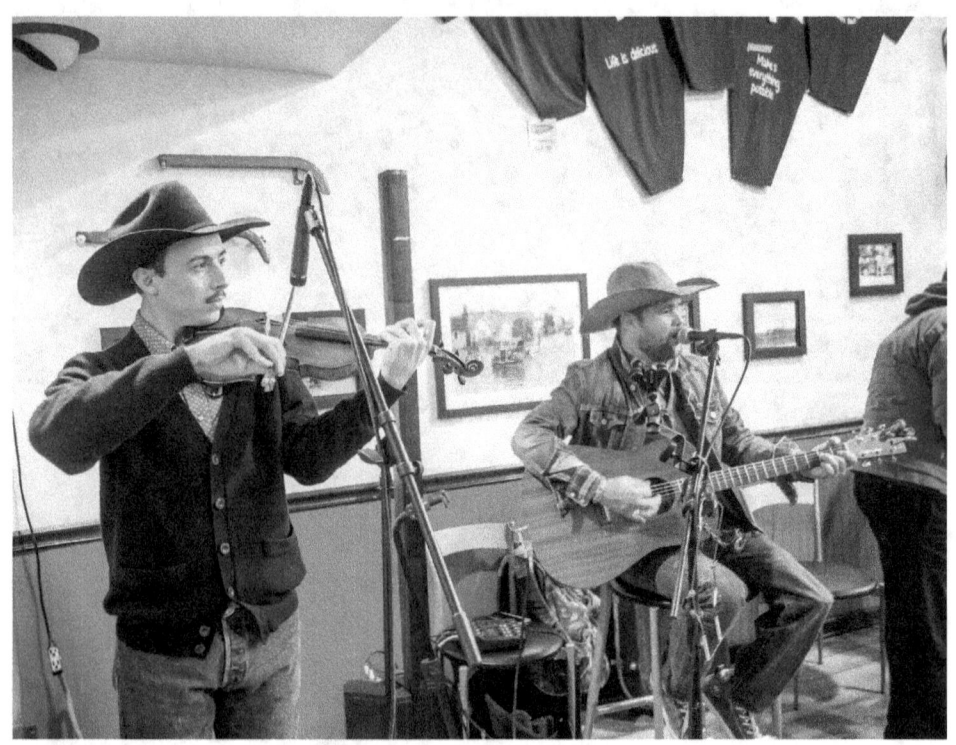

Good cowboy music

William J Wood Jr

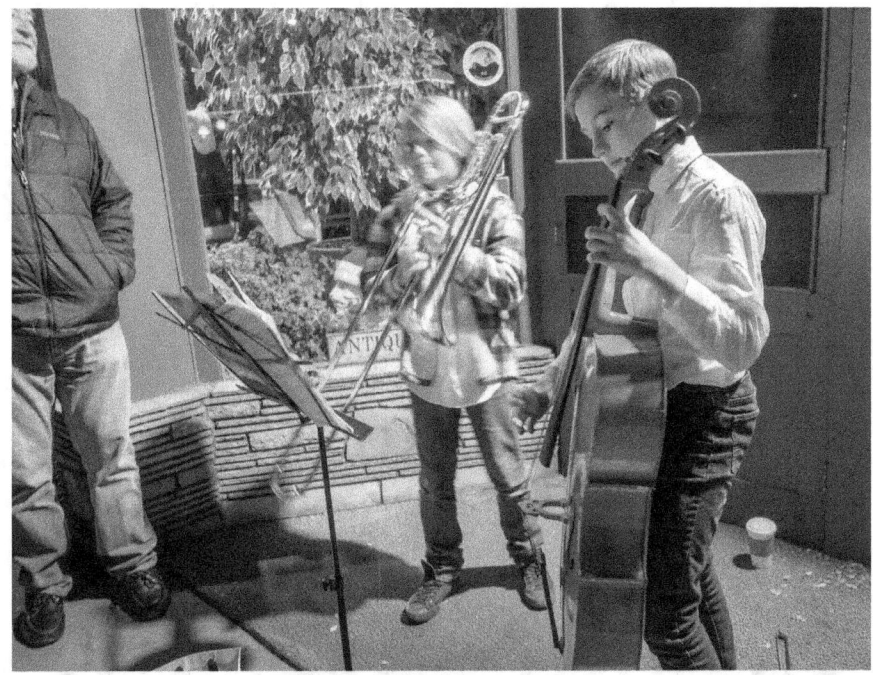

Sidewalk trio

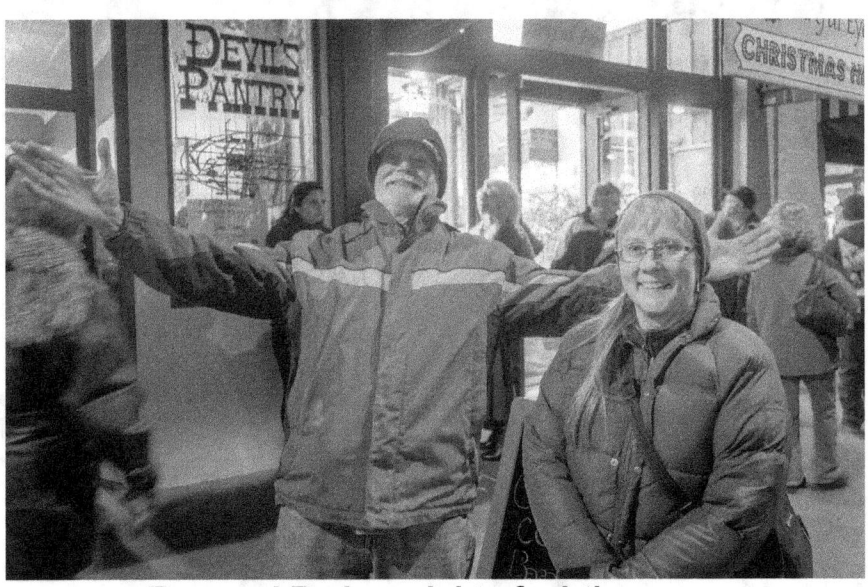

Tom and Barb, a night of mirth

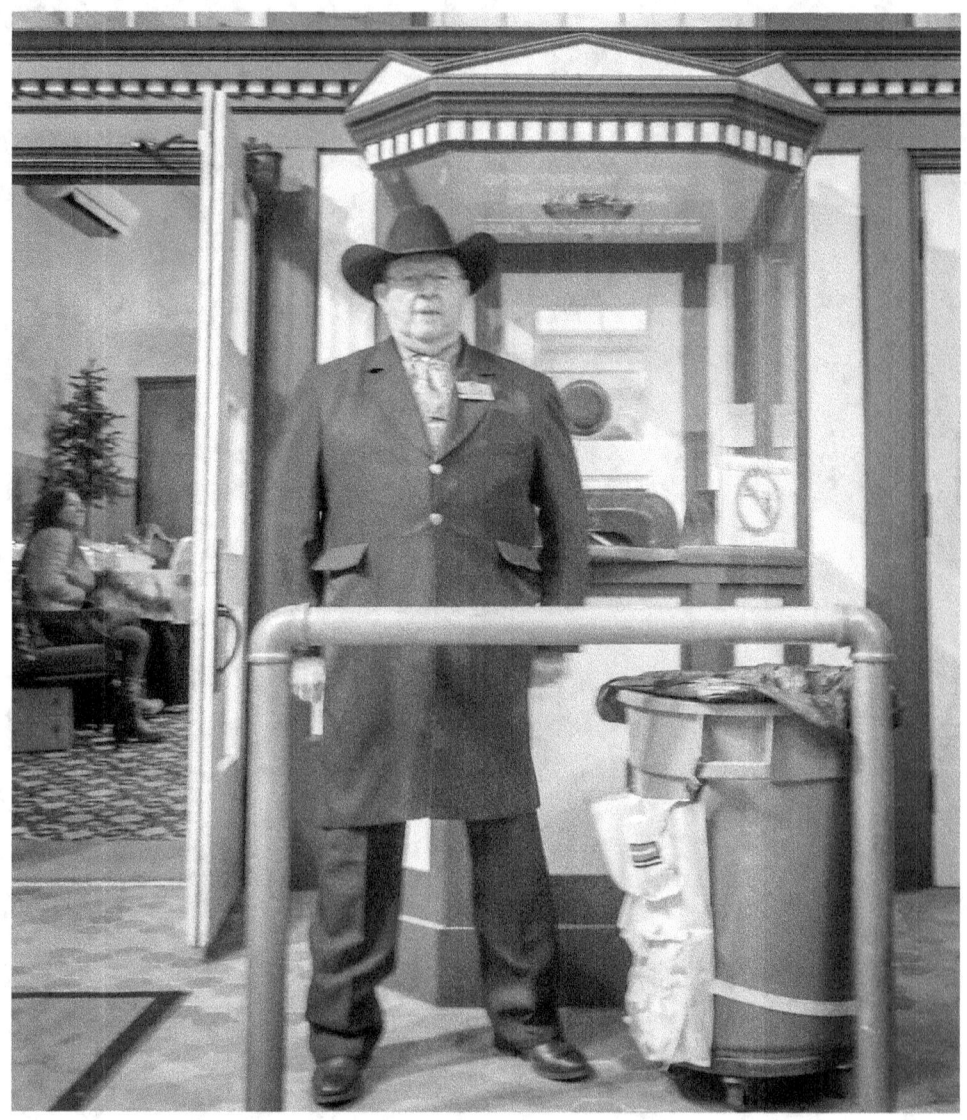

Where d'ya think you're goin?

Chapter 12

Those Who Serve

We donned hiking gear and piled into Tom and Jean's car. Tom's cousin, Honduras Jim, met us at the trailhead. Trail 261 led to the peak of Granite Mountain, a 7,628-foot Proterozoic pluton punched through the Bradshaw Mountains. After a few hundred yards, Jim said, "I think that juniper is around here somewhere." He was referring to the "Grandfather Juniper," a behemoth alligator juniper saved by the Granite Mountain Hotshots during the 2013 Doce Fire. Firefighters climbed out on burning branches and doused them with their canteens. The picture is famous: a human pyramid of grinning firefighters, smoke-blackened, in front of a building-size, multi-trunked juniper. If you stayed for the credit roll after seeing the movie, *Only the Brave*, you saw this picture. All but one of those firefighters would perish eleven days later in the Yarnell Fire.

Jim was unsure of the exact location of the Grandfather Juniper. We climbed a rocky trail that blessed us with long views. Three miles in we stopped for lunch. Barb and I had become fans of foil-wrapped flavored tuna packages. They pack well. Another mile through a forest of dead, grey juniper skeletons brought us to the summit. Here, the view was across the valley of the quad-cities through crisp blue air to the Black Hills. It was a perfect hike with not a single death plunge.

It seemed a strange coincidence that *Only the Brave* was showing in theaters. Tom went with us. On June 30, 2013, nineteen members of the crack firefighting troop, the Granite

Mountain Hotshots, died in the flames of the Yarnell Fire. Yarnell is 28 miles southwest of Prescott. It sits at 4,780 feet elevation, the last gasp of the transition zone of the Colorado Plateau before the drop to Wickenburg and the northern edge of the Sonoran Desert.

On that fateful day, a small fire in the Peeples Valley spread toward the town of Yarnell. Several firefighting crews were called in to protect the town. An unexpected 180-degree wind shift caught the Granite Mountain Hotshots on an upslope. The fire raced toward their position at over twenty miles-per-hour, too fast to outrun. They deployed shelters, aluminum foil and fiberglass cocoons, which can withstand up to 300°F heat. The fire over the Hotshots generated 1200°F.

The movie was gripping. Josh Brolin nailed the part of Eric Marsh, the hard-guy crew boss, Supe, who created an elite team out of a group of local firefighters. Granite Mountain was the only municipally funded hotshot crew in the country. Aside from knowing the wrenching conclusion of the movie, I was uncomfortable seeing how much *Lebowski* (Jeff Bridges) had aged, because that meant I had aged a similar amount. In fact, I've noticed all my friends are aging. I'm going to start hanging out with young people.

After the movie, Tom told us some of the Hotshots had been at his house doing fuel reduction the week before the Yarnell Fire. He also told us they left a controversial issue out of the film. Over the radio, people heard Marsh and his second-in-command arguing about the wisdom of leaving the safety of the "black," the already-burned terrain, and heading down-slope.

Tom invited me to go to his OLLI class. The Osher Lifelong Learning Institute is a community education arm of Yavapai College. OLLI offers all kinds of classes: hiking, history, religion, politics, writing, music, gardening, and a class on the Ford Edsel. Tom's class was political discussion. The topic for the day was Trump's decision to move the U.S.

Embassy in Israel to Jerusalem, an act that enraged Palestinians and possibly undermined the peace process. It's a debatable topic, which is what happened with a lively, engaging discussion among a group of well-informed seniors with strong opinions. I kept my mouth shut for a while since I was a guest.

Another issue discussed was the bourgeoning *Me Too* movement. Some women had worked careers in the *Mad Men* era of the 50s and 60s. They all had stories. I couldn't resist stirring the pot. I asked, "Have any of the women here ever flirted with a co-worker?"

I felt warm hands on my shoulder. A sultry voice from behind said, "Oh no. I would never do that." The warm hands belonged to an attractive redhead with a mischievous grin. She recounted an incident. Driving in LA traffic, she noticed a man staring at her from a limousine. He followed her for a while. She was getting agitated until she looked at him and realized it was Cary Grant.

The Prescott scene was growing on me: festivities, convivial Chautauqua, sunshine, Victorian houses, plutons and Martian atmospheres. It put me in the mind of the time I lived in Atlanta's Little Five Points neighborhood, a Victorian oasis of gothic-south sweetness surrounded by neighbors with the genteel oddness of Faulkner and Flannery O'Conner. My neighbors, Kemo and Rachael, had moved there from a commune and had a new baby. Their home, a parade of interesting characters, was a welcome escape from medical school ego wars.

One time, a prominent civil rights activist was visiting. A lively discussion erupted. I played devil's advocate, as is my nature. The activist, a large black man resembling James Earl Jones, looked hard at me with voodoo eyes and said, "You could kill somebody one day." I thought about that as he launched into a story. A woman had been stalking him. She would stand outside his window for hours.

He said, "So I didn't wash my ass for three days. The next time she came around I pushed my dirty butt against the window and yelled, you want summa this sister?"

I thought, "And he's telling me I could kill somebody!"

Tom and Jean invited us for dinner to their place, a beautiful craft house overlooking the lights of Prescott. Tom suggested we stay overnight so he and I could get drunk. I insisted the cat come with us. I didn't want her to stay by herself in the RV. That was OK, but then we would need car transport as we couldn't take the cat on the scooter. The conclusion was Barb and I would ride Smax to Tom's house then ride back to the RV after dinner.

We wore our down parkas, as it would be below freezing on the way home. Jean prepared a delicious Portobello mushroom lasagna. After a full active day and lasagna and some wine, I didn't quite make it through all the pictures of Scotland and England. Jean grew up in Nottingham, next to Sherwood Forest, the home of Robin Hood.

In their close-knit intentional community, Tom and Jean have weekly communal dinners and diverse group activities. They travel frequently with friends. A group, all in RVs, travels to *Habitat for Humanity* builds in the States and Mexico. I envy the life they have made. I enjoy my quiet country home, but I don't have many nearby friends.

My post-prandial slump vanished on the ride home through clear, frigid air. Tomorrow would be Wickenburg.

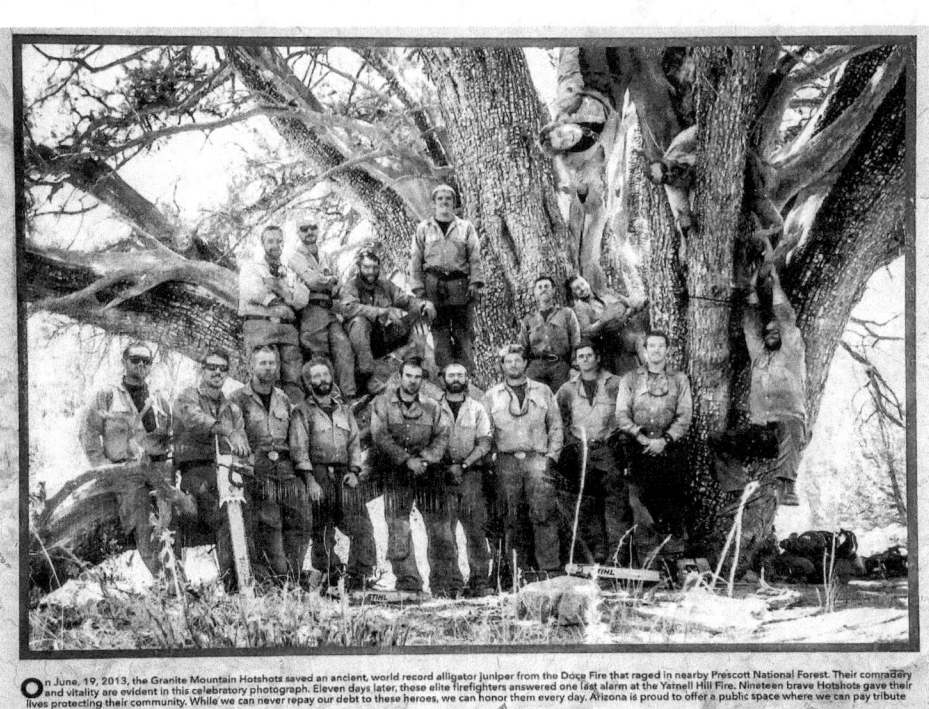

Granite Mountain Hotshots

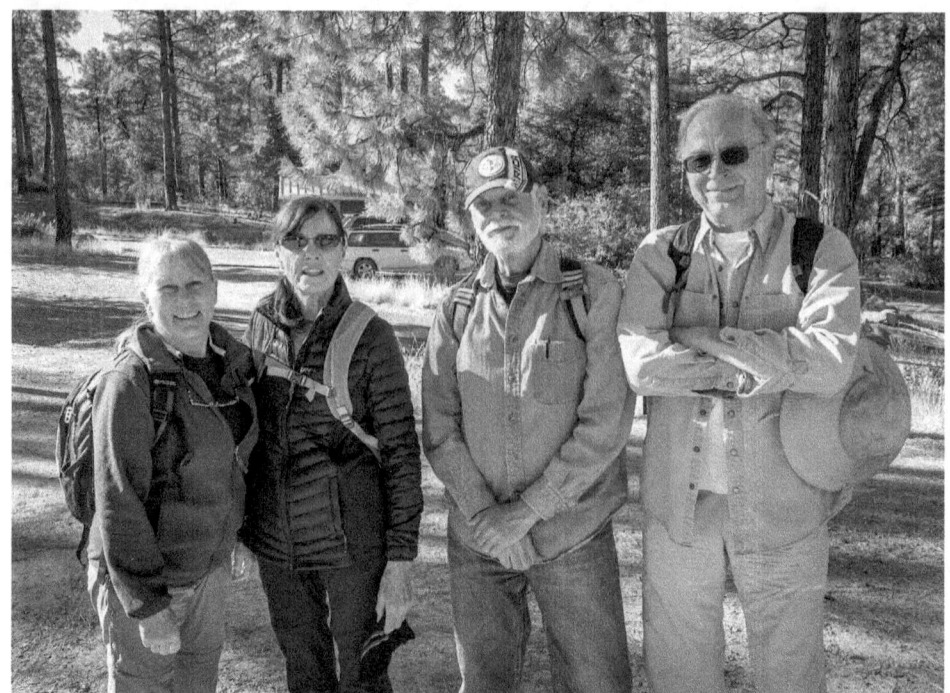

Granite Mountain hike. Barb, Jean, Tom, Jim.

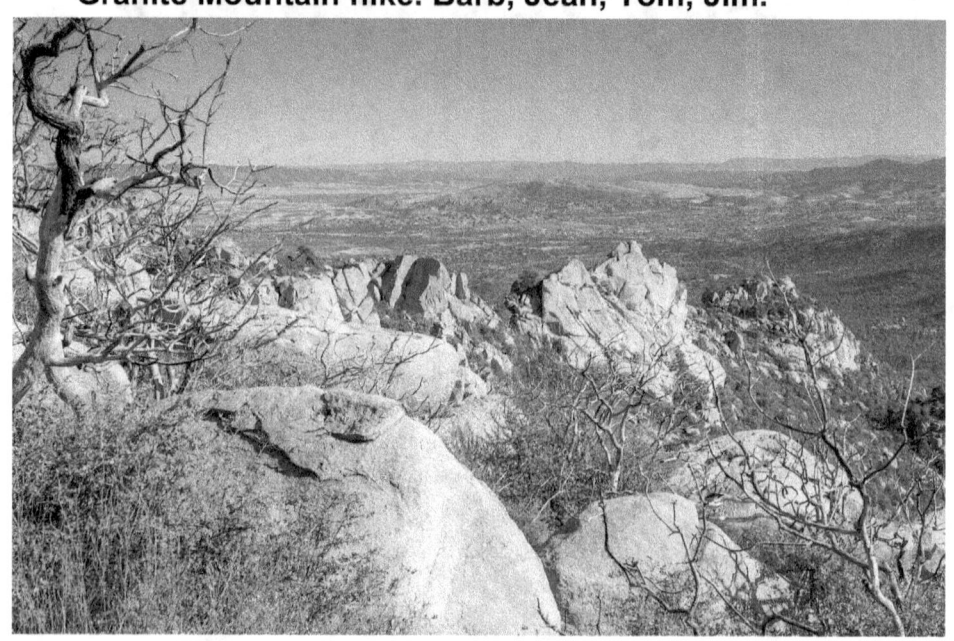

Prescott from Granite Mountain

Chapter 13

Wickenburg

We stopped in Yarnell to see the roadside memorial to the Hotshots. It was wind-worn, perhaps by winds like the one that had fanned the flames over the trapped firefighters. Before the summit of Yarnell Hill, we pulled into the Granite Hotshots Memorial State Park. A ranger informed us our RV was too big for the small lot. Tom had told us the three-mile trail to the memorial was left rough and undeveloped, so hikers would experience the hard work of firefighting.

State Route 89 descended like a roller coaster to the bajada of the desert. We dropped our golf bags at the Wickenburg Country Club. We can't carry bags on our scooter and we don't like to have to drive the RV to transport the bags every morning. Aren't clubhouses for housing clubs? We crossed the Hassayampa River on our way to the Aztec Village RV Park. Much of the river runs underground. The Yavapai call it the "upside down river." Legend has it that anyone who drinks from the Hassayampa can no longer tell the truth. You could call it the River of Politicians.

The Aztec RV Park was rustic, in the parlance of our day. Permanent trailers housed families of sweet-faced Hispanic kids. Most visitor sites were empty. We picked a quiet, shaded spot looking over a fence at muscled roping horses grazing on green pastures. I would come to appreciate this quiet woodsy haven.

In the 1860s, a German prospector, Henry Wickenburg, founded the Vulture Mine. Vulture? The mine was a bonanza of gold and silver. Five thousand miners flooded into town. They couldn't survive on the spiny cacti of the Sonora. They needed fresh food. A yarn-spinning veteran of the few Civil War skirmishes in Arizona, Jack Swilling, took a lesson from the old Hohokam canals coming off the Gila River. He built a small irrigation farm to provide for the miners. Swilling could not have foreseen that his small farm patch would rise from the desert like a phoenix to become the sixth largest city in the nation.

Swilling suffered chronic pain from a skull injury and a bullet in his back of unknown origin. Alcohol and morphine kept him going. His partner in the irrigation business was Charles T. Hayden, grandfather of Carl T. Hayden, Arizona's torch-bearing senator who would champion the Central Arizona Project. Swilling and two companions headed out from Black Canyon City to bury their friend, Colonel Jacob Snively, killed by Apaches. Three men, matching the description of Swilling and his friends, robbed the Wickenburg stagecoach. The Swilling party was arrested and sent to the infamous federal prison at Yuma, part prison, part oven. Swilling died in his cell before the real robbers were caught.

Wickenburg's downtown blocks cater to the cowboy tourist. The original train depot houses the visitor's center. Life-size bronze statues of real Old West characters stand frozen-in-time at points along the walking tour. Push their buttons and they spiel out the history of Wickenburg in authentic western patois. "Well, thut train was a-gawin so slow ya coulda herded geeses in front of it." We walked the town and ate at a festive Mexican restaurant.

The next two days we golfed. By mid-morning temperatures were in the 70s. We were both rusty, but what the heck. The charming desert course had long trails between holes. In the quiet afternoons at the Aztec, we read, watched movies, and worked on projects.

An enormous trailer pulled into the spot next to us. It took an hour for the guy to get it situated just right. Our neighbors, retired farmers from Indiana, had been wintering in Wickenburg for years. After the husband's hip replacements they no longer trailered their horses; instead they towed a Polaris UTV, a utility vehicle, the Cadillac of retirees. Half the parking slots in Wickenburg sported UTVs. Maybe there is one in my future if my hips and knees give out. Sorry Smax.

If you're a horse person, go to Wickenburg. Several RV parks in the area have arenas. In town there are daily roping demonstrations. There are more riding trails than mountain bike trails. When I was a kid, we went to dude ranches for our vacations. My favorite horse was a strawberry roan. I forget the name. I haven't ridden a horse in years. The last time I rode, I smashed my boys on the saddle, no doubt due to poor riding skills. I live next to horses and I enjoy seeing them for what they represent.

One time I stopped by the town of Halfway, a sleepy picturesque ville in the shadows of the Wallowa Mountains in eastern Oregon. I was on my way to backpack in the Wallowas. I stopped to visit a retired surgeon I knew. Gordon had made his fortune as an ENT surgeon in Portland. Bit by bit, he bought irrigated pastures in his old hometown and put together a herd of two hundred cattle. Gordon came out from his house and shoved a scotch-on-the-rocks in my hand as we hopped into his pickup for a tour of the S7 ranch. He was proud of his fenced, irrigated green pastures. "I like to grow things." He pulled up to a trailer home and honked. Fred, Gordon's foreman, came out hitching his pants.

Gordon said, grinning, "Bill, here, is going to walk into the Wallowas."

Fred's eyes grew big. "Whyn't you take a horse?"

I explained, "Fred, if I ride a horse all day my butt gets really sore."

Fred shot back, "Well if I walk all day my feet get sore!"

Jared Diamond, a professor of geography at UCLA, wrote a seminal book, *Guns, Germs and Steel*. Diamond was in New Guinea walking with a local, Yuri, who asked him,

"Why are you rich and we are poor?" The book is a masterful attempt to answer that question. Why did civilization arise and amass greater power in some parts of the world, but not others?

Diamond argues the answer is in geography more than anything else. It was geography that blessed Europe and North Africa with wheat, barley and large domesticable animals: cattle, sheep, pigs and horses. The unobstructed east-west passage from Europe to Asia allowed for cross-cultural influences in the developing civilizations. Herd immunity to common diseases evolved. In the New World, European colonizers dominated the horse culture of the Natives due to "steel" and "guns", superior weapons technology, and "germs," immunity to diseases imported from the Old World.

Before steam and internal combustion engines, horses and oxen supplied the horsepower for transportation, agriculture, industry and war. We are only a few generations away from a time when horses served many of our needs. We still admire the gentle, strong ungulates that were once our constant companions. The sound of hooves pounding reverberates in our cultural DNA. Disposable income supports the modern horse culture. Never ridden, my neighbor's horses constantly graze and occasionally frolic. They are rescued horses, lovingly cared for by Rhonda who brings them alfalfa in the winter.

Anywhere in America as you leave the urban boundary you see horses. They are everywhere. Contemporary horses don't pull plows. They don't carry the mail. Owners ride them, when time allows, on trails or in parades or in rodeos or in dressage. We allow the fleetest to compete in races while we wear silly hats. Like our other pet species they are for companionship, our need for connection to a disappearing pre-industrial state of nature. If only they could talk.

A road-worn class C motor home squatted next door. The elderly owner came out with a huge white dog, a

Kuvasz of Hungarian origin. The man was from Alaska. For the last thirteen years he had cared for his wife who died from a debilitating illness. Now, in the home stretch of his trail of years he was free to migrate south for the winter. I mentioned my fear of driving a big RV on snow. He had driven a thousand miles through snow coming south. He missed an important turn because the sign was buried in a huge snowplow mound. I'm a wimp. The dog was not supposed to be friendly, but as we talked it walked over and allowed me to pat it. I'm good with dogs. I might be a dog whisperer.

Wickenburg had been pleasant, warm and relaxing in our hidden camp. Phoenix was a short drive. We would again stay with our friend Bob at his gracious central Phoenix home. Last year we helped him with some home improvement projects.

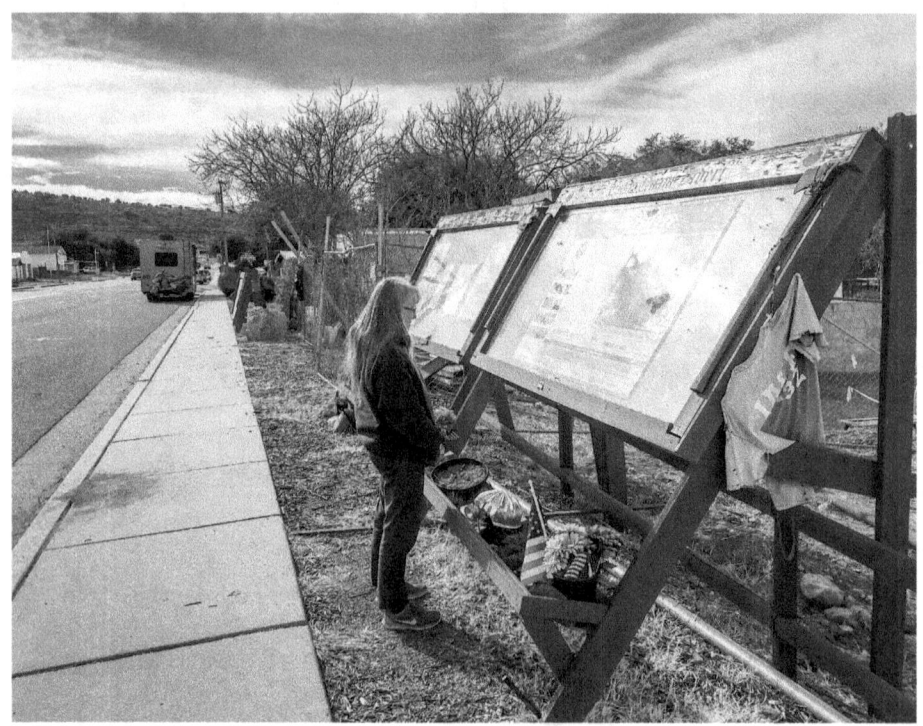

Hotshot's memorial in Yarnell

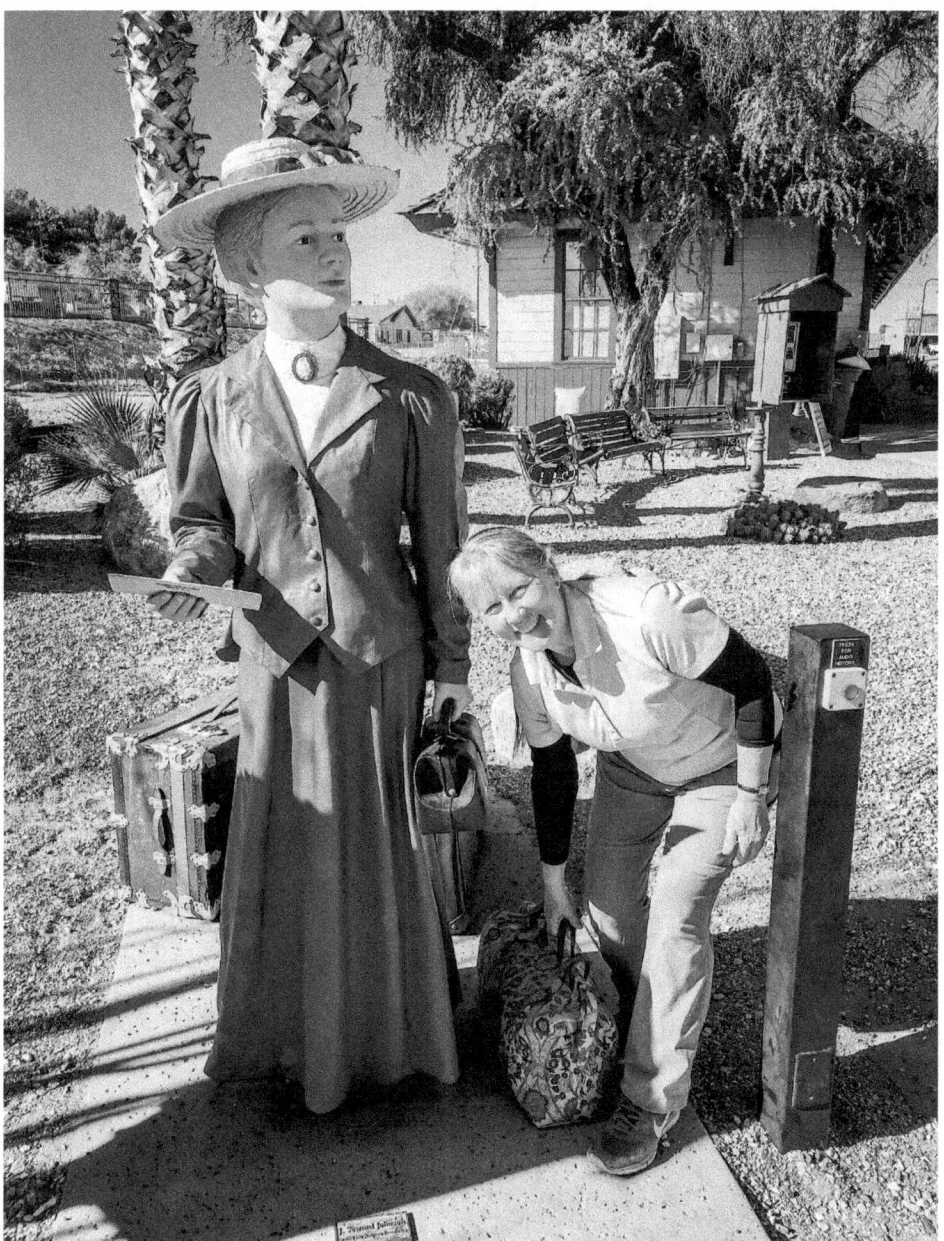

Take your bag, Ma'am?

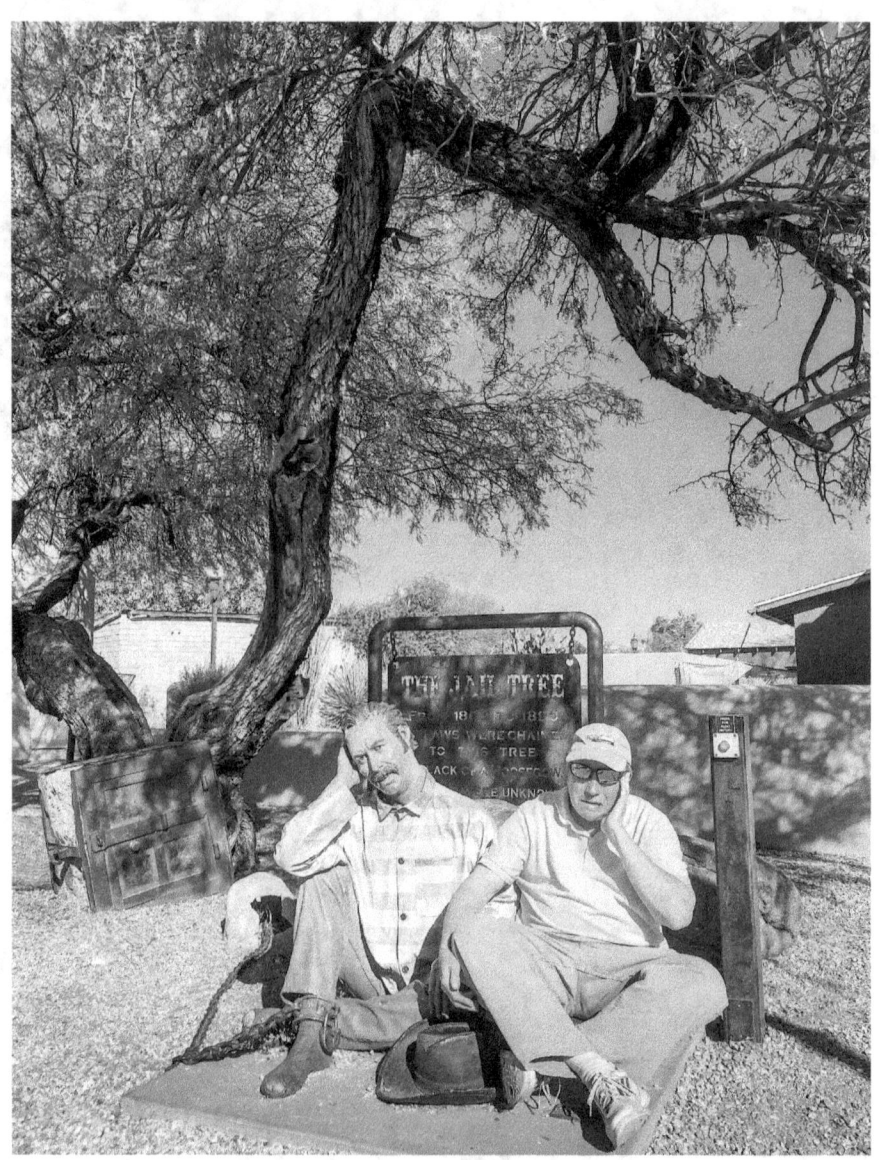

Sorrow at The Jail Tree

Chapter 14

Phoenix Stories

Barb and I did our residencies in Phoenix. Mine was surgery; hers was internal medicine. The non-negotiable agreement with residency programs is that freshly graduated doctors work prodigious hours on evanescent salaries for education at the side of experienced staff physicians. The Phoenix Integrated Surgical Residency, the "Pisser," shared the Phoenix VA Medical Center, the Phoenix Indian Medical Center and Good Samaritan Medical Center. My starting yearly salary was $13,000.

I often worked a full day, followed by a full night, followed by another full day, 36 hours straight, before going home to my own bed. My chief year I was on-call every day for the entire year. The old saying was: "The only bad thing about every other night call is you miss half the cases." Now, residents don't work such herculean hours.

On March 4, 1984, Libby Zion, an 18-year-old college freshman, presented to New York Hospital with flu-like symptoms and odd jerking motions of her extremities. An intern and a second-year resident admitted her after discussing treatment plans with her primary care doctor. She was taking an antidepressant, phenelzine. The residents ordered meperidine, commonly given to treat spasms. She became agitated so restraints were ordered. Her temperature rose to 107°F. During attempts to lower her fever she went into cardiac arrest. She died from a rare condition known as serotonin syndrome. Several physician expert witnesses at the trial stated they had never heard of this pharmaceutical complication.

Libby's father, Sydney, was an attorney and a former writer for the New York Times. He wrote an editorial piece stating, "You don't need kindergarten to know that a resident working a 36-hour shift is in no condition to make any kind of judgment call, forget about life-and-death." In the civil trial, jurors cited the hospital as negligent for having junior residents in charge of forty patients.

We often had over sixty patients on the surgical wards at the Phoenix VA with a single resident covering at night. In 1989, the New York State Health Commission recommended residents not work over 80 hours per week nor more than 24 consecutive hours. A meta-analysis of 959 physicians found that working continuously for 30 hours dropped clinical performance scores by 1.5 standard deviations, similar to being drunk. The Accreditation Council for Graduate Medical Education, the ACGME, which presides over all medical residency programs, adopted an 80-hour work week and maximums for shift-length. The AGCME recommended strategic napping though no studies have measured the actual fatigue mitigation of naps.

Most studies have shown little to no change in patient mortality under the new work rules. Enforcement is difficult. Many residents and programs ignore the guidelines. There is no whistle-blower law for residents, so there is fear of reporting non-compliance. The medical profession at large has concerns that resident training has suffered under the new rules.

I received rigorous training at my program with a thousand surgery cases under my belt. I also gained weight and became so fatigued during my chief year I woke up tired every morning. If someone had offered me time off during my training, I would have jumped at it. I've overheard colleagues of my generation grousing about how residents aren't as well trained or as tough as us iron men of yore. I don't know. My main thought, as is my thought for many things, is it's not my problem any more. Retirement is like an autumn of problems falling to the ground.

My favorite rotation was the Phoenix Indian Medical Center. We got to do a lot of cases at PIMC, but more than that I came to admire the dedicated staff physicians. The career Public Health Service (PHS) doctors who mentored me were a different breed from the private practice doctors. They weren't paranoid about getting more cases so they could pay for McMansions or vacation homes. There was a sense of mission and duty and purpose. The staff surgeons were skilled and experienced. The Chief of Surgery, Dr. Frank Zweimer, had served years in India where he developed expertise treating leprosy. His knowledge served us well treating Native Americans who have higher rates of amputation than any other ethnic group due to a high prevalence of diabetes.

Dr. Robert Norton, a Harvard graduate, volunteered to work at a PHS Hospital in Can Tho, South Vietnam, during the Vietnamese War. *Look* magazine quoted him: "I didn't go into medicine to stay in one part of the world and make money while people on the other side bleed to death." Dr. Norton was a skilled plastic surgeon and also a birder. I had to cover the service during the Christmas Count. He taught excellent technical skills in his elegant, faintly mocking, humorous style.

During the Gotterdammerung of residency one does not have a lot of time to watch the news or read the newspaper. One day in the surgery lounge, Dr. Norton asked me if I knew what was happening in Cambodia. I didn't. He was shocked that none of the world powers had intervened in the Cambodian genocide. The Khmer Rouge savagely executed or starved three million people. Years later, in Phnom Penh, I visited Tuol Sleng, the prison where the Khmer Rouge tortured their victims before hauling them to the Killing Fields.

The horror seemed embedded into the physical structure. I felt ill for two days.

Just now I Googled for information about Dr. Norton and found that he had retired to Port Angeles, where my family had hiked to the Elwha Dam. I fear he may no longer be among us. A belated thanks to you, sir.

The Indian Health Service provides health care and dental care to 2.5 million members of the recognized tribes. In 1955, the IHS was under the Bureau of Indian Affairs. Now it is an operating division of the U.S. Department of Health and Human Services. With a 2017 budget of $5.1 billion, the IHS yearly cost-per-patient averages under $3,000, less than half the national average of $7,700.

During residency, Barb and I went to Alaska to hike and camp at Denali. There is an IHS Medical Center in Anchorage. I wondered if they might be interested in hiring me. The friendly Chief of Surgery sat me down and explained someone would have to die before there was a new position open.

On the flight to Anchorage, a large man with a cowboy hat sat next to me. He was also a Texan, so we got along. I told him I was about to graduate from my residency and thought it might be nice to work in Alaska. He interrogated me about the details of my training and life history. At the airport he showed me his fine hand-tooled leather luggage from the famous King Ranch. Six years later, the series *Northern Exposure* aired. The tag line was a New York Jewish doctor, fresh out of residency, had to repay his tuition by serving in a small town in the hinterlands of Alaska. I'm 94% certain that my cowboy friend from the Anchorage flight was Barry Corbin, a Texas-born actor, who played the part of the retired astronaut in the series. I have wondered if Corbin related my personal story to the show's creators. It's something I've been curious about and, likely, always will.

Our last year in Phoenix, Barb worked for the Phoenix Epidemiology and Clinical Research Branch of the National Institutes of Health. This branch researches diabetes and obesity. Most of the volunteer research subjects are members of the Pima tribe, descendants of the Hohokam who built the ancient canals. The Pima, now called the Akimel O'odham, are the People of the River. The Papago, near Tucson, are the Tohono O'odham, the Desert People. Conquistadors coined the term Papago, which means "bean eaters."

In the 1800s the Pima had irrigation farms around the Gila and the Salt Rivers. The tribe graciously supplied food and livestock to Gold Rush 49ers and U.S. troops en route to California. The Pima have the highest rate of obesity and diabetes of any ethnic subgroup. Evolving in the desert, their physiology adapted to a low calorie and low fat diet. Historic photos show brown, weathered Natives with zero body fat. Feed them McDonald's and they balloon up. Barb and I made friends with many Pimas. I can speak a few phrases of the language. A group of Barb's patients came to our wedding and gave us gifts of sand paintings, which now hang in a place of honor.

I dropped by PIMC years ago when I was in town for a melanoma conference. Few of the employees I had known were still there. I couldn't find my old friend Peter, a Pima who weighed at least 400 pounds. He was the hospital operator and always gave me a big smile when I entered the building. "Hey Dr. Wood, *shop-kai,* how are you?"

The hospital had an old-fashioned PA system that anyone could access from a telephone, like the camp megaphones in the movie *MASH*. There was a regular meeting called the "Talking Circle," a support group for Native issues. One time, I got on the PA system and announced a meeting of the "Silent Squares." I got in trouble, but Peter cracked up like it was the funniest thing he ever heard. After that, we were good buddies.

Peter showed me his car, a Ford Fiesta. To fit his enormous frame into the car, he installed a 4-inch diameter steering wheel. Peter had knee surgery when I was rotating on the Orthopedic Service. His gown was two bed sheets pinned together. When we saw him on morning rounds, the attending surgeon told him not to bear any weight on the operated leg. Down the hall, I turned and saw Peter staring at me. When he had my attention, he grew a big smile and lifted his good leg off the ground. I miss the human atmosphere of PIMC, so different from the condescending bureaucracy that lords over corporate-controlled medicine.

During last year's stay at Bob's place in his verdant neighborhood of central Phoenix, we helped him with a home improvement project, a new credenza. This time, he had a pair of brand new Sony Bluetooth speakers still in the box. We went to work. The controls for the speakers were extremely complicated. It took a while to figure out. I talked to Bob the other day. He hadn't used the speakers since we left. He couldn't remember how to sync them.

Bob likes watching Fox News programs. Like most military veterans, he has no use for sissy liberals who never experienced combat. He and Barb started binge watching news programs beginning with Hannity. I couldn't take it. Before Laura Ingraham came on, I fled to the RV.

Beyond Fox News, we had a great time with Bob. We pulled his BeLite Ultralight Aircraft out of the garage to exercise the engine, but we couldn't start it. It looked like there were bubbles in the fuel line. Bob is a fellow photography buff. He also likes metal working. He has a top-of-the-line lathe with computer controls. In Vietnam he bought Minox cameras, the original spy camera. No one makes the 9.5 mm film any more, so Bob is fabricating his own film slitter.

We went out to dinner with a second Bob, my long-time friend from high school and college-roommate, and his wife, Sandy. Los Dos Molinos is my favorite Mexican restaurant in Phoenix. The decor is all bright colors and lights and cactus, like a Day of the Dead parade. The building was a hacienda owned by legendary cowboy star Tom Mix. Bob #2 told me there was a rumor that Los Dos Molinos was over-spicing their meat. He had a bad experience at the one in Chandler. I asked about that when I made reservations. The woman assured me there was no extra spice in the food. Good enough.

Bob #2 had given me detailed edits on my first photography book, *Harvesting Photons*. I wanted to pay him back, so I presented him with a new Amazon Fire. He could read the book on it. We had a great dinner talking about the old days and the new days. Sandy shared a lot of fascinating history about growing up in a mining town. Going with friends to a restaurant under the stars in Arizona is the best experience anyone can ever have.

We planned to spend two weeks in Tucson visiting with family and friends. My heart always draws me back to my old home town, and it always will.

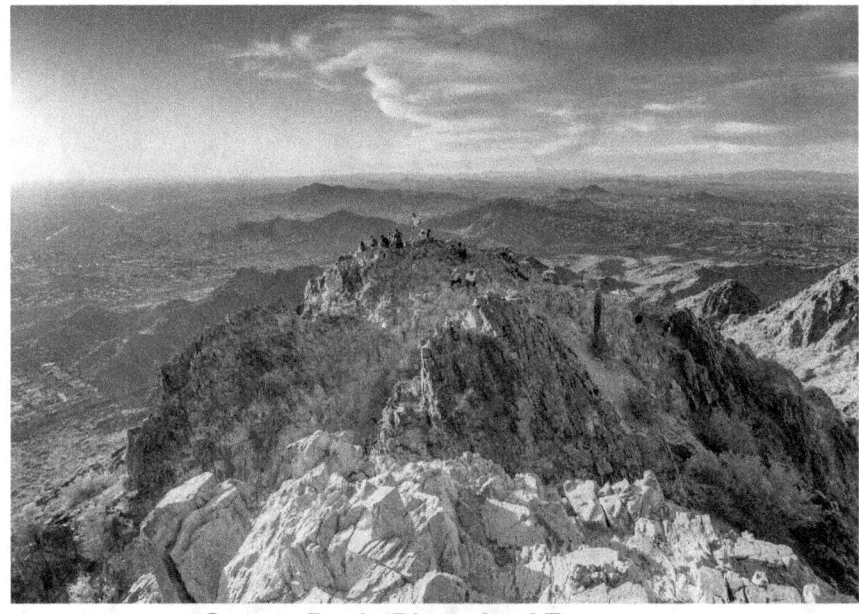

Squaw Peak, Phoenix, AZ

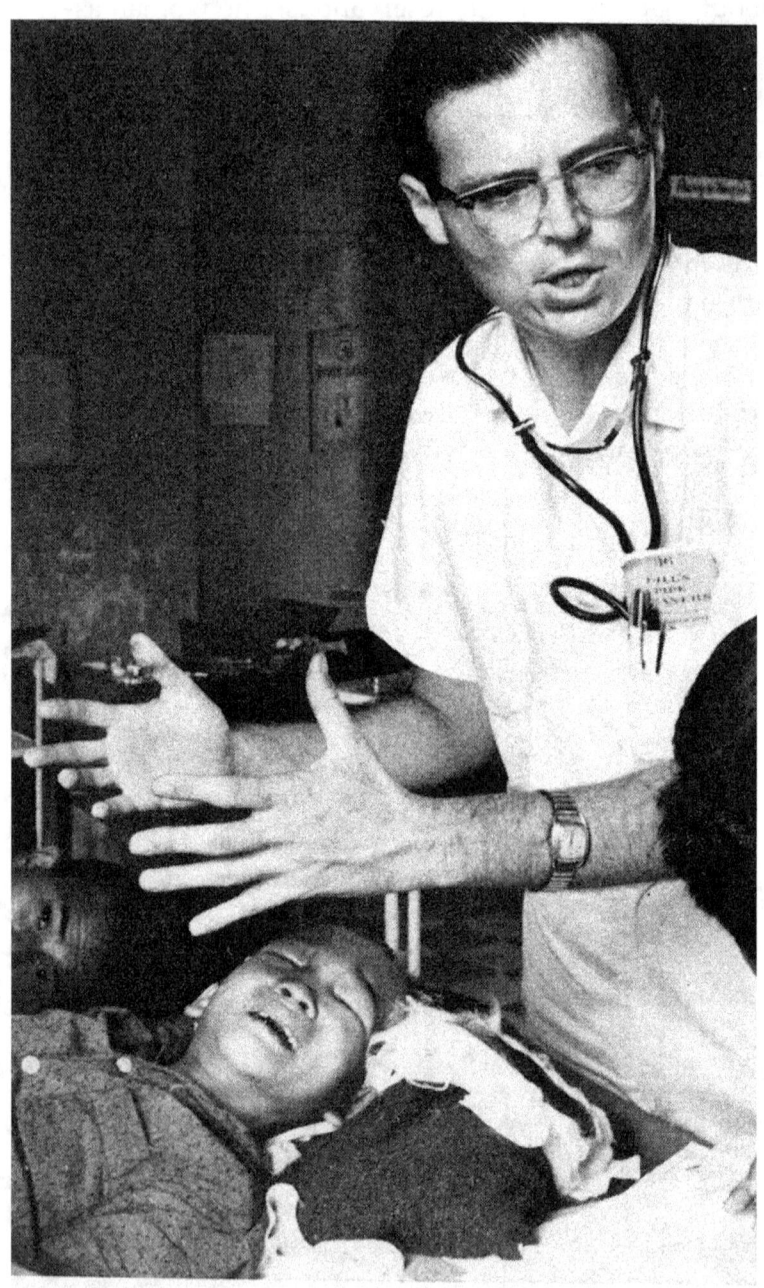

Dr. Robert Norton at Can Tho, South Vietnam

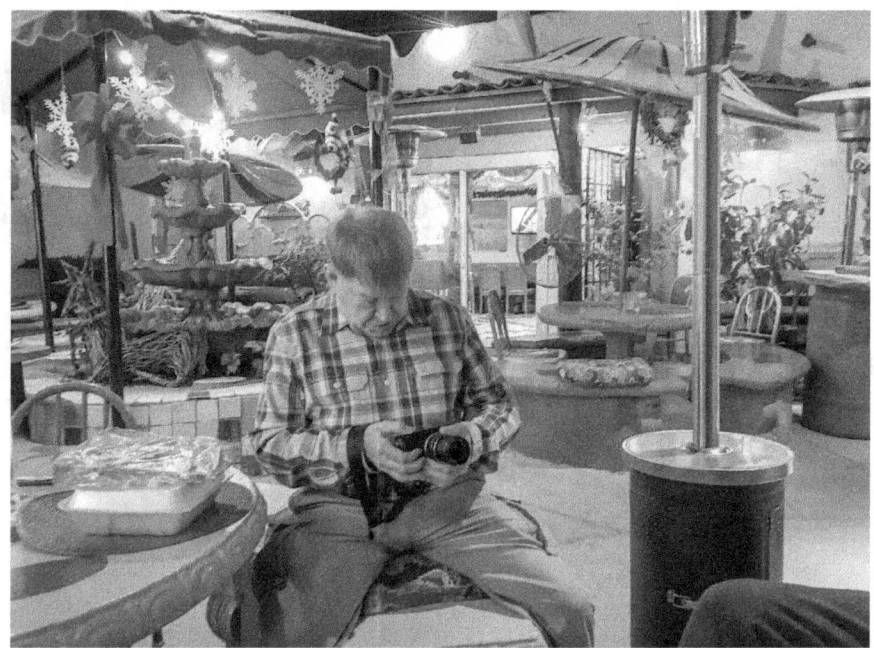

Bob at Los Dos Molinos

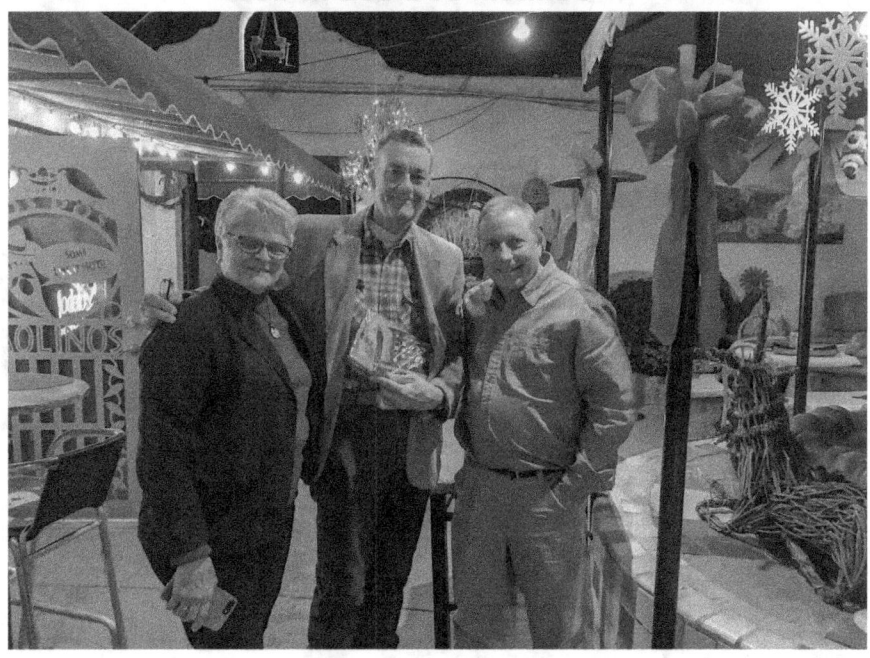

Bob (#2), Sandy and me

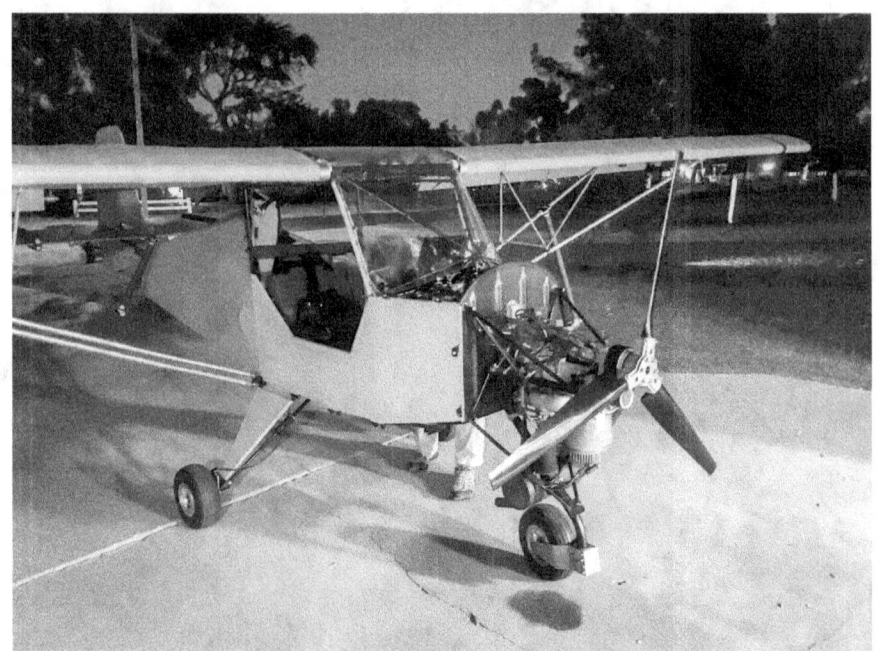

Bob's BeLite Ultralight

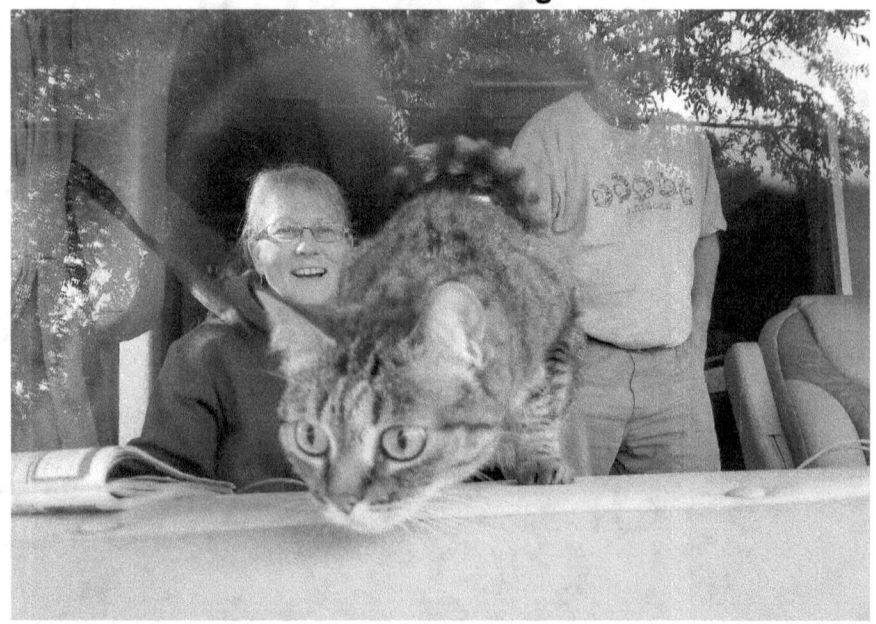

Bob's picture of Waffles

Chapter 15

Tucson Stories

The last Society of Surgical Oncology (SSO) meeting I attended was in Phoenix in 2009. This meeting is the yearly focal point for cancer surgeons. Powerful professors, heads of departments and leaders of the academic surgery world attend these meetings. They play political chess, give out awards, make speeches, and observe the crop of young surgeons eager to work their way up the academic ladder. During my two-year fellowship, following residency, I was in the mix of ambitious young surgeons. I presented my research at meetings and went to the alumni rooms. My chairman did his best to find me a university position and offered me an associate professorship in Houston. One problem was I disliked Houston. Barb disliked Houston. The other problem was I wanted to live somewhere in the West around mountains and deserts, the places I loved exploring.

None of the handful of medical schools in the western states wanted me. I ended up going into private practice in Portland, Oregon. I fancied I could do research in a private practice setting. The research available to non-university MDs is industry-sponsored studies. I did a study on a radiologic scanning agent for liver tumors. It didn't work well. My industry handler was disappointed I wasn't enthusiastic about promoting the product.

At the SSO meeting in Phoenix I searched for my fellow Fellows, graduates of the Surgical Oncology Fellowship at MD Anderson. We would get together at these meetings and catch up. Most of them were at medical schools, which is a different lifestyle than private practice. They rounded on patients with teams of residents and medical students, and published papers to keep their tenure. A few pursued research. As years went by, fewer and fewer of my old group showed up at the SSO. This time, I only found one, a professor at a prominent Canadian medical school, who was miffed that I didn't remember the names of his children after twenty-five years. He evinced no interest in my practice or my family. After shaking hands, he looked away scanning the crowd with his ambition radar at full intensity and said, "Let's schmooze."

After the meeting, I felt in need of cleansing. On the drive to Tucson, I called my old best friend, Jay, and invited him to join me on a backpack down Mount Lemmon. He wasn't sure if he wanted to do such an ambitious route. I told him I would go solo if no one wanted to come. When I got to town, Jay talked me into a shorter route down the mountain. He knew the trails. Several other friends were up for it. We gathered at my mother's house. I had my old green Kelty pack. The foam hip belt was rock hard after years in an outdoor storage space.

The Box Camp Trail began at Spencer Canyon on the upper slopes of Mount Lemmon. We planned to camp at Hutch's Pool on Sabino Canyon Creek, dropping 4,600 feet in 8.7 miles. Compared to hiking uphill, hiking downhill is half as hard on one's heart and lungs, but five times worse on the knees. Every step on a downhill requires arresting the momentum of the combined weight of hiker and pack.

At the trailhead, I inspected Klaus' pack. I'm calling him Klaus since he is sensitive about his identity. Klaus had packed way too much stuff. I threw out at least half of his food and gear. I didn't go through Rick's pack. Rick (Tucson Rick, not Santa Fe Rick) had a tendency to over-pack. I say "had" because he reformed after this trip.

The route climbed gently through snow patches and Ponderosa Pine for the first mile. The initial descent was comfortable, but soon we hit steep switchbacks on a primitive trail over boulders. At mid-day we crested a ridge. Tucson's fungus of metropoliteana spread through the valley below.

Everyone was in good spirits. Klaus brought out his new phone, at the time one of the first models of internet cellphones. His plan was to do fact checks on the many vigorous debates and arguments. He couldn't get a signal. Jay, never one to back off from a source of humor, kept asking Klaus every fifteen minutes, "Do you have a signal yet? Do you have a signal yet?" Klaus never got a signal.

By late afternoon my knees were shot. Each step was a little jolt of pain up the old leg sticks. Rounding a corner, we saw an animal. "What is that?" I thought it was a mountain lion cub. It charged us. It was a fox. Growling, the fox clamped its canines around my hiking pole and shook it like a caught rabbit. I took a one-handed picture while fencing with it. It released me and charged Guiliana, who also fended it off with her pole. There was no doubt this was a rabid animal. It staggered off the trail and we moved quickly, poles in hand.

At sunset we plodded into the riparian basin of Sabino Canyon. We made a big fire and set up tents. The stars came out and sung a song about Mexico. A night in the desert can cure all ills. There was only one problem. Rick and Ralph were still somewhere up the trail.

We ate dinner and gathered around the fire. Hours went by. Someone said Rick had been stopping a lot. The thought hit me they would pass the rabid fox in the dark. Jay suggested I go check on the fox, which didn't surprise me. When I got to the area, sure enough, two red eyes glowed in my headlamp cone. Mr. Fox was away from the trail. I saw lights high up on the switchbacks a mile away. An hour later Rick staggered into camp and collapsed into his tent. He hadn't eaten dinner the night before, nor much breakfast. He had tanked. Ralph had shepherded Rick down the mountain with frequent stops. They saw no fox.

Rick slept in his tent the next day. Jay and I explored Hutch's Pool, our favorite campsite in high school days. We looked for the spot where the Old Colonel had seen the mountain lion. The Old Colonel was our friend who wore a Confederate Army uniform, complete with a functioning Colt Navy revolver, as hiking attire. On one trip, before bedding for camp, the Colonel pointed across the firelight and told us he had seen a mountain lion staring at him when he woke on a solo trip. Andy Ringenberg and I tied a rope to a nearby bush. In the middle of the night we rattled the bush and yelled to the Colonel, "Get your gun, there's a mountain lion."

The Colonel came out of his tent with his Colt revolver at arms length, wearing only his period-correct long johns with seat flap. "You show yourself Mr. Lion. I ain't a-feared of you. I kin out-fight and out-fuck any man alive."

The Colonel was a terrific actor. He and Jay were stars in the high-school drama department. Andy and I burst out when we could no longer hold it. The Colonel is now a professor of western history. Jay thought he could recognize the old campsite, but nothing matched my memory. Things change after forty years.

Something happened to me on the hike out. The desert acquired a gauzy glow in the morning sun. It cradled me and siphoned my nagging insanity that comes from expecting justice. From the Sabino Canyon Visitor Center, I drove Jay up the mountain to retrieve his car. On the way down I pulled in at Windy Point Vista to shoot the sunset. Jay drove by on the highway, but he didn't see me trying to flag him. I remember his profile staring straight ahead. I remember it because it was the last time I saw him.

A few months later, on returning from a Boy Scout camp with my son, Barb took me outside and told me Jay's wife had called. He had died. Jay's friend, Giuliana, found him in a chair with a book over him. The grief was sudden and intense. Jay was in great shape. He played soccer. I took a chair into the forest and cried for my friend of many years and many adventures, or maybe I cried for me.

Tucson can't hold on to its writers. Tucson authors enjoy the spiritual magic of the desert and benefit from the stimulating cultural milieu of a university town. When they become rich and famous, they move away. Harold Bell Wright left. Barbara Kingsolver moved to Virginia, became a locavore, and was named as one of the "Virginia Women in History." Richard Grant, author of *American Nomads* and *God's Middle Finger*, decamped to Pluto, Mississippi. Even Charles Bowden, who graduated from Tucson High School and reported for the Tucson Citizen, moved to Las Cruces, New Mexico toward the end of his life.

Bowden was an admired and prolific writer. Much of his fame came from his investigations into the Mexican cartels: *Down By the River: Drugs, Money, Murder and Family*; *Murder City: Ciudad Juarez*; and *The Global Economy's New Killing Fields* and others. I haven't read those books. Evil sociopaths no longer interest me. I refuse to read Cormac McCarthy any more. When I was young, I thought existential despondency was cool. Now, I just find it despondent.

Bowden went to work for the Tucson Citizen to earn enough money to buy a Colnago racing bike. Lanky and strong, he was a fearsome rider. None of the other reporters wanted to take on the sex-crimes stories. Bowden discovered a talent for speaking to crime victims. The evil void of murder fascinated him. When he felt contaminated by the despair of the victims, he took long hikes in the soular laundromat of the desert. He discovered a market for nature writing. He became friends with landscape photographer Jack Dykinga and author Ed Abbey. I've read most of his nature books: *Frog Mountain Blues, Blue Desert, Killing the Hidden Waters* and others. He wrote about desert ecology and water issues and mining. He wrote about the Papago and the feared Sand Papago and their life in the arid Sonora.

Bowden, friends called him Chuck, was a gritty endurance hiker. He hiked many backcountry rambles in Mexico, Arizona and Utah. Most of the weight of his pack was books he liked to read in camp. One time he and a friend hiked forty-five miles from the Mexican border at night just to see what it was like for illegal aliens.

Frog Mountain Blues is Bowden's panoramic about the Santa Catalina Mountains, the setting of our hike down Mount Lemmon. The ancestors of the O'odham went into the Catalinas every spring to harvest fish and frogs. After years of brilliant nature writing, Bowden returned to reporting the dark stories about sicarios and murder.

From our RV camp next to the Superstition Mountains, east of Phoenix, Barb and I traveled Highway 79, a beautiful back road, across the desert to Tucson. We stopped at the roadside memorial for Hollywood cowboy Tom Mix at the very spot where he drove off the road and was killed by an unsecured luggage trunk breaking his neck.

In Tucson, as before, we parked in Mom's side driveway in front of the jumping cholla. We made an appointment to have our hydraulic jacks repaired. The issue was our cat. Waffles couldn't stay in the Photon Bus during the repair. Mom did not want the cat staying in her house. "I'm OK with dogs." I was upset that she was unwelcoming to my beloved pet. Waffles had been confined to the RV for a month. Luck is having the right friends. Rick (Santa Fe Rick, not Tucson Rick) was in town. He came over and fixed our hydraulic jacks. There was corrosion around the fuse.

The week was pleasant. Mom took Barb to the theater with her group of friends. None of the friends liked to drive, so Mom always chauffeured the group. That was an ongoing issue. To repay Rick for fixing our jacks, I helped him repair the road at his rental house. We built a check dam where a flash flood had washed away part of the road and spread a small mountain of gravel.

Lori, Rick's former renter, dropped by while we were working. She had built a custom Santa Fe style house on the edge of Sabino Canyon. She was planning to rent it. Half joking, I asked if the driveway could accommodate an RV. Later, she called and asked if Barb and I would like to house-sit for her over Christmas. We could hike into Sabino Canyon from her front door and the cat was OK with her. I jumped on it. Mom was upset that we wouldn't be spending another week at her house. I was upset that she was upset. This is family. We promised to come over for dinners, which sort of smoothed things out.

Lori spent years designing and building her dream house. The bone-white interior stucco walls were full of art and decor, including originals by R.C. Gorman. She had a friend who was a friend of Gorman. The "Picasso of American Indian Artists," Gorman was a legendary Navajo artist known for his stylistic paintings of Navajo women in elegant curves of brilliant color: reds, oranges and purples stolen from high-desert sunsets. These alluring dark-eyed women stared at me from Lori's walls. When Gorman died in 2005, New Mexico Governor Bill Richardson ordered the flags flown at half-staff.

The view east was over the deeps of Sabino Canyon to Thimble Peak. At night I saw the lights of trail runners climbing Blackett's Ridge. Several days we hiked into the canyon. Sabino Canyon is Tucson's playground. I detest the word playground to describe a natural area. It promulgates the ethos that the world was created for the benefit of the human species. This is the anthropocentric mindset that Aldo Leopold railed against in his Land Ethic. A better word is sanctuary.

On Christmas morning we headed up high, in altitude, on the Esperero Trail. Sabino Creek became a green stripe in the canyon shadows. An ocean of housing developments washed up against the foothill slopes of the Catalinas. On a previous hike, we had noticed a solitary adobe mansion perched high above Rattlesnake Canyon. A local couple on the trail informed us the owner of the mansion lived in New York and was involved in Russian television. He hardly ever visited. The half-mile private driveway to the mansion was made of hand-placed brick parquet.

We were due at my brother's house for Christmas dinner. Looking down from our high point, I saw that Bird Canyon Creek headed west into a neighborhood. It looked like a shortcut. We hiked down the creek and soon ran into the first of multiple no-trespassing signs. We were running late, so I argued to press on. The shortcut was a long mile through boulder pour-offs and a running stream. We came to a riprapped boulder cliff. On top, a brick parquet driveway spiraled up the mountain to the mysterious Russian's mansion. A large guardhouse menaced before an iron-staved gate. I studied the guardhouse to see if any AK-47 barrels protruded from killer holes. A sign posted inside the gate said, "IF IN DISTRESS, CALL 911." What the hell? One side of the gate was against a granite cliff wall. The other side had industrial barbed wire. We climbed boulders that allowed us a millimeter of crotch clearance above the razor wire. This was an oligarch's Checkpoint Charlie.

Walking through the neighborhood of xeriscaped homes felt like an escape to freedom. Two cute young sisters ran out to show us their Christmas presents. One had a toy sewing machine. I asked her if she could fix a button on my shirt. Her smile vanished as her eyes widened. She said, with all sincerity, "I'll have to ask my Mom."

My brother, Jim, has a well-appointed outdoor kitchen on a covered patio that looks toward the Rincon Mountains where summer monsoons put on lightning shows. Jim and his wife, Laurie, are seasoned barbecue chefs. The prime rib and award winning scotch were just the thing to wipe out thoughts of Russian oligarchs. This was Christmas in America, you election-meddling vodka-heads. Jim's two-year-old granddaughter stole the show. For the grandkids, Jim had made a presentation stage with blue curtains and a working mic on a stand. When the granddaughter walked up to the mic and sang songs like a natural, we almost fell out of our chairs.

The week was a dream in Lori's dream house. I could gaze forever at that view of the canyon and the mountains, painted at night by an Arizona moon. Barb sensed I was falling in love with the house. She put a knife in me. "We are not buying this house!" When dreams die they evaporate and leave a salty residue.

New Year's Eve loomed. The mysterious Klaus is my friend and a veteran of Geezer trips. He is a magician and proprietor of the *Mystery and Magic Dinner Theater*. He will be upset that I have hinted at his identity. Klaus constantly gets calls for people wanting reservations to his weekly show. On our Geezer trips, these calls, furtively answered by Klaus, interrupt our lively conservations, which enrages Rick who lets forth with verbal torrents. "Turn off that damn phone!" I phoned Klaus and was glad he answered and took our reservations for his big gala New Year's performance.

At some point in the age cycle, Barb and I quit going out for New Year's Eve. I hoped I wouldn't fall asleep at our table. Balloons, like at a political convention, covered the ceiling of the ballroom. Conversations rumbled in low thunder from the sold-out tables. Klaus had looked like petite death at the weekly Friday breakfast of our Tucson friends. He complained of getting calls for reservations at 4:00 am. I told him to try doing that for thirty years instead of just one week. There had been an issue with the vendor ripping him off on the pouring charge for the champagne.

Outside the ballroom, he looked less frazzled in his magician's tuxedo. He pulled me aside and told me in a low voice that my credit card number had bounced. Klaus explained that his policy was to cancel unpaid tickets, but since he was my friend, he let it ride. All my friends are interesting. I guess it's a criteria.

It was a great party and a magic evening. Each table had costume top hats and tiaras and confetti poppers. The loopy characters in the who-done-it mystery had the crowd howling. Klaus brought up embarrassingly flattered audience members to be sawn in half or hypnotized into chickens. It was Vegas without the six-hour drive. We bonded with our tablemates, a family that had driven up from Nogales with two well-spoken teenagers. A week later I called Klaus to rectify the credit card. When he recognized my voice he said, "Is this Dead-Beats-R-Us?"

It was time to hit the road. We made reservations in Tubac, forty miles south, near the *Tin Cup* golf course. We would visit the Mission San Xavier del Bac on our way out of town. One of these days I need to figure out how to quit leaving Tucson.

William J Wood Jr

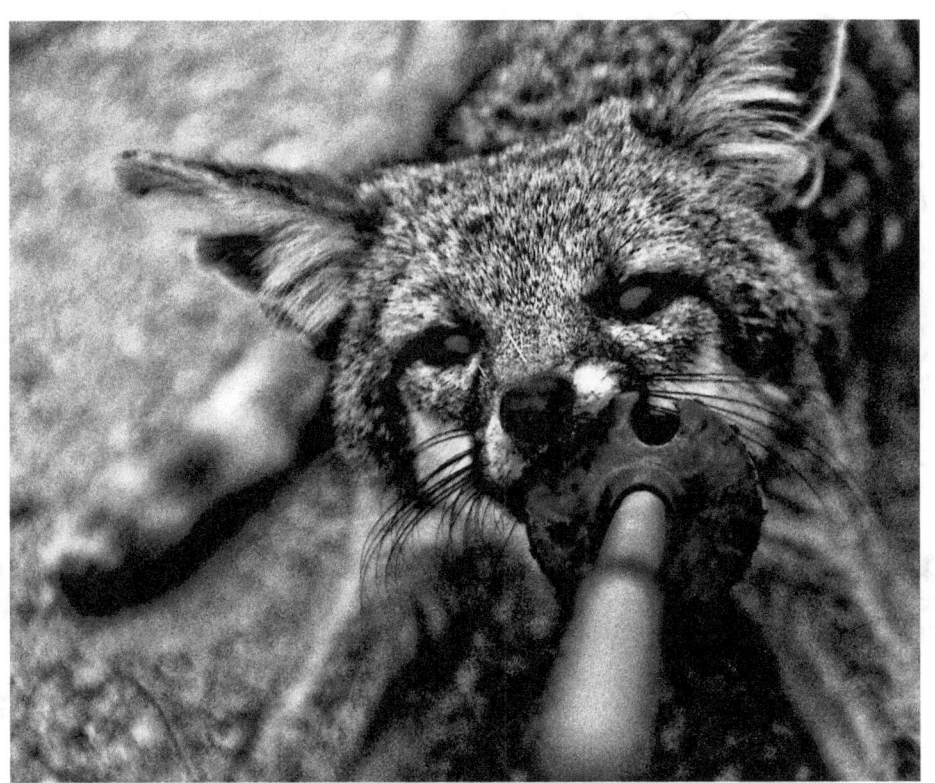

Rabid fox attacks

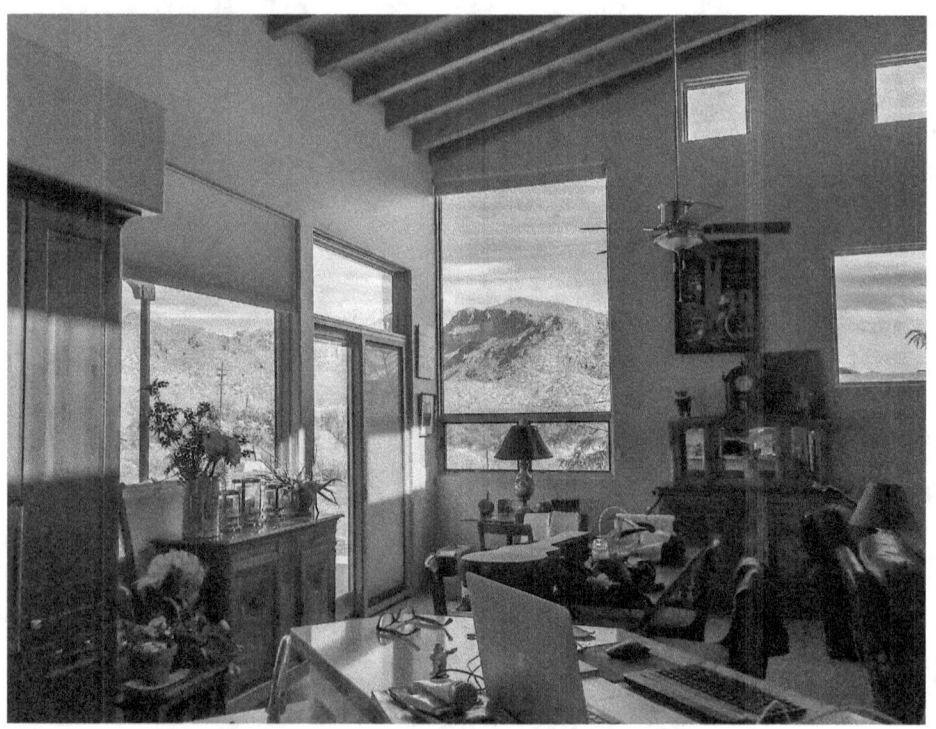

The house I fell in love with at Sabino Canyon

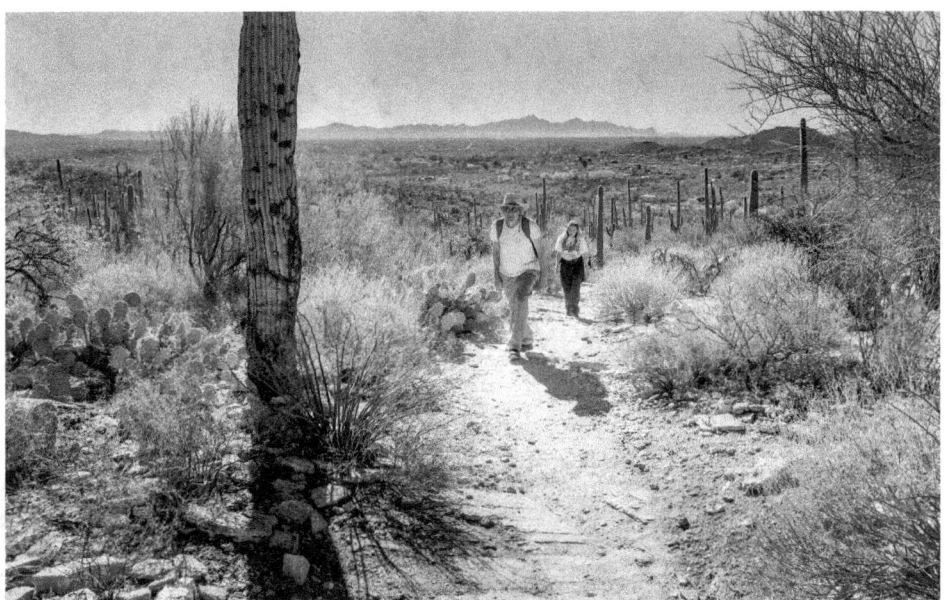
Hiking Sabino Canyon

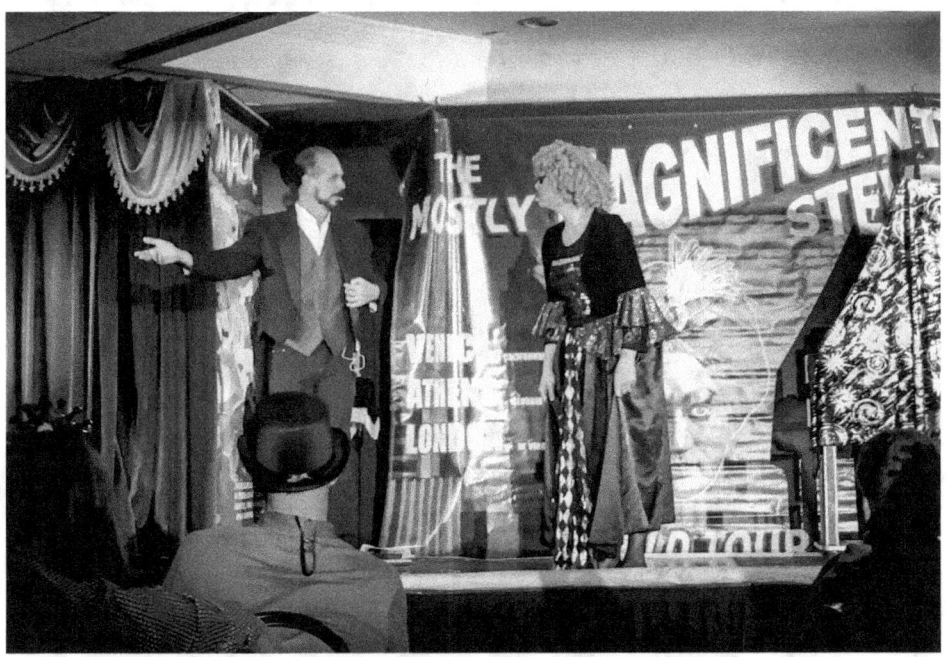
The Mystery and Magic Dinner Theater

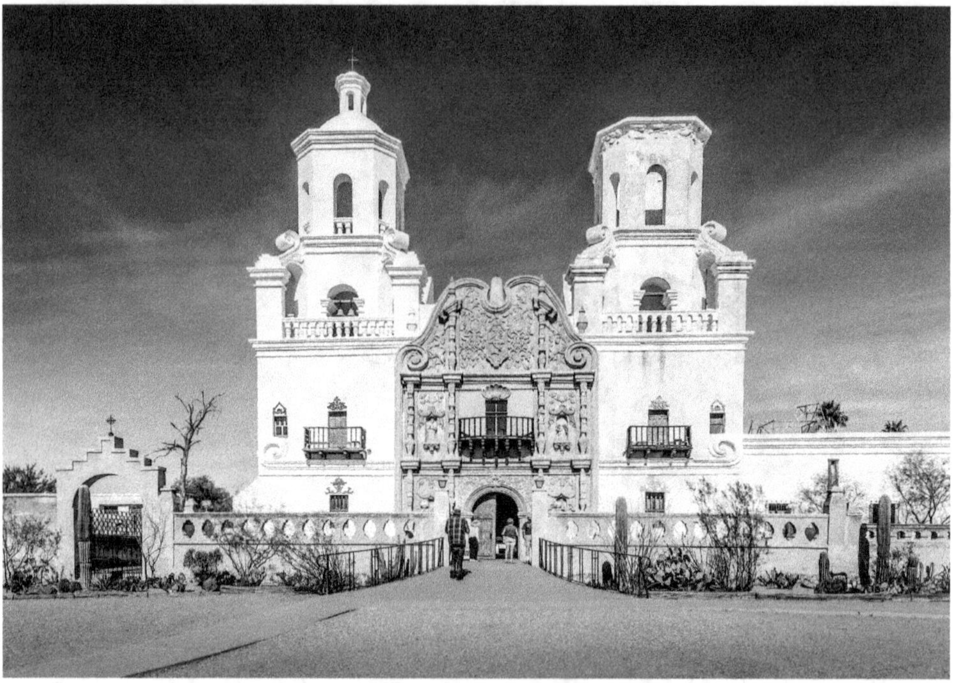

Photographing the American West

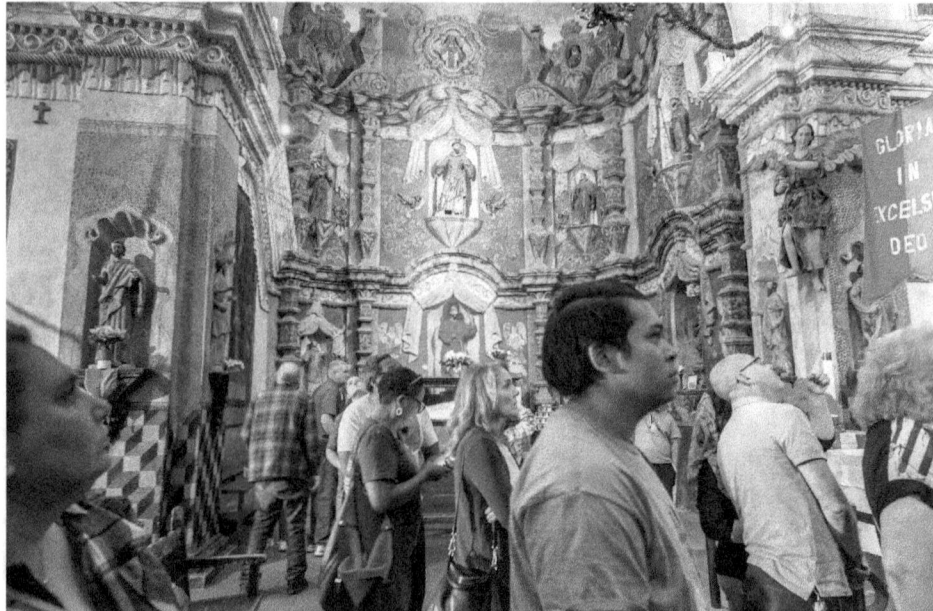

Mission San Xavier del Bac

Worshippers at the Mission

Chapter 16

No Country For Young or Old Men

In the spring of 2011, the Geezers gathered for a trip into the Chiricauhua Mountains in the southeast corner of Arizona. For the Apache, these high peaks and cool streams were a refuge from the surrounding desert. Geronimo, the legendary chief, surrendered to General Nelson Miles in 1886 at Skeleton Canyon, in the shadow of the Chiricauhuas.

We knew these mountains well. Just inside the boundary of the Coronado National Forest, we saw a sign we had not seen before. The sign read: TRAVEL CAUTION. SMUGGLING AND ILLEGAL IMMIGRATION MAY BE ENCOUNTERED IN THIS AREA. Like the Whack-A-Mole game, illegal border crossing routes sprouted in ever more remote areas as the Border Patrol shut down the better-watered routes, like Nogales or Douglas. The first night we kept a wary eye and listened for sounds in the dark forest. By the second day, the beauty of the jagged rhyolite pinnacles and the roaming wild turkeys erased any thoughts of illegal aliens. In this birder paradise, I was more attuned to finding Trogonidae: the Eared Quetzal, the large iridescent turquoise-colored bird of Aztec royalty, or a less-rare Elegant Trogan. These legal Mexican avian immigrants, who can fly over a border wall, send birders into orgasm. My old mentor, Dr. Robert Norton, had told me about the Quetzal. He told me about many birds, including the parasitic-nesting cowbirds.

My mammology class at the University of Arizona came out here to the Southwest Research Station to trap rodents and bats. I missed the best ever Chiricauhua trip. Rick's (Santa Fe Rick) bachelor party was a camping trip into these embracing mountains. Magically, Klaus packed in a chef-worthy grilled fish banquet that became a legendary Geezer story. I missed that camp and will regret it to my grave.

We saw no illegal aliens. The only incident worthy of fear happened during our nightly campfire debate. One of our group, who shall remain unnamed, pressed his argument by firing a revolver into the air. The lively debate stopped, then nervously resumed.

Will and Kim, ex-Tucsonans, drove from Missoula to join the trip. I was glad to have Will with us. He is a hydrologist and an informed naturalist. Will and I hiked in Cave Creek Canyon, a famous birding spot. The Chiricauhuas sit at the junction of the border of three large ecosystems: the Sierra Madre Occidental, the Sonoran Desert and the Chihuahua Desert. This conjunction supports niches for a wide variety of birds. Will named most of the birds we spotted or heard. Acorn Woodpeckers were all over the place.

Our group made several stops on the way back to Tucson. In the border town of Douglas, we lounged in the elegant Gadsden Hotel, named for the Gadsden Purchase that annexed southern Arizona into the United States. There is a famous chip in the marble stairs leading from the lobby to the second floor made by Pancho Villa's horse. I couldn't reconcile the sight of Douglas with my distant memories. More than half the automobiles on the streets were white-and-green Border Patrol SUVs. Many businesses were shuttered. Other than the absence of bombed-out buildings, the town looked like a war zone.

Kim asked us to stop by Huachuca City so she could visit her brother. Kim is a woman who exudes such maternal sweetness it is impossible to say no to her about anything. Her brother, Kit, developed a serious mental illness years ago. Kit's wife had a similar condition. They were both doing fine. Kit, who looks like he could have played one of the bounty hunters in the *Wild Bunch*, makes sought-after custom leather saddles. He toured us around his studio and explained all the instruments. Kit takes a year to make a masterfully tooled saddle that is a work of art. Get your orders in now.

After Jay's passing, we friends began meeting for breakfast every Friday at the Tucson Racquet & Fitness Club. The breakfast is now an institution. The Slavic-accented waitress knows how everyone likes his or her orders. We out-of-towners are expected to show when possible.

Discussing the Chiricauhua trip at breakfast, a woman walked up and said she overheard us. She had grown up on a ranch just outside Huachuca City. She told us a story. Her neighbor, a rancher, looked out his window one day and saw four men hiking with large, black backpacks. He called the Border Patrol. A week later the mayor of Nogales, a friend of the rancher's, drove out and told him the cartel had marked him for death. The rancher sold out and moved to Texas. Compared to the days when adventurous high schoolers would bomb over the border to Nogales for a night of revelry, the borderlands now have an air of grim wariness. This is Cormac McCarthy country: no country for young or old men.

A year before our Chiricuahua trip, 58-year-old Robert Krentz, a rancher in the San Bernardino Valley east of the Chiricauhuas, drove out in his ATV to check water lines. He had his dog and two guns. At 10:30 am Krentz sent a garbled radio transmission to his brother. The brother thought he heard the words "wind" and "illegal alien." Twelve hours later a search helicopter located Krentz, dead from gunshot, slouched on his still-running ATV. His dog was dead. The killer's tracks disappeared near the border.

The border wall in this part of Arizona is X-shaped steel beams, no barrier to foot traffic. Krentz was a kind man who left water spigots on his land for wandering illegals. Once, he gave two women and their children a ride into town. Two weeks before, Krentz' brother had called the Border Patrol after he witnessed bureros, dope smugglers, who were caught with 290 pounds of marijuana. Some believe Krentz' murder was a revenge killing.

Residents in the San Bernardino Valley and nearby towns of Portal and Rodeo report multiple break-ins. They construct security fences and carry arms anytime they leave home. Two weeks after our trip, the large Horseshoe II fire broke out near our campsite. Locals claim illegals set the fire to draw attention away from their routes.

On the Geezer trip, north of Sierra Vista we passed through a checkpoint. This was my first. When asked if we were U.S. citizens, we said, "Yes." One time I drove out to Kit Peak, in the Tohono O'odham reservation, to shoot the sunset. Coming back after dark, a sudden, intense white flash from the roadside blinded me. A mile later I hit a checkpoint. Same question. Same answer. Barb and I had to go through a checkpoint on I-19 every day returning from the Tubac Golf Resort to our camp at Amado.

In 1904, seventy-five horse-mounted guards patrolled the entire U.S.-Mexico border. Their job was to prevent illegal Chinese immigrants from entering. Nitroglycerin-wielding Chinese laborers built the transcontinental railroad. They were rewarded with the Chinese Exclusion Act of 1882. Many workers fled south to Mexico. A hydrologist I know told me he was surveying in the Sierra Madre south of the border and noticed intricately constructed stone dams on streams. His Mexican guide told him the Chinese constructed the dams to irrigate their poppy fields. The Chinese, excluded from the land of trains, supplied the first heroin epidemic in the film-noir era of Los Angeles.

Founded in 1924, the U.S. Border Patrol guarded both the Mexican and Canadian Borders. At the start of WWII, the Patrol had 1,500 staff. After the September 11 attacks in 2001 the Border Patrol became part of the new Department of Homeland Security. The number of agents mushroomed to 21,394. The CBP, U.S. Customs and Border Protection, is the agency responsible for guarding our borders. ICE, U.S. Immigration and Customs Enforcement, investigates smuggling and trafficking and performs deportations. Funding for the CBP was $12.4 billion in 2013, a 91% increase from its 2003 budget.

The CBP divides the border into sectors. The Tucson Sector, the busiest, covers most of the Arizona border. Four thousand agents work out of eight stations in this sector. Most agents work at the border, but some staff the nine interior checkpoints that screen traffic. Legal Hispanics have complained about racial profiling at the check points. Sometime I would like to dress up in a Pancho Villa costume and see what happens.

In the wake of the Krentz murder, anti-immigrant sentiment raged in Arizona. The legislature passed a bill, SB 1070, the Support Our Law Enforcement and Safe Neighborhoods Act. The Act allowed law enforcement officers to determine a person's immigration status when there was a "reasonable suspicion" the individual was an illegal immigrant. Illegal aliens over 14 years of age had to register with the federal government and carry documentation. Legal aliens had to carry proof of citizenship. Are not all of us who aren't Native Americans considered legal aliens? In the eyes of Sheriff Joe Arpaio and the Maricopa County Sheriff's Office, the MCSO, functionally this law made racial profiling legal, even though a last-minute amendment, HB 2162, stated police may only investigate incident to a "lawful stop."

One of the bill's drafters argued that since the law contained the phrase "may not consider solely race, color or national origin," that it was not legalizing racial profiling. So an officer would have to report that the subject looked like a Mexican AND looked at him funny. On our passes through the I-19 checkpoint, the officer waved us through as soon as he saw our white faces.

In 1973, the California Border Patrol pulled over Felix Umberto Brignoni-Ponce and his two passengers for no other reason, according to the officers, than they looked Mexican. The passengers were illegals. California charged Brignoni-Ponce with knowingly transporting illegal immigrants. He appealed all the way to the Supreme Court based on violation of his Fourth Amendment right to protection from unreasonable search and seizure. The Court held that his Fourth Amendment rights were indeed violated. Brignoni-Ponce, a Puerto Rican, did not take a lesson. He was arrested five more times for carrying illegal aliens and spent three years in jail.

The usual suspects lined up on their usual sides to oppose or support SB 1070. Tens of thousands demonstrated in protest. Multiple proposed boycotts from other states threatened a $90 million loss to Arizona convention and hotel companies. Major League Baseball came out against it, probably because a quarter of the players were at risk for being late to a game. Linda Ronstadt said, "Mexican-Americans are not going to take this lying down." That would have been enough for me. Los Angeles threatened to quit buying power from Arizona producers. This supports my long-held position that California treats Arizona like a cur dog.

Unhappy police officers, cities Tucson and Flagstaff, and an ACLU-backed class action group filed seven lawsuits. The United States Department of Justice filed a lawsuit against Arizona. It is unusual for the DOJ to sue an entire state. The federal suit declared the Act was invalid because it interfered with the immigration regulations "exclusively vested in the federal government." The state of Arizona countersued.

In 2012, the Supreme Court ruled on Arizona v. United States by a 5-3 majority that Sections 3, 5(C) and 6 of SB 1070 preempted federal law. These sections included the documentation mandate, arrest without warrant and the restriction against applying for employment without federal work authorization. However, the Court upheld allowing state police to investigate immigration status for "reasonable suspicion." In 2016, the last tooth fell out of the Act when Arizona ended its practice of requiring police officers to demand papers from suspected illegals. The policy change happened as a settlement in a suit brought by the National Immigration Law Center.

Arizona likes colorful characters. Joseph Michael Arpaio, the self-proclaimed "America's Toughest Sheriff," served as Maricopa County Sheriff for 24 years. He gained national fame, or infamy, in his early career for constructing a concentration camp prison in the desert called "Tent City." Cooling fans in the tents rarely worked. During a heat wave the temperature in the tents rose to 145°F. He issued pink underwear to inmates and forced them to listen to an in-camp radio, KJOE, that broadcast endless Frank Sinatra. "Cause it's witchcraft, wicked witchcraft." He revived the chain gang concept. When asked about conditions in the camp, Arpaio replied, "It's 120 degrees in Iraq and the soldiers are living in tents and they didn't commit any crimes, so shut your mouths!"

He was a local hero to some. The people re-elected him five times. To others he was a sadistic, paranoid, self-aggrandizing asshole. The New York Times labeled him, "America's Worst Sheriff." During his reign, the MCSO was lax in investigating sex-crimes and crimes involving Latinos. Sheriffs failed to investigate a Hispanic 14-year-old's claim of rape by her uncle, even though his semen was in her rape kit specimen. After repeated rapes she got pregnant. Her settlement was $3.5 million. The MCSO improperly cleared, reported as solved, 75% of active cases with no arrests or investigations.

In 2007, the Phoenix New Times published an article about a grand jury investigation of Arpaio. The same night the Times article came out, deputies arrested owners Mike Lacey and Jim Larkin on trumped up charges. Their settlement was $3.75 million. Arpaio teamed up with a corrupt and later disbarred Maricopa County Attorney, Andrew Thomas, to investigate his political opponents, including judges, administrators and county supervisors. He targeted Mayor Phil Gordon and Arizona Attorney General Terry Goddard. Twelve lawsuits brought by Arpaio's targets cost the county over $13 million in settlements and over $44 million in legal expenses.

Arpaio and his buddies played funny money with the MCSO budget, enjoying luxury hotels and haute cuisine. They had the local broadcast news film the arrest of 18-year-old James Saville for plotting to kill Arpaio with a pipe bomb. It was a fake entrapment. Saville got $1.1 million.

Sheriffs regularly invaded Latino neighborhoods in saturation patrols hunting for illegals. A federal court informed Arpaio he did not work for the immigration service. Cries of racial profiling piled up into a class action lawsuit overseen by U.S. District Court Judge G. Murray Snow, who should be named "America's Toughest Judge." Snow stood firm to repeated defiance and mockery from Arpaio and the MCSO. Arpaio accused Snow and the DOJ of conspiracy and started a criminal investigation he called the "Seattle Operation."

After many years of legal attempts to harpoon America's toughest sheriff, a U.S. District court convicted Arpaio of criminal contempt in 2017. But the old aphorism did not hold. Arpaio is big, but he did not fall hard. President Trump pardoned Mr. Arpaio, who announced he will run for Senator Jeff Flake's seat. Said Arpaio, "I got a little disturbed about how some people in the Senate were treating the president." My question is when will the movie come out?

We had fun golfing in Tubac on the "Tin Cup" course for three days. The eighteenth hole is an island green surrounded by water. Barb felt intimidated on the tee since the nearby outdoor cafe was full of patrons watching. She whacked a worm-burner into the water that skipped several times then popped out on the middle of the green.

We camped at the De Anza RV Resort, a converted greyhound racetrack in Amado. We went to a fish fry dinner. The scene gave me the creeps. I felt like I was at a nursing home patronized by an overly polite young wait staff. Time to hit the road. We headed toward Las Cruces, New Mexico, a town I had heard much about but had never seen.

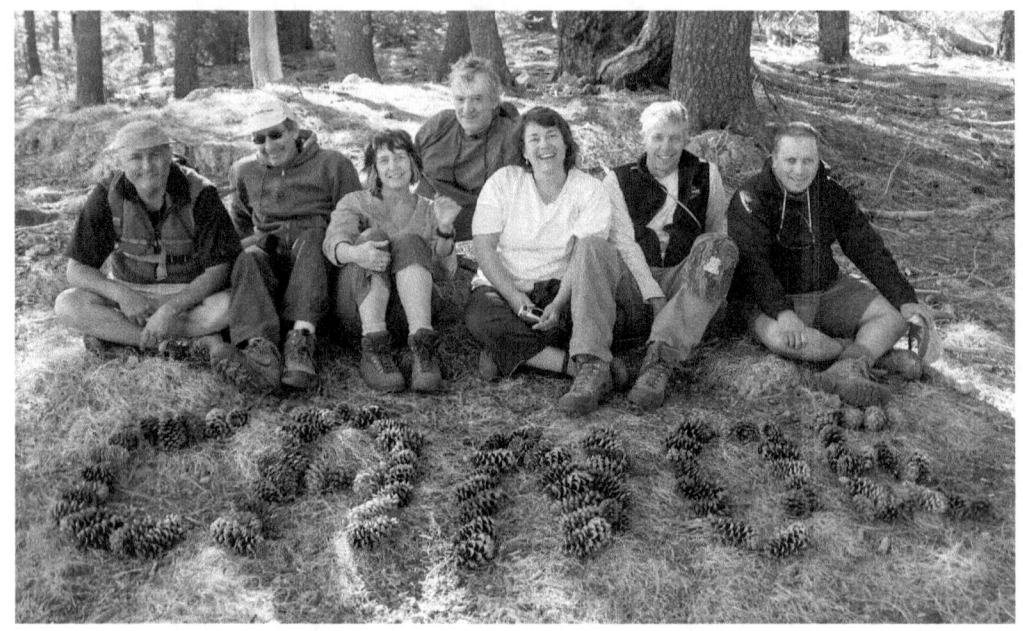

The Geezers in the Chiricauhuas

William J Wood Jr

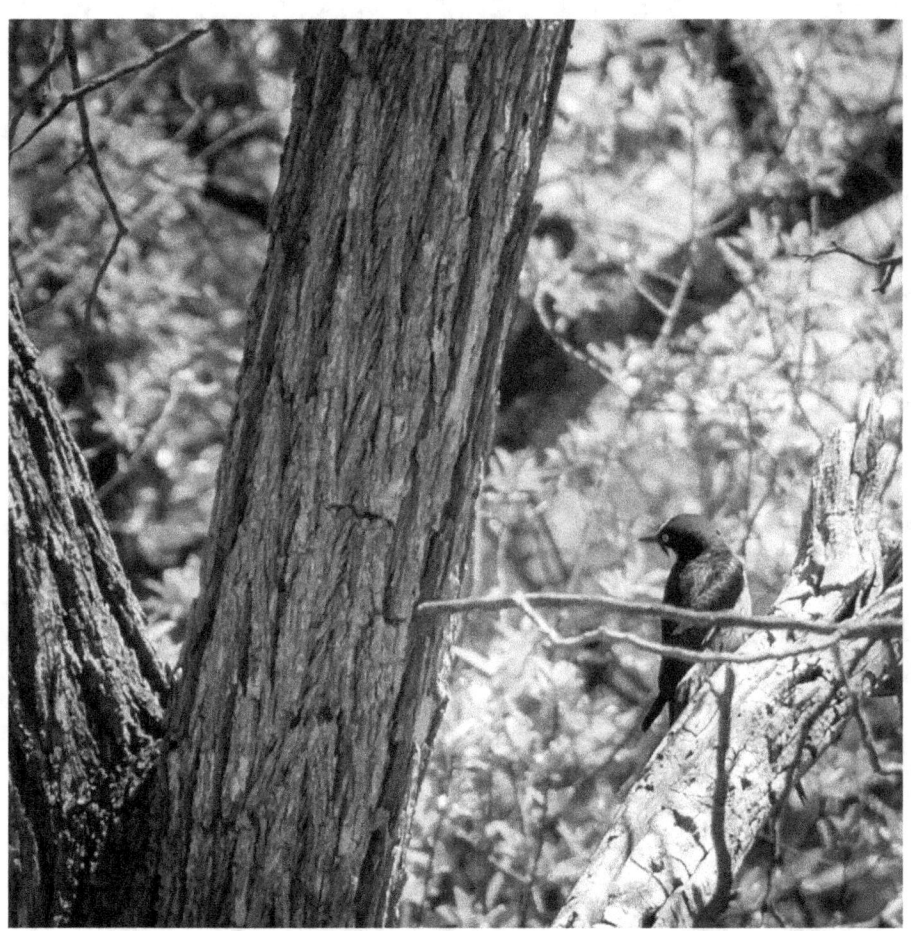

Acorn Woodpecker

Photographing the American West

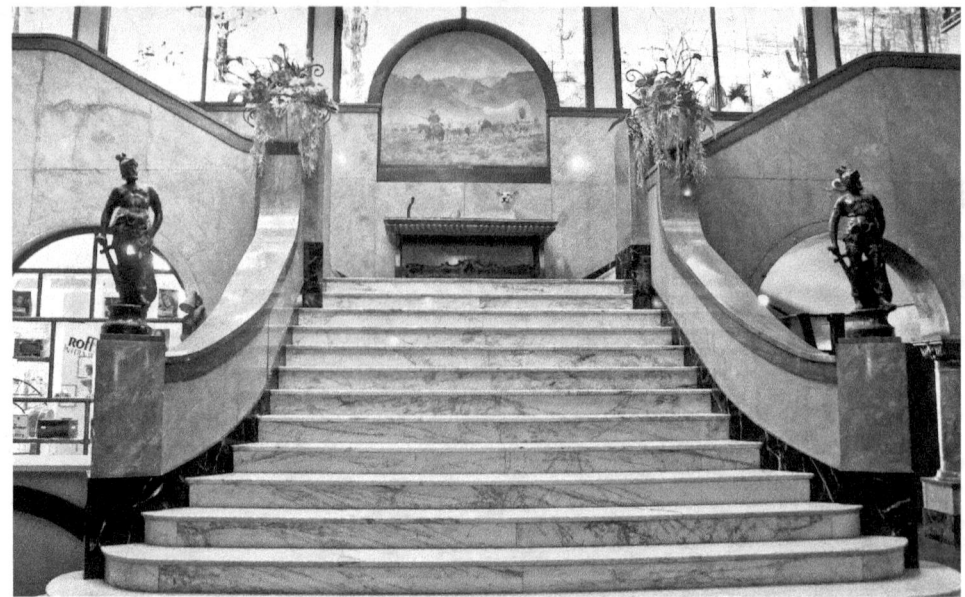

Gadsden Hotel, Douglas, AZ

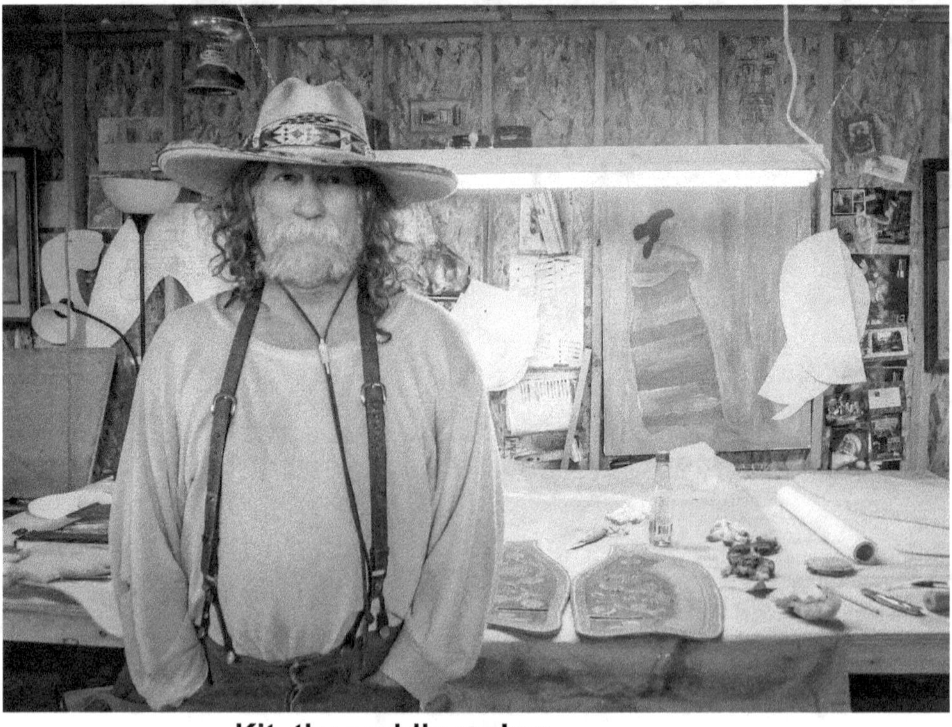

Kit, the saddle maker

Chapter 17

When I Was a Kid, They Called Me Billy

We left the remote for our Amazon Fire at Lori's house. We had to swing back through Tucson anyway to connect with I-10. It was afternoon when we got out of town, so we stopped overnight in Wilcox. The park was a gravel lot the size of several football fields with maybe ten RVs scattered in random sites. The big-bearded man camped next to us had a dozen rigged fishing rods and a big black Harley in his toy hauler. He was from Arkansas and boy did he like to fish.

After a quiet night, we decamped early. Wilcox looked tired in the morning light, as if saying "Just fill your gas and move on." I remembered Christmas lights at night on Wilcox' Main Street cheering me while driving back from the Gila Mountains.

Whoever invented curios gets a gold star carved from a seashell on their forehead. My affinity for curios, combined with the sign, U GOT 2 STOP, made the Continental Divide Trading Post on I-10 irresistible. Outside the Post, Volkswagen Minibuses surrounded a concrete teepee. My kind of place. The Divide had it all: day-glow hand-painted skulls, cowboy lamps, moccasins, coffee mugs, T-shirts, wind chimes, crockery: everything vital to survival in the 21st century. You got to stop!

In Las Cruces, the couple next to us at the Hacienda RV Park had a 42-foot Class A with a hydraulic lift on the back for a Harley. You see lots of Harleys in RV parks. The friendly retirees were from Arlington, Texas. They made the same trip every year to watch the MLB spring training games in Sun Valley, outside Phoenix.

After breakfast, we rode out to the Dripping Springs Natural Area at the base of the Organ Mountains, the trademark spiked peaks that backstop Las Cruces. The trail to the spring cut through soothing amber waves of Agropyron trachycaulum, slender wheatgrass. Up the hill from the weeping spring stood a lonely structure, the old sanitarium. After failing to build a dam across the Rio Grande and getting kicked out of the bank he had founded, The First National Bank of Las Cruces, Dr. Nathan Boyd built the sanitarium for his tubercular wife in 1917.

Macabre stories hang over this area like an ammonia fog. Hikers report sightings of ill people with pus-draining wounds roaming the brush around the sanitarium. Spirits fade into shadows and vanish. Locals believe the ghosts to be patients who waited for a slow death in the rudimentary wards. Overnight campers report nightmares.

El Ermitano lived in a cave, La Cueva, north of the springs. Giovanni Maria de Agostini, an Italian Maronite, never stayed long anywhere. He roamed throughout Europe in his youth in the early 19th century. He visited most of the countries in South America. Catholics at Cerro Monje in Brazil celebrate Agostini with a yearly festival. An unknown person, maybe a local native, stabbed El Ermitano to death in his cave. Realizart Produadalo, a Brazilian film company, shot footage around the area for a documentary, *The Hermit of La Cueva*.

The next day we went to the New Mexico Farm and Ranch Heritage Museum. Four stars (or whatever the maximum is) to this spacious, immaculate museum. The indoor exhibits detailed the history of New Mexico, from the Paleolithic to the present. My favorite was the panels commemorating the lives of the old ranchers in the area. Deane F.

Stahmann, 1900 - 1970, farmed with science. He discovered geese went well with pecan orchards. The geese ate the weeds and fertilized the trees. One year he sold 20,000 pounds of geese feet to China. There was gold in those geese feet and thanks for the fertilizer. In the outdoor pens we saw steers, sheep, goats. An informative emporium explained the types of old farm equipment, now sleeping under rust. On certain days you can run a milking machine.

We toured the Museum of Nature and Science and the M. Phillips Fine Art Gallery in Las Cruces' spacious downtown walking mall. Close to our RV camp, we enjoyed historic Mesilla Plaza. Mesilla was once the territorial capitol. The town refused to grant land to the railroad. Nearby Las Cruces complied. It's the saga of the old West. No gottie railroad, no gettie economic boom. Billy the Kid's least favorite bar squatted in a corner of the plaza. Instead of a whiskey neat in the old courtroom, the judge poured Billy a hanging sentence.

Billy the Kid's (1859-1881) given name was Henry McCarty. He made up the pseudonym William H. Bonney after escaping Arizona Territory following his first killing. Had he stayed for the trial, chances are Bonney would have been found innocent for killing in self defense a local bully, Francis "Windy" Cahill. During his escape to New Mexico, the Kid almost died after Apaches stole his horse. He got involved with the Lincoln County War. A posse coming to seize cattle in payment for a debt killed Bonney's employer, rancher John Tunstall. The Kid joined the Lincoln County Regulators, a group opposing Tunstall's enemies. Killings ensued on both sides. Governor Lew Wallace offered Bonney clemency for his testimony about the gruesome murder of a local lawyer by the anti-Regulator group. Bonney testified, but the promised clemency was not granted so he escaped from the Lincoln County Jail. On the run, he killed a man, Joe Grant, who was gunning for him.

Following a ranch-house armed siege, Sheriff Pat Garrett captured Bonney. At the Mesilla Courthouse, the judge sentenced Billy the Kid to hang. He again escaped from the Lincoln County Jail, killing two deputies. The determined man hunter, Pat Garrett, sat in an unlit room in a house of Bonney's friend, who he had been questioning. The Kid walked in unannounced. Billy couldn't see into the dark room. He said, "Quien es? Quien es?" Pat Garrett shot him through the heart. Years later, a group of men gunned down Pat Garrett outside Las Cruces. The apparent motive was a beef over a goat herd. None of Billy the Kid's eight killings were in cold blood. Except the killing of the deputies, all his shootings occurred in active fights with armed opponents. He killed the deputies to escape hanging.

Death by knife or gun was common in the old West. It still happens. On the trauma service at Good Samaritan in Phoenix we received multiple victims from a large Latino wedding that got out of control. I did an emergency thoracotomy on a man with a knife wound. With my fingers as if holding a bowling ball, I tamponaded three holes in his right ventricle and sutured around the holes. The procedure was unsuccessful.

Our days in Las Cruces were relaxing and free of violence. I had always wanted to see the town of Roswell because of the alleged UFO crash in 1947. The morning sun hid behind dark skies as we merged on NM 70 north. A cold spitting rain ushered us into the White Sands National Monument. We hiked in rain gear. My aunt told me that my cousins had sunburned their skin off as kids at the Monument. Gypsum sand, a rare matrix, gives the dunes their bleached white shine. Rain dissolves the gypsum crystals into a solid coat, stabilizing them. I grabbed shots of undulating ghostly dunes under black-bellied clouds.

We drove through Lincoln County, peaceful now. Roswell was not what I expected. Instead of the charming adobe of most New Mexican towns, Roswell looked like a west

Texas town, like Pecos where my grandparents had lived. A cold rain pattered our roof overnight. We didn't bother with the UFO museum. The next day we headed to Santa Fe, driving through the lonely scrublands of the Pecos River Valley. The only picture I took was of an unusual sculpture at a rest stop.

We picked up hedge clippers on the way. In Santa Fe we parked down the street from Rick's house and attacked the encroaching tree limbs in his Driveway From Hell. It didn't work. Later at home, I Turtle Waxed the RV sidewalls, but the scratches were still visible.

It's funny how timing gets weird. Rick had to leave his house after dinner to fly to Connecticut to pick up his wife, Mimi. They would drive back to Santa Fe in her car. Mimi's elderly mother, in Taos, was not doing well. We would have the house to ourselves. Trips are where life mixes with the ether.

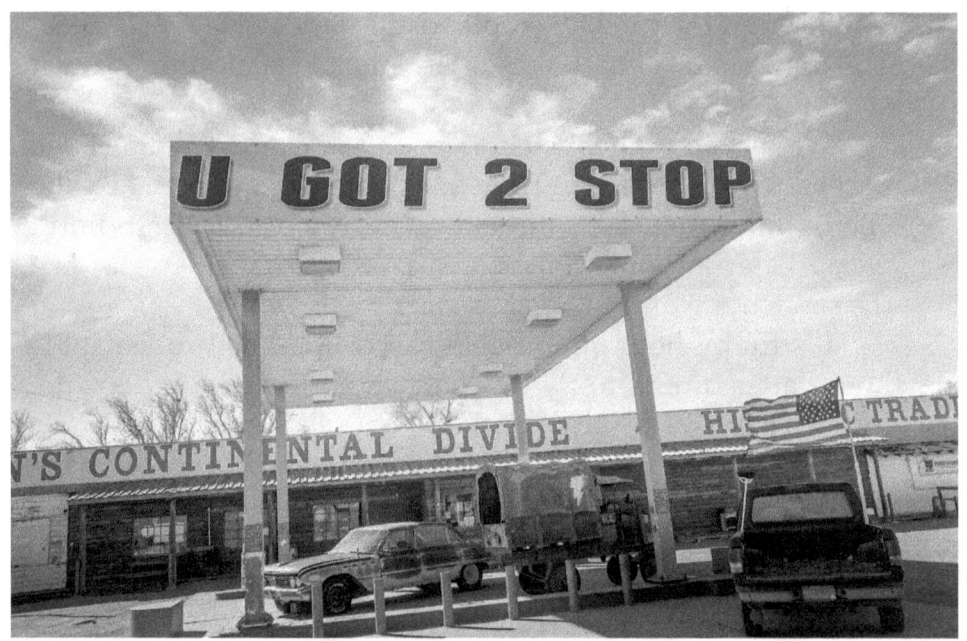
You got to

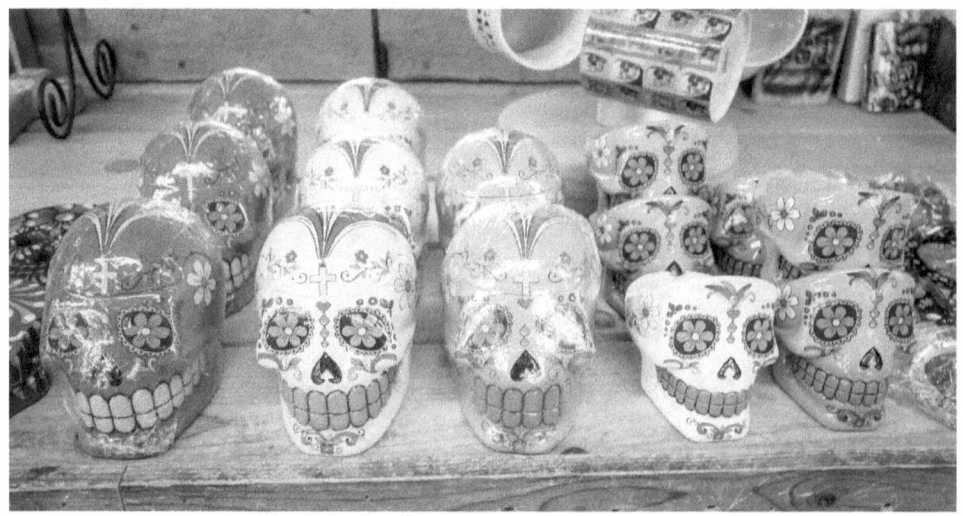
My kind of place

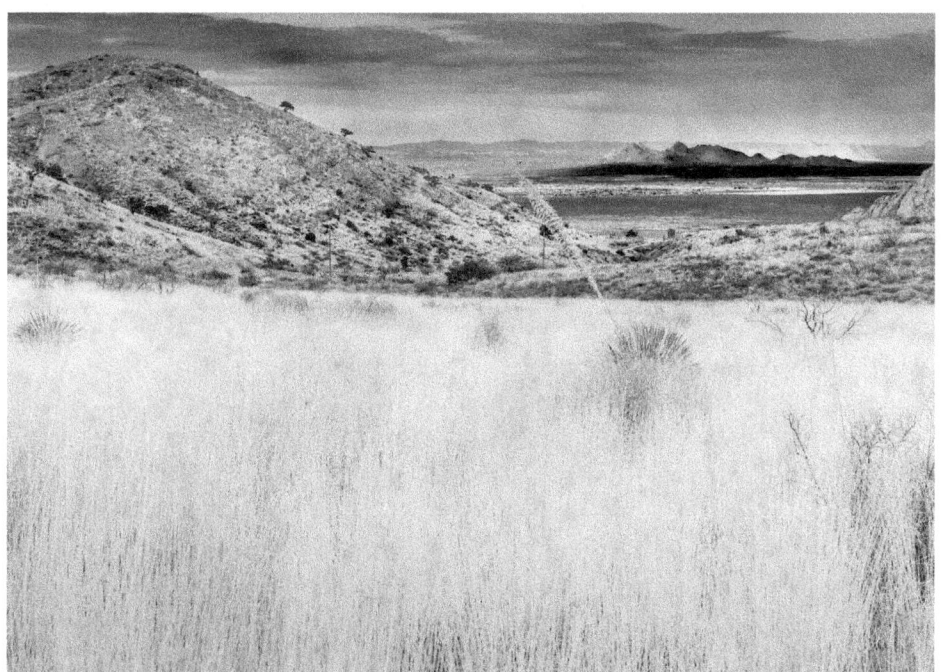
Dripping Springs Trail. Slender wheatgrass.

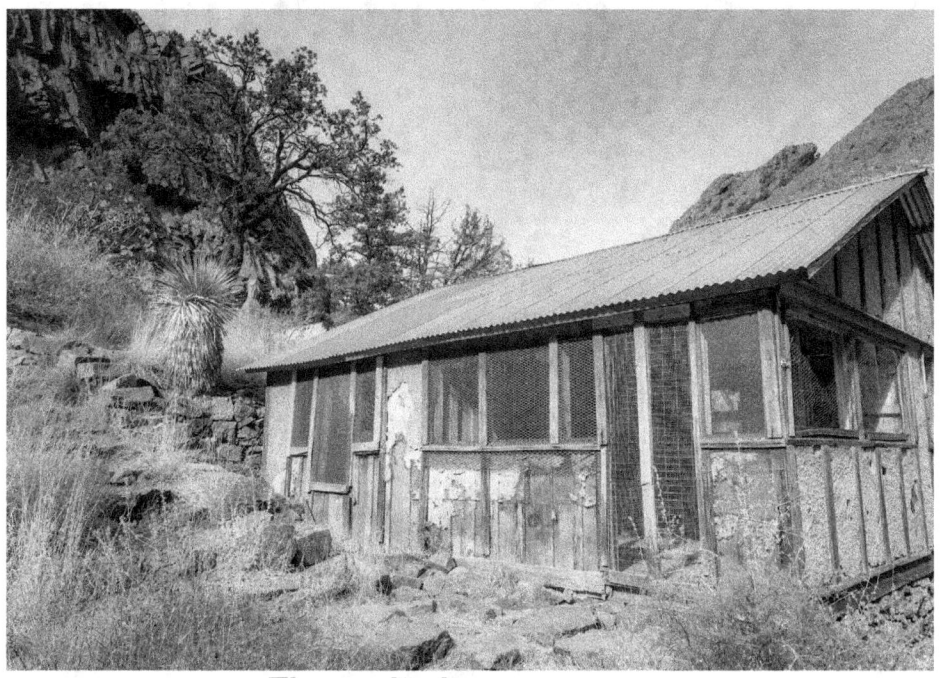
The sanitarium

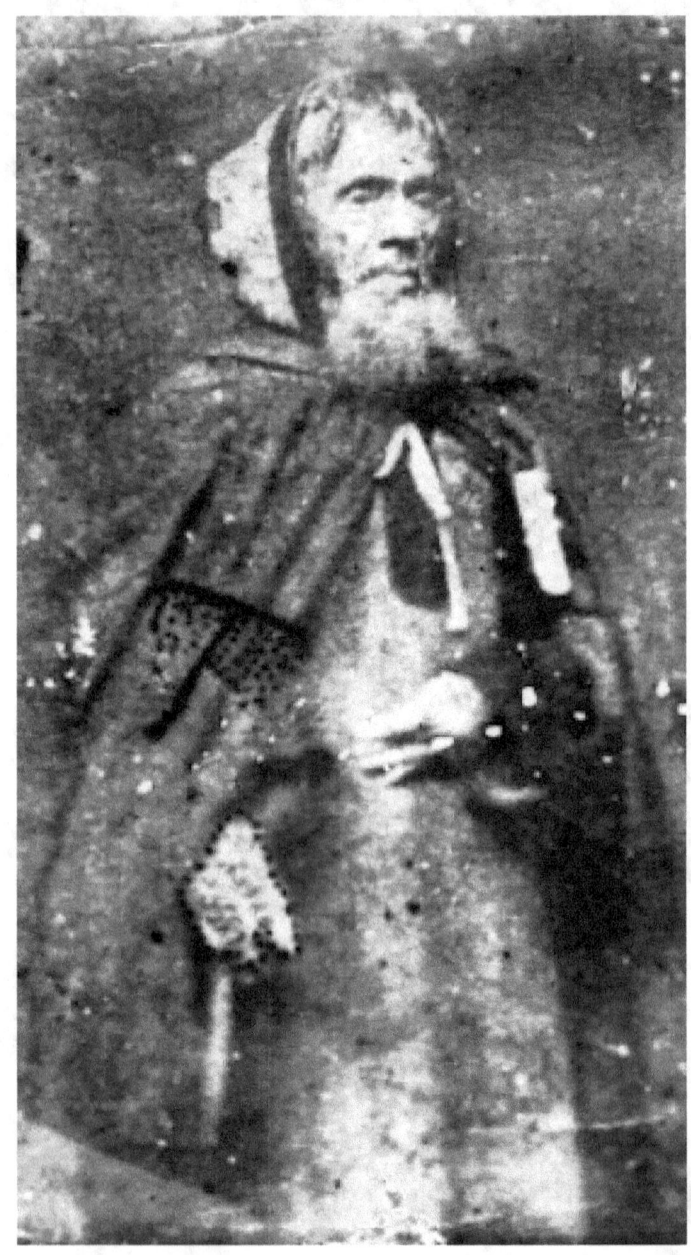

El Ermitano

William J Wood Jr

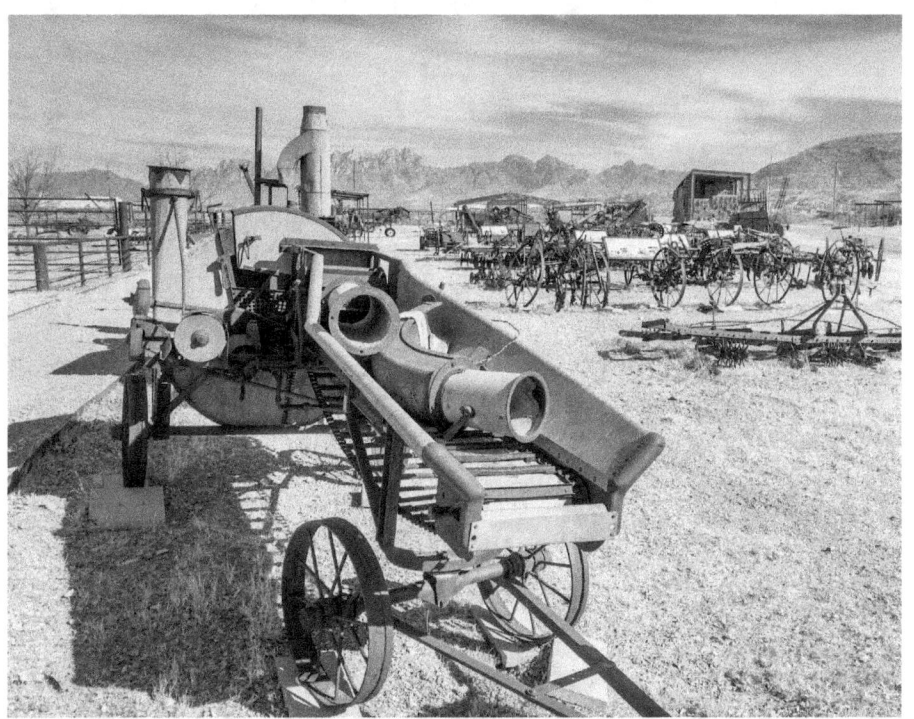

New Mexico Farm and Ranch Heritage Museum

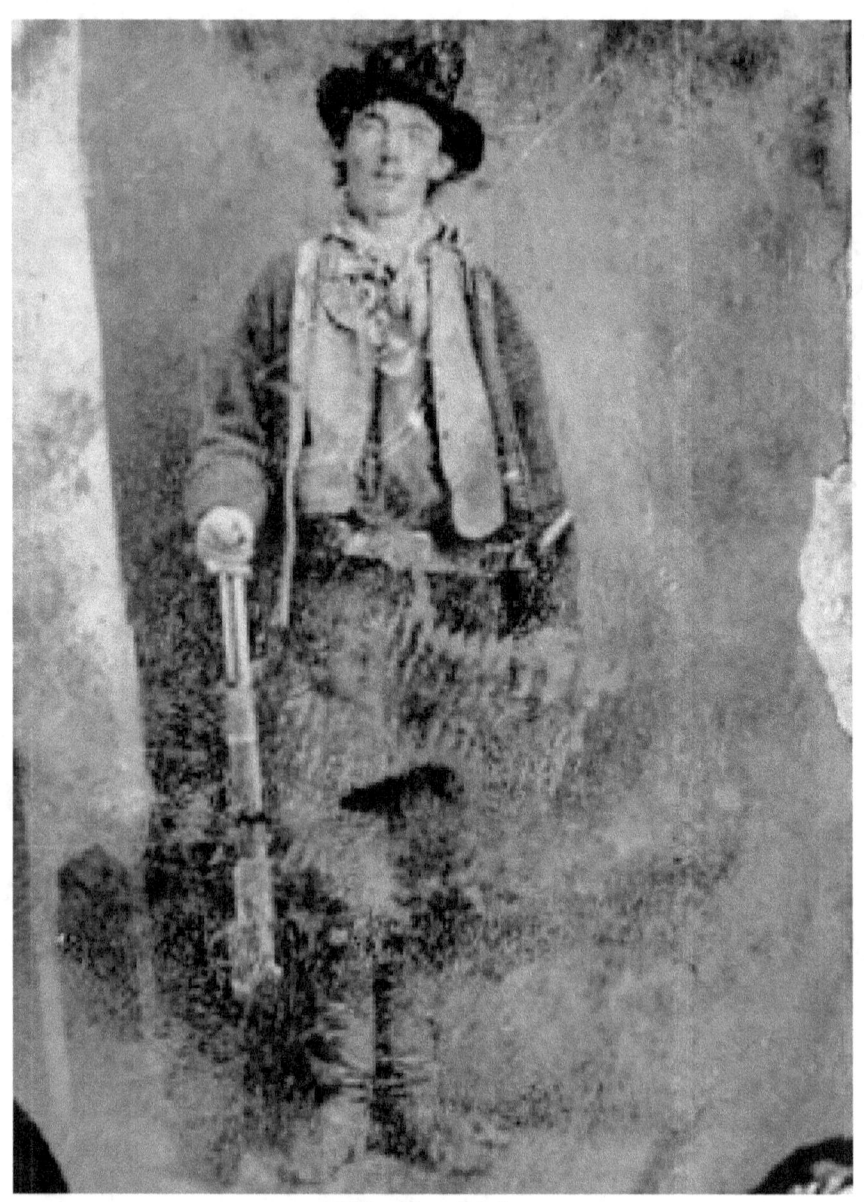

Billy the Kid

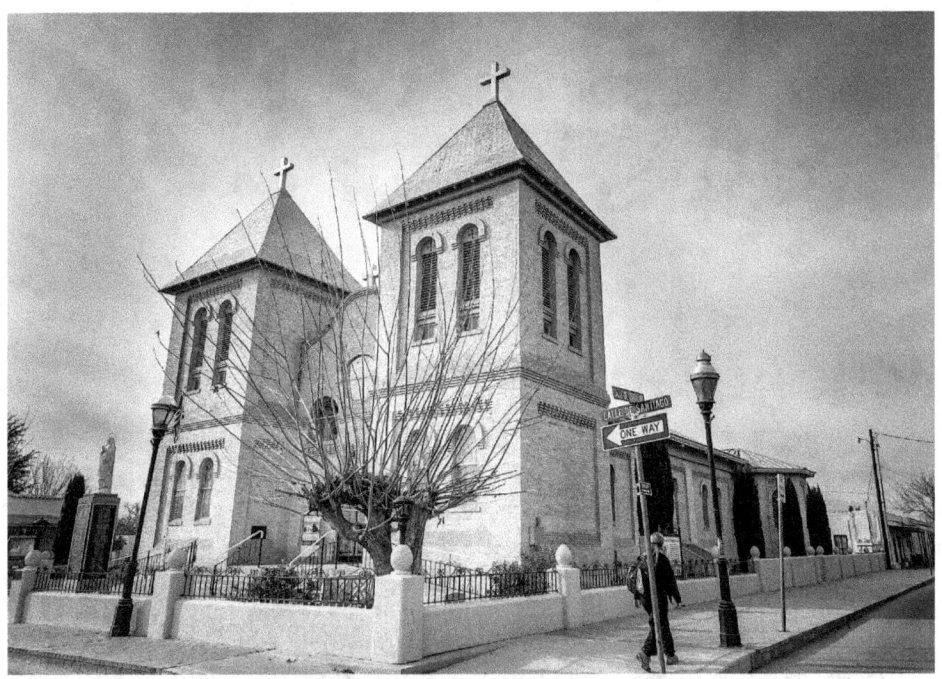
Mesilla cathedral

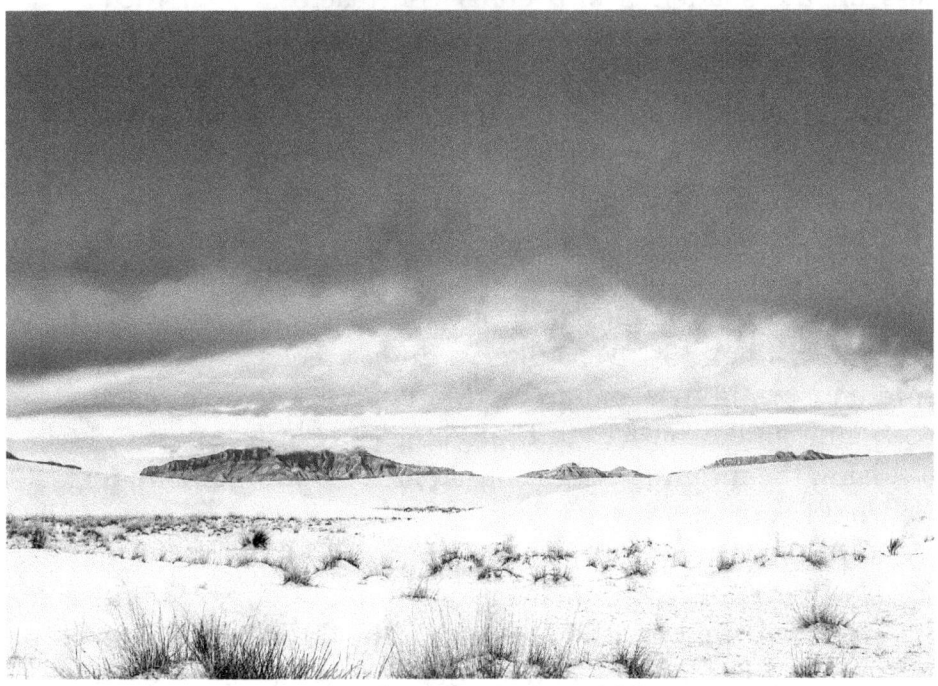
Gypsum sand, White Sands National Monument

Chapter 18

Folk Art and Terrorists

In the Driveway From Hell I cringed as tree branches rasped my sidewalls. Rick had dinner with us, then left to catch his flight to Connecticut. We had done a lot of hiking and touring on the trip, so we were content to be homebodies for a few days.

Rick's neighbor, Keith, ran a shade tree mechanic business on the shadeless old tennis court across from Rick's house. I asked Keith if he could change the oil in the RV. He agreed, but I noticed he had lots of projects already going, so I did it myself. I harbored the thought that changing oil on an RV was a major project. It wasn't, but I was still overly proud of myself for getting it done.

The hydraulic jacks on the RV made it easy to access the oil pan. Keith lent me a pair of jack stands so I wouldn't get crushed if the hydraulics gave out. I bought 8 quarts of Mobile One synthetic 5-20W, a filter, a filter wrench, a variety of different size funnels and an oil drain pan. I watched several You Tube videos on RV oil changing. The hardest part was accessing the moronic tight location of the oil fill tube under the front hood.

Keith and I enjoyed several long conservations during our stay. I discovered a well-informed, far-ranging, inquisitive mind. Dig that. Keith built sets for the thriving film making industry in Santa Fe and worked as an extra. Rick told me Keith was hoping to get out of the mechanic business.

Rick lives next to Museum Hill, home to several museums and the Santa Fe Botanical Gardens. The hill overlooks the central city and the southern end of the Sangre de Cristo range. Last year I dashed up Museum Hill to photograph an amazing sunset. Rick had given us Culture Passes that had free entrance to most of the museums. We started at the Wheelwright Museum of the American Indian.

The Wheelwright is the love child of a friendship between a transplanted Bostonian, Mary Cabot Wheelwright, and a Navajo medicine man, Hastiin Klah. In the 1920s Wheelwright recorded Klah's narration of the Navajo Creation Story. Focused on Navajo religion, the two realized a museum would be the ideal protectorate for recordings, manuscripts, tapestries and sand paintings. Klah died before the 1937 grand opening. In the 1970s, the Navajo tribe repatriated all religious items due to concern of non-Navajos pretending to teach the tribe's traditions.

Architect William Henderson designed the entrance of the Wheelwright to evoke a Navajo hogan. We walked through rooms of extraordinary beadwork. A different section held myriad displays of Indian jewelry that progressed through the history of the art from the early days when the Spanish taught silversmithing to Natives, to the modernist, high-art present.

Next stop was the Museum of International Folk Art, the MOIFA, founded in 1953, that ancient year of my birth, by Florence Dibell Bartlett, the civic minded daughter of a Chicago hardware store owner. To quote Bartlett, "The art of the craftsman is a bond between the peoples of the world."

We walked through the marquis exhibit on Tramp Art. Most of the creators of these unique pieces were not tramps, but rather laborers and farmers, who pulled out pocket knives in their leisure hours. The common theme in the carvings, made from cast-off wood items, is repetitive notching. It was unnerving to think about the time devoted to the more exquisite carvings.

The Girard wing blew my mind. Ten thousand crafted objects, sculpture, tapestry, dolls, paintings and miniatures occupied every available space. Miniature collections as large as a living room brought to life scenes of villages, historic battles, native home life and even Hell. When I shot photos at eye level, I heard Rod Serling in my brain: "You are now entering a world of..."

A temporary exhibit, Crafting Memory: The Art of Community in Peru opened a flood of memories from our time working in the Andes and the Amazon jungle. Many of the pieces related to the Peruvian War on Terror. In the 1960s, Abimael Guzman, a philosophy professor at San Cristobal University in the Andes, founded a political party based on Maoist ideology: the Sendero Luminoso, the Shining Path. Common to other South American countries, Peru suffered from centuries of conflict between a ruling elite of conquering Spaniard descendants and an impoverished indigenous criollo population. In the 1980s the Senderistas pressed an armed insurrection in the manner of Mao's Red Army: conquer the countryside and the cities will fall.

Our friends, Stan and Sharon, did a three-year surgery mission in Peru. In 1993, they took us to Pucallpa, a town in the equatorial jungle of the Ucayali River. We stayed with their friends who ran a Christian-based vocational school, TEC, outside the town. The friends told us about the days of the Shining Path. They often saw bodies along the roadside. The TEC missionaries vacated Peru for several years. An armed force invaded the school, but chose not to burn it.

At TEC we received a radio transmission asking if any doctors were available. A man in a village up the river had suffered a gunshot wound. After a comforting pep talk, Barb and I volunteered. In a pecky-pecky boat, we puttered up miles of overhung riverbank through Heart of Darkness scenery. As was often the case in Peru, the story of the gunshot was a purposeful myth. The man had no gunshot wound, but rather an ileostomy performed by local surgeons after he perforated his bowel on a chicken bone. He didn't have the money to pay for an ileostomy closure. If I had had surgical instruments and lidocaine, I could have operated on the picnic table. Alas.

Back at TEC, the theory was the man might have been a Senderista on the run. He was not from the local area. Government troops had captured Abimael Guzman a year ago and were hunting down the remnants of the Shining Path. Televisions in public areas broadcast a continuous live feed of Guzman pacing in his cell.

Over twenty years, 70,000 people in the Andean provinces died from torture, massacre or "disappearance." Terrorist bombings reached as far as the upscale Miraflores shopping district in Lima. Several of the exhibits at the MOIFA showed the Rondas, the government-backed militias formed by towns to oppose the terrorist's rule. Here I was a tourist on a beautiful day in Santa Fe circling back to another time and another place. We moved on.

Rick and Mimi appeared after their three-day hellish cross-country drive through snow and ice. Their hotel in Oklahoma looked like a meth den. We made them a nice dinner and watched one of my favorite movies, *Paul*. Filmed in New Mexico, *Paul* is about an alien, voiced by Seth Rogen, who escapes capture and joins two British UFO enthusiasts on a wild ride through the West in an RV. Maybe the RV part influenced me. The wife of a friend of ours ran the Greer Garson Studio in Santa Fe, where some scenes were filmed.

I felt awkward invading the home of my friends who had just driven across the continent. We were running short on time. Mimi encouraged us to stay as she was leaving to deal with her mother in Taos. We shoved off the next morning. From this point, we would replicate last year's trip with stops at the Petrified Forest and Death Valley. I was tiring of long drives and short stops. Experience refines desire.

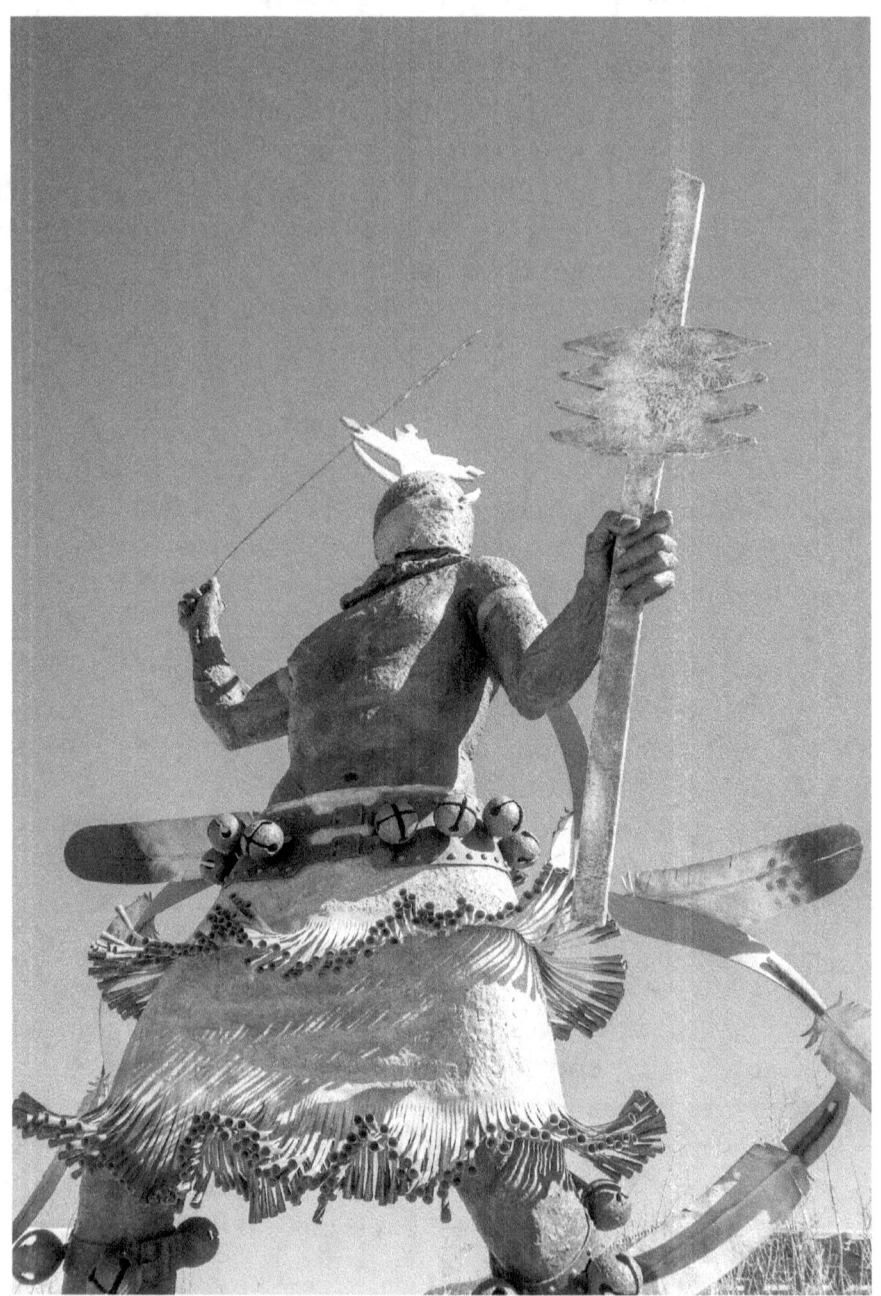

Milner Plaza, Museum Hill, Santa Fe, NM

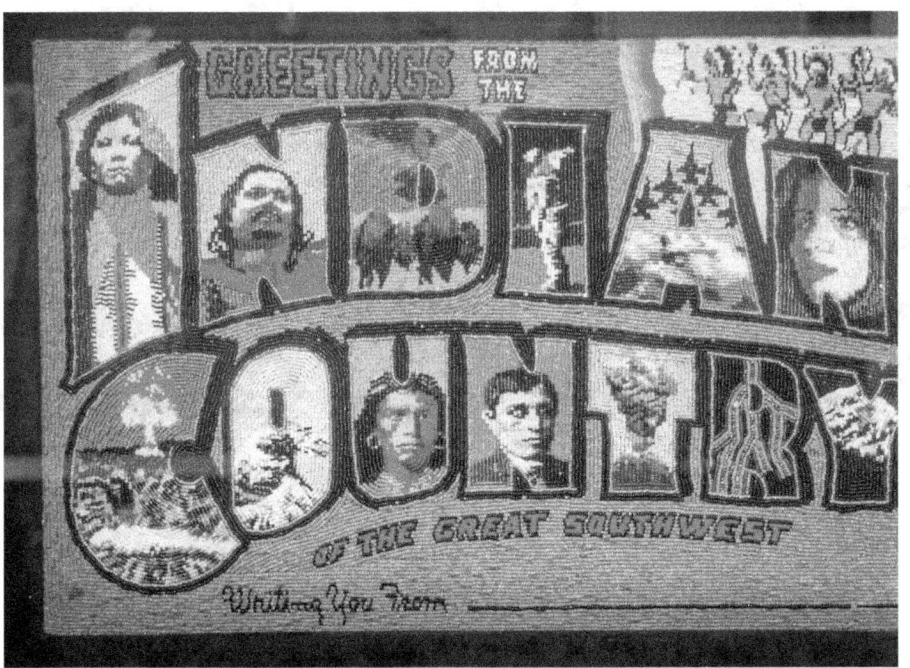

Beadwork at the Wheelwright Museum

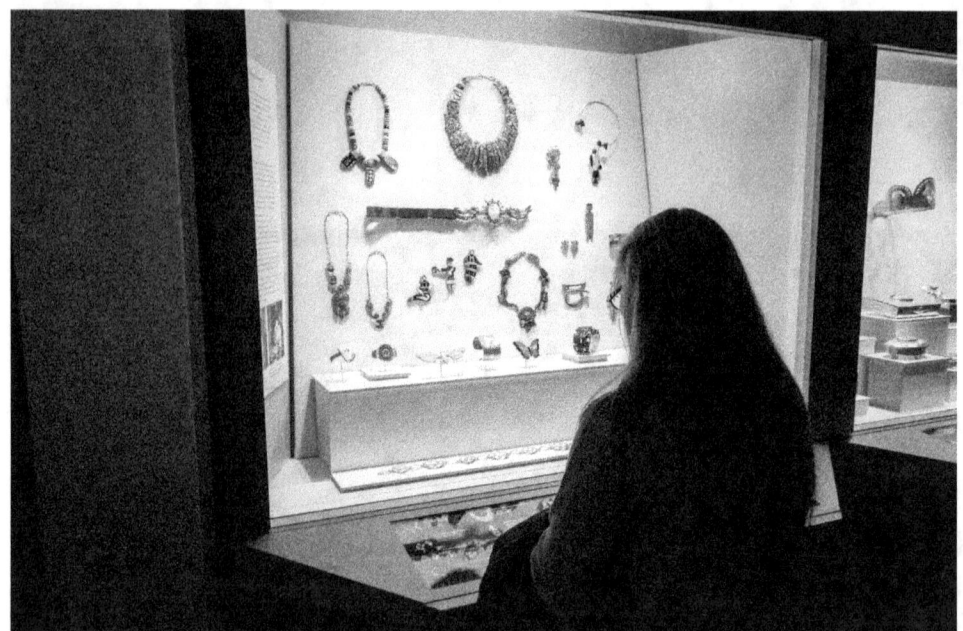
Indian jewelry, past to present

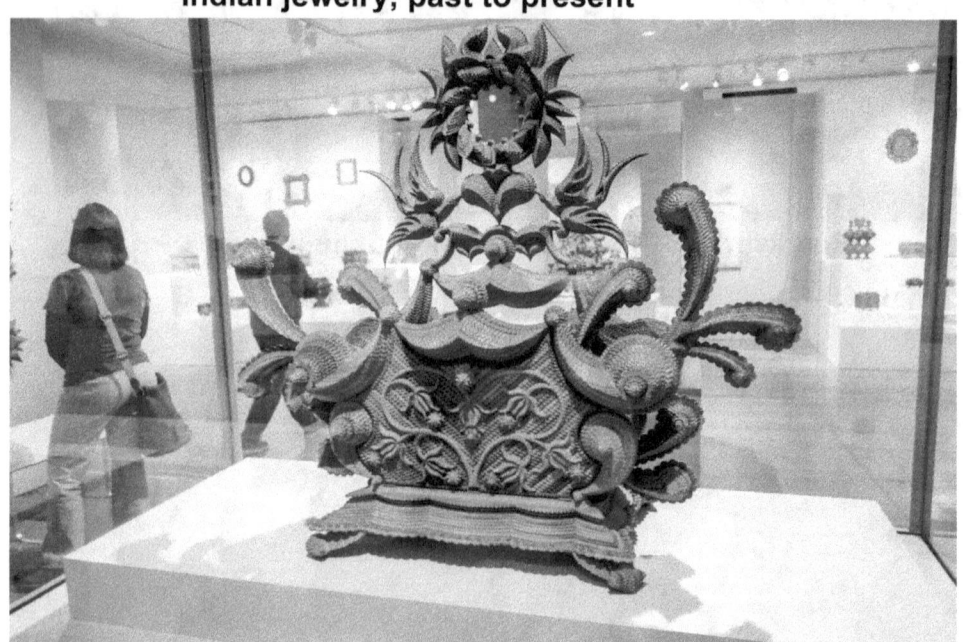
Tramp Art at the MOIFA

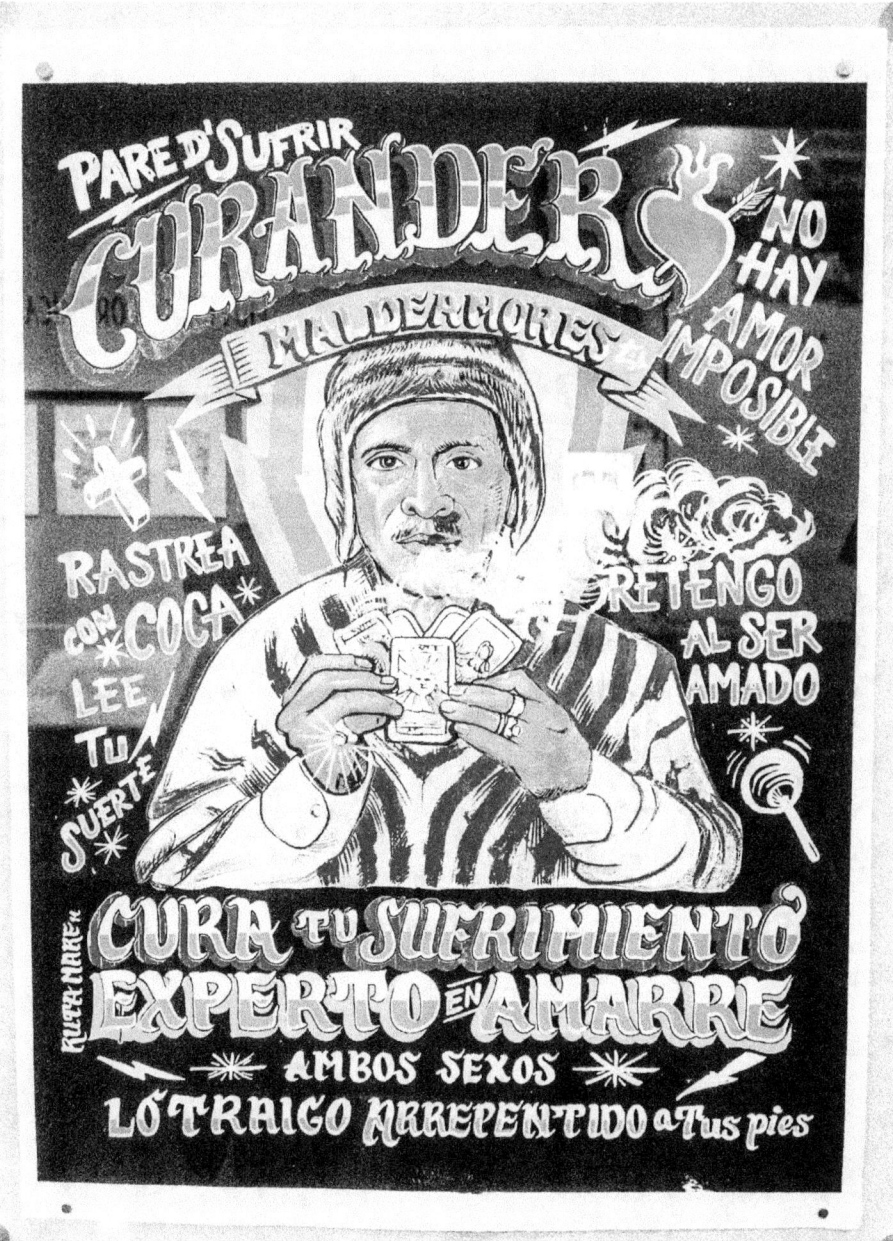

Peruvian art

Photographing the American West

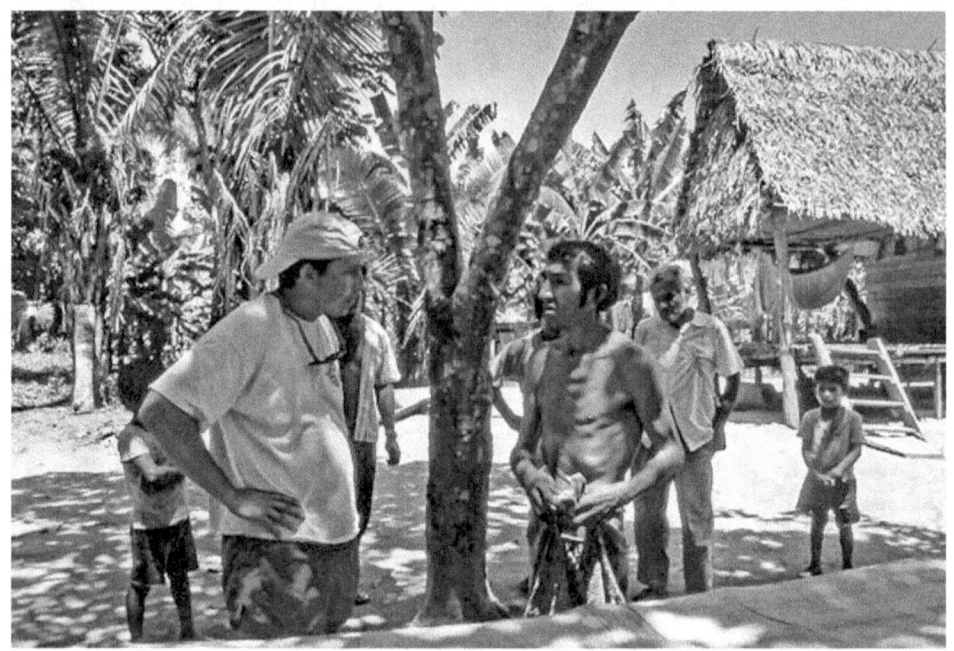

In Peru. "No tengo los instumentos."

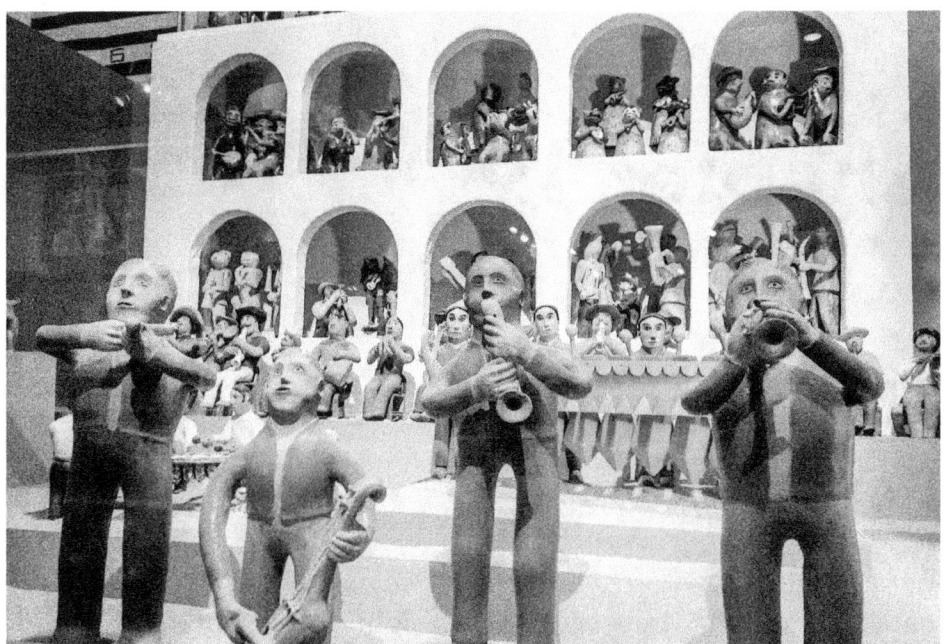
Folk art at the MOIFA

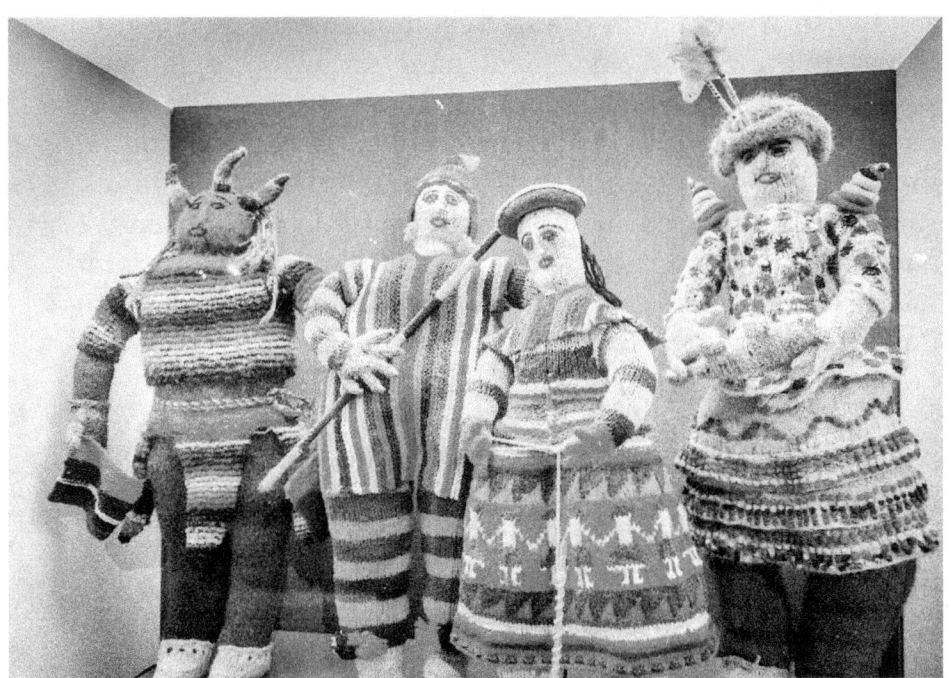
"The art of the craftsman is a bond."

Chapter 19

The Curse of the Petrified Forest

From Santa Fe we arrived at the Petrified Forest National Park near closing time. We went straight to the south end of the Park to the Giant Logs trailhead. Last year we ran out of time before we could get to this trail.

I wish I was a 19th century explorer. Those guys got to name anything they saw. Lieutenant Amiel Whipple, who surveyed the area looking for an east-west route in 1853, named an arroyo Lithodendron Wash. Looking at any of the thousands of dry washes in Arizona, one would not think such a distinguished name would apply. Come to think, I have never named my pond. I will do so now. I proclaim that body of water, Anasparadisus Meditare, Duck Paradise Pond. I propose the Petrified Forest staff rename the Giant Log trail, Accresare Acinus.

The trail lived up to its current name. Mature trunks of Araucarioxylon arizonicum slumbered in crystalline repose, dreaming of their glory days in the Triassic. Few logs were intact. Most were short, feet-long segments of the mother log. The interiors sparkled in a gamut of dazzling gem color: red, ochre, green, white, purple and cinnamon. They transfixed and focused the mind. "I wants it. I wants it. My precious."

How many valuable petrified fossils have souvenir-hounds pilfered? The origin of the factoid is uncertain, but beginning in the 1980s an oft-published estimate was 12 tons per year. Park Superintendent Brad Travis and paleontologist William Parker took photos of the popular high-density sites, like Crystal Forest, and compared them to historic photos. Most looked identical. Some even had more exposed fossil due to erosion. There is pilferage, but nowhere near 12 tons.

People have been sending stolen rocks back to the park. Some feel guilty. Others send back rocks stolen by relatives or friends. Some hope that sending the rocks back to their original site will remove the curse. The curse? A belief has blossomed that stealing petrified wood from the Park will bring a curse.

Bad Luck, Hot Rocks, a book by Ryan Thompson and Phil Orr, investigates the origins of the "conscience pile," the car-sized pile of returned rocks. Many rocks had letters of explanation:

> *I am writing this letter in hopes of easing my conscience and saving the most important thing of my life, my marriage. I removed three rocks which my husband discovered hidden in my brassiere. Being a true Christian he has constantly told me of my wrong doing. I am keeping one rock to remind me of the lesson I learned. I am enclosing twenty cents for you to buy another rock to replace the one I am keeping.*

> *I'M NOT superstitious, but a year later my husband was killed in an airplane crash not far from your facility. I just want to get rid of this reminder.*

> *The final straw was when I stepped thru the ceiling of our new house. I've had enough. I'm sending it back.*

> *We found out my step mother had kidney failure, then our dog died. Please take these pieces back before we have more bad luck.*

> *DEAR MR. RANGER, I AM SORRY I TOOK THIS. I AM ONLY 5 YEARS OLD AND MADE A BAD MISTAKE. ANDY.*
>
> *Please put this back so my husband can get well. I tried to keep him from taking it. Distraught Wife.*

In some returns, the guilt-ridden included detailed descriptions of the exact location of the rock. The policy is not to relocate the rocks. According to Superintendent Travis, disturbance of the replacement site would invalidate any future scientific study. This may stretch the science card a little. Pothunters have ruined thousands of archeological sites in the Southwest. Disturbance severely lessens the information gained from an archeological survey. But rocks? Really? *A phytosaur slept here. He awoke and fled into the forest.*

I looked through my mindless collection of "pretty rocks" in my library. There was a piece of petrified wood. I have no memory of collecting it. Perhaps this explains the multi-year curse that has made my life pure agony.

Rabid souvenir hunger wiped out one national monument. The Fossil Cycad National Monument, established in 1922 in the Black Hills of South Dakota, contained the largest collection of 120 million-year-old cycadeoids, an early flowering plant. They look like fossilized pineapples. Visitors made off with every single fossil. Congress demonumentized the site in 1957.

The belief that everything and anything discovered in a natural state is up for grabs seems to be part of our cultural marrow. Hikers stole fossilized dinosaur footprints in Death Valley. Someone chiseled out 3,500-year-old petroglyphs near Bishop, CA. Motorists nicked a baby buffalo in Yellowstone!

A true idiot, Casey Nocket, a San Diego woman, traveled to seven national parks and painted her cute, faux-art figures on rock faces. She signed her graffiti as "Creepytings," perhaps appropriately. Darwinianly, she posted selfies with her creepy doodles on the internet. The federal court sentenced her to 200 hours of public service and a $275 fine. I would have made her clean up the defilements.

We stayed in Holbrook overnight. The next day we stopped in Kingman. Holbrook was Holbrook. Kingman was Kingman. Last year we lucked out in Death Valley and got the last open full service spot at Stovepipe Wells. This time, no one answered at the reservation number. If we couldn't get a site at Stovepipe, we would face a long drive out of the park. My strategy was to stay in Beatty, Nevada, just outside Death Valley. We would drive early to Stovepipe. If no sites were available, we would have time to drive into central California.

The Space Station RV Park in Beatty had good reviews on Google with 4.3 stars. "On-site small market with the only place in town to buy fresh veg & fruit. Fresh coffee in the morning. Stayed here for a night 2 yrs ago." We drove through the camp. Derelict RVs shouldered each other in cramped sites. Trash was everywhere. It looked like the only place in town to buy fresh meth. We retreated to the Death Valley Inn RV Park, clean and well groomed. I showed the manager my photo of a UFO over nearby Rhyolite. She said, "We see a lot of those around here."

At dawn we headed out for Death Valley. Rhyolite, Nevada is a ghost town east of the Park. Last year, I shot star photos among the ruins on a frigid, windy night. When I developed the images, I got a surprise. A UFO, a row of lights with an inverted cup dome, hovered over the old Charles Schwab Bank. In daylight, Rhyolite was less spooky. The macabre ghost sculptures, the *Last Supper* by Belgian artist Albert Szukalski, seemed out of place against the backdrop of the high desert. Belgians! There were no sculptures of urinating boys.

On Daylight Pass, the long descent through the Amargosa Range, I pulled over to shoot a dust cloud scudding across the floor of Death Valley. Luck be a lady at a reservation desk, we got the last available full service site at Stovepipe Wells, just like last year. The curse of the petrified wood must not travel. As a bonus, there was a zombie in the back seat of our neighbor's car. What more could we ask for?

When we rode Smax through Furnace Creek the next morning, the temperature was a balmy 70s. Sixteen miles later and a mile higher at Dante's View, the air was frigid, below freezing. We froze. A stiff leg hike brought us to a glorious panorama over Badwater Basin. Across the valley the Panamint Mountains glowed. Telescope Peak, in the Panamints, was one of the victims of the idiot from San Diego. After my hands regained motion, I got shots of the entire valley stretching north to infinity. Barb traded me her heavier gloves for the ride down. Thawing was both pleasant and vital.

The next day, past Bakersfield, we harvested our fifth windshield chip. We got it repaired at the Safelite shop in Modesto, the most dangerous city in California. Seemed peaceful. It was evening when we pulled into my brother John's home in Stockton for a few days of his gracious hostelry. John led me through an off course route at his home golf course. We ended up playing 20 holes.

Time was growing short. Barb had to resume her commitments to social organizations in February. I was not looking forward to the rain in Oregon. I wanted one more camp, so we made reservations at Bodega Bay, where Alfred Hitchcock filmed *The Birds*. I had never been there. I liked the name Bodega.

William J Wood Jr

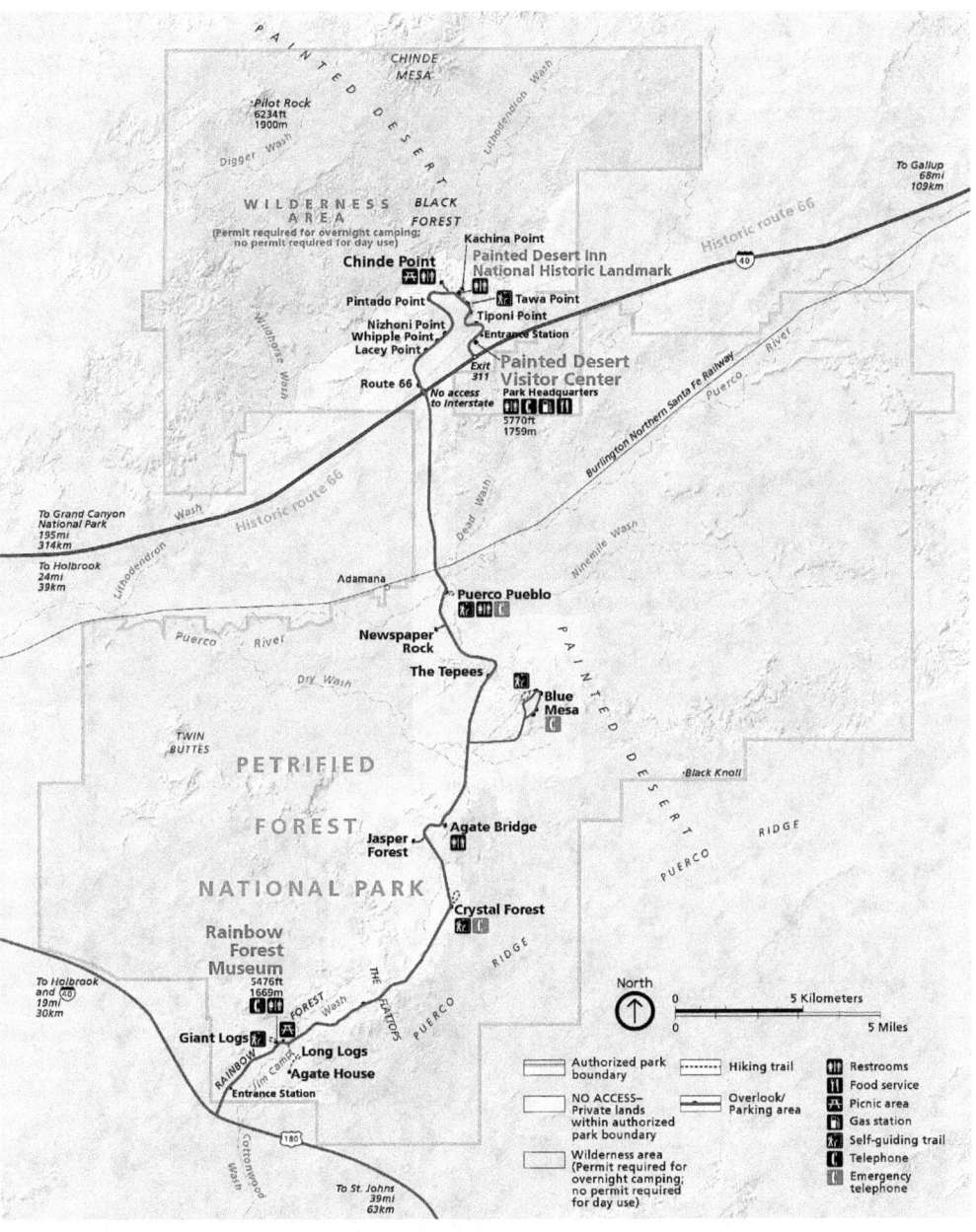

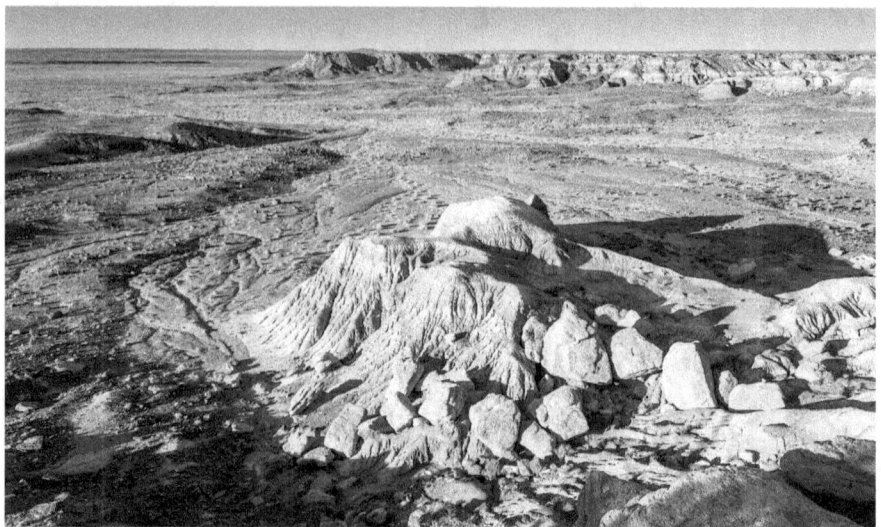
The Jasper Forest

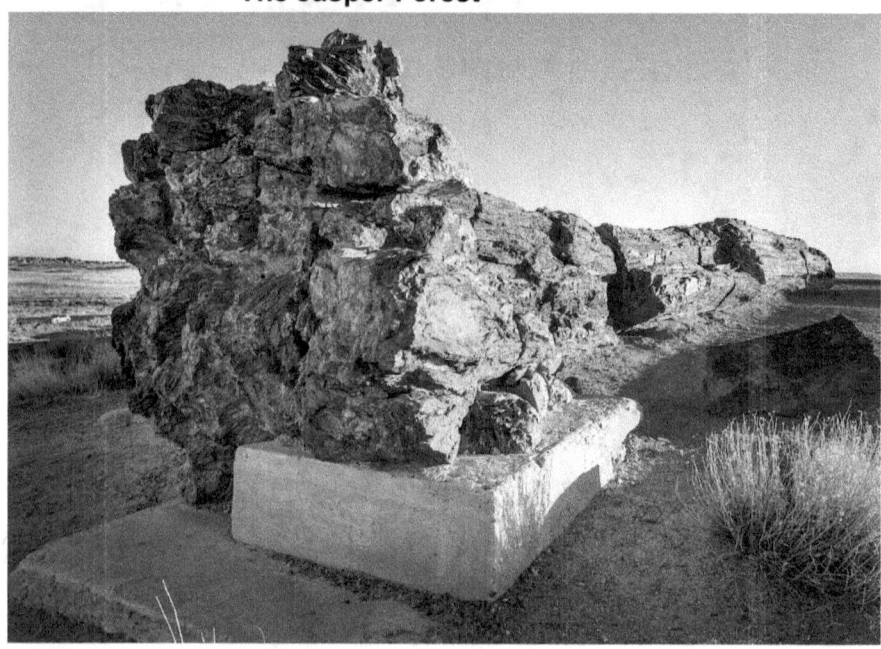
Rare intact log

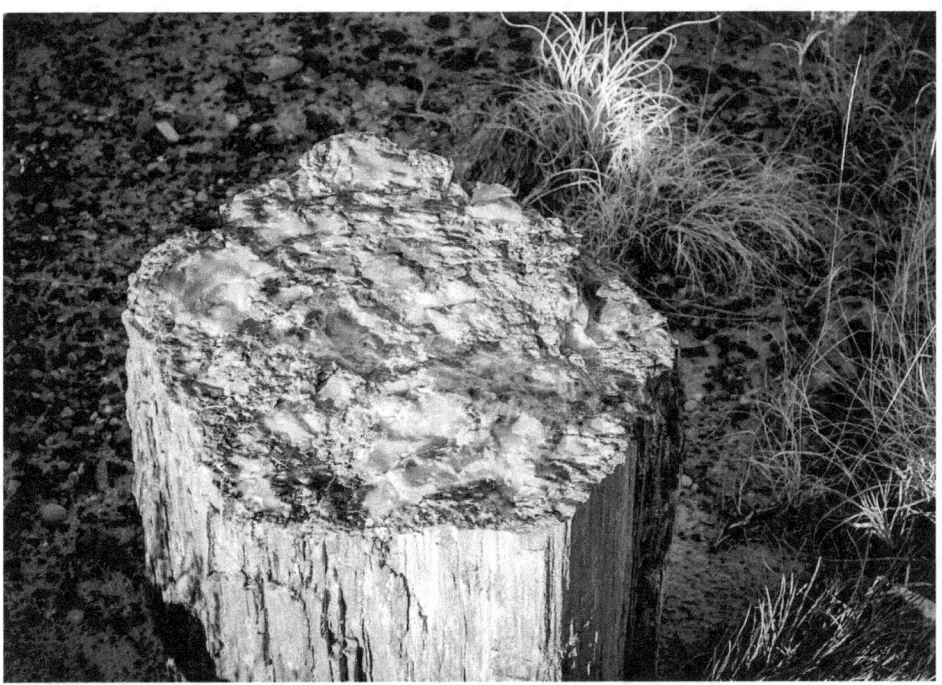
A gamut of dazzling color

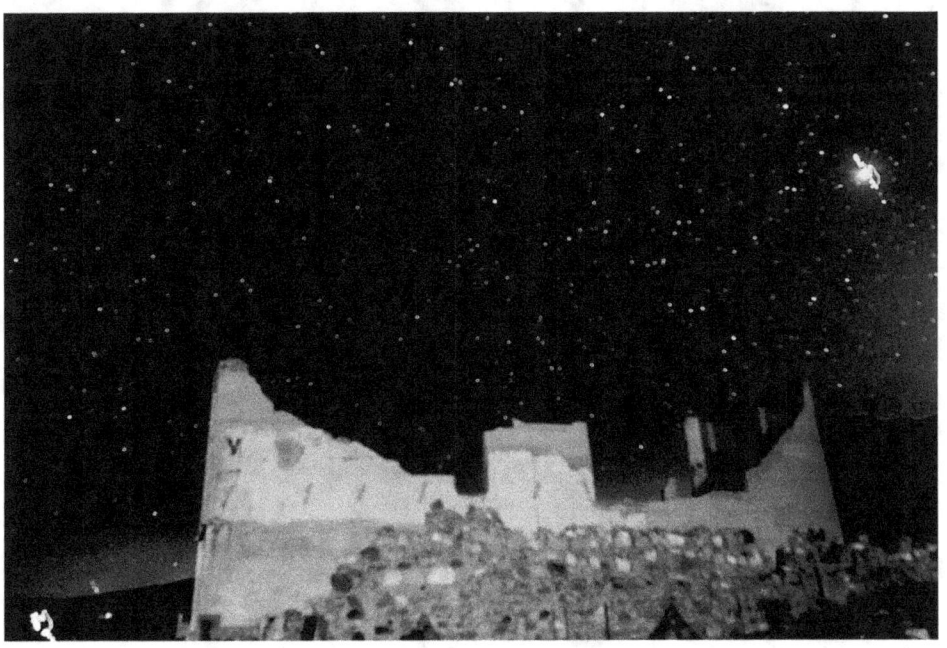
UFO over Rhyolite, Nevada

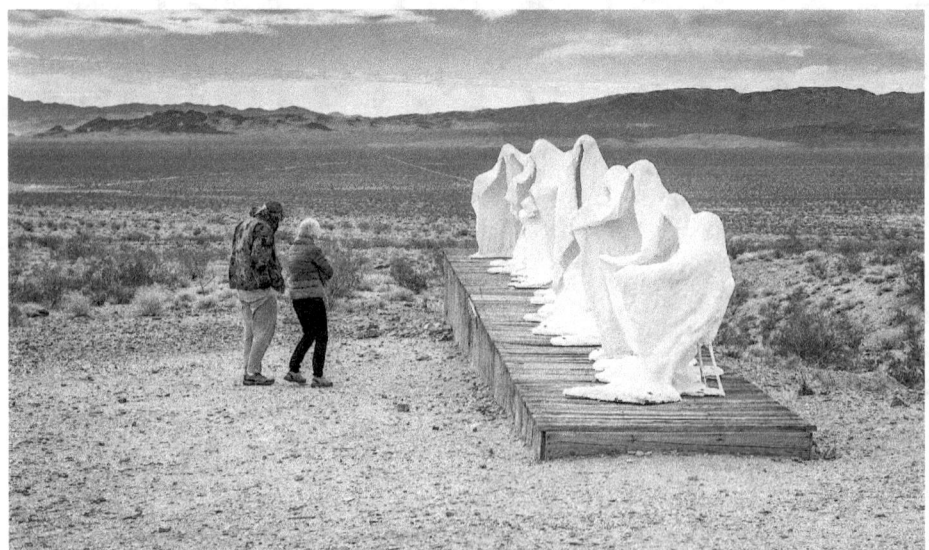

The Last Supper in Rhyolite

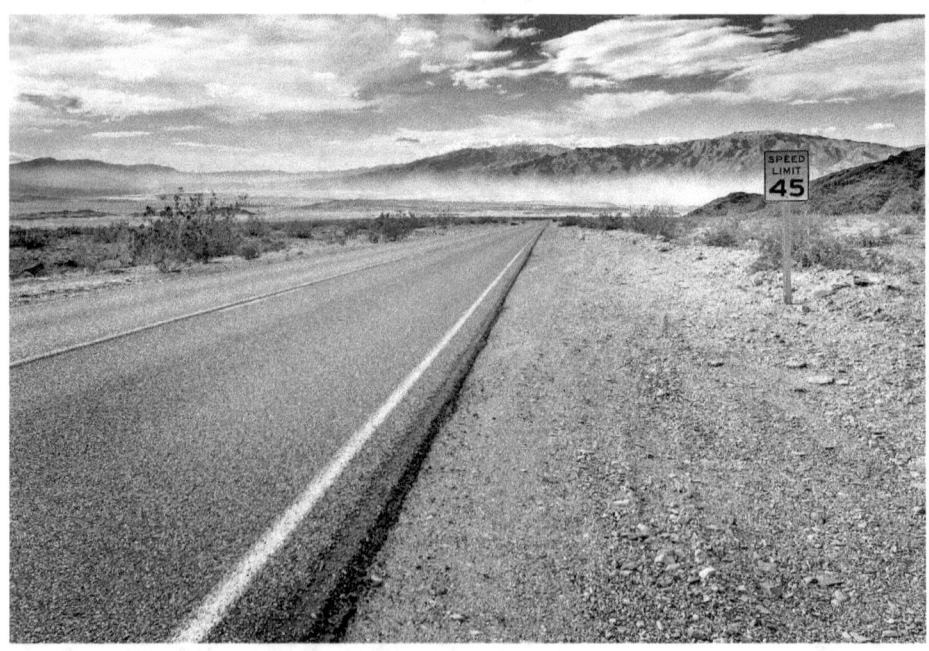

Dust storm in Death Valley

William J Wood Jr

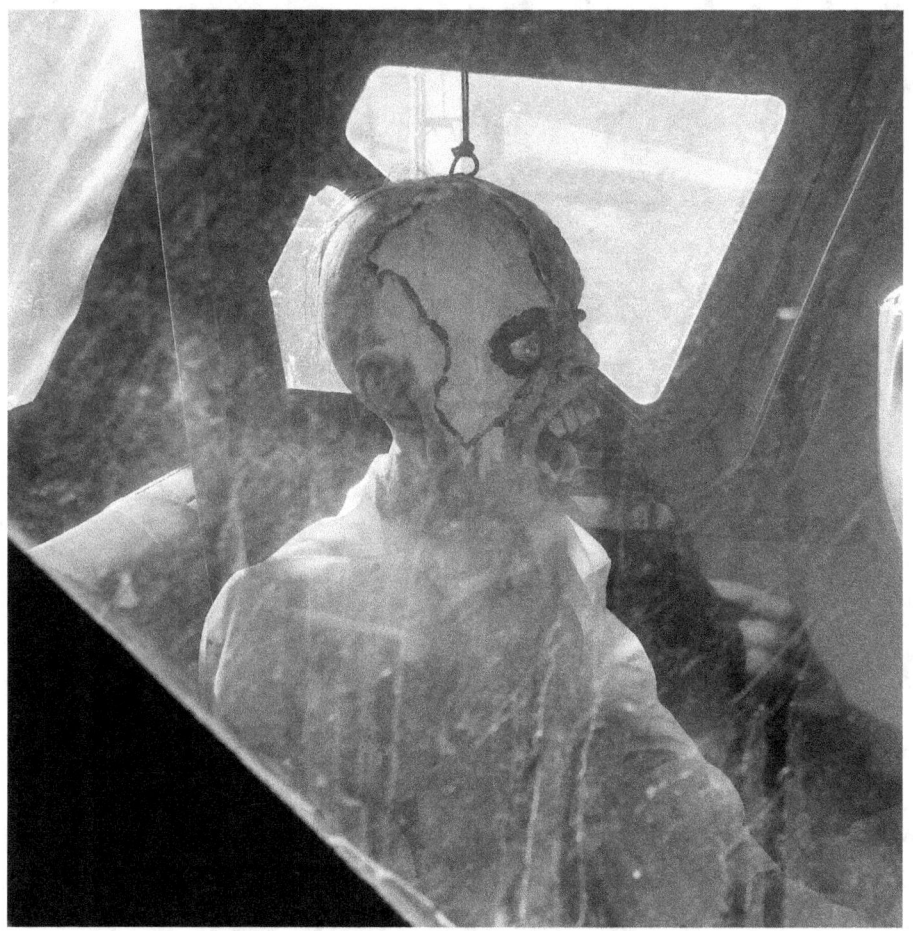

Friendly camp neighbor

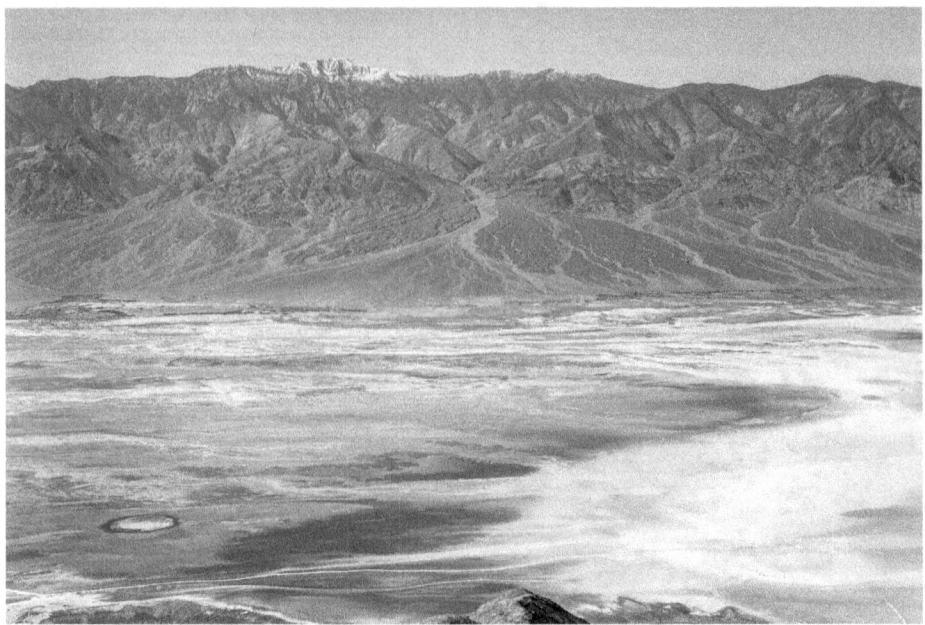
Badwater Basin and the Panamint Mountains

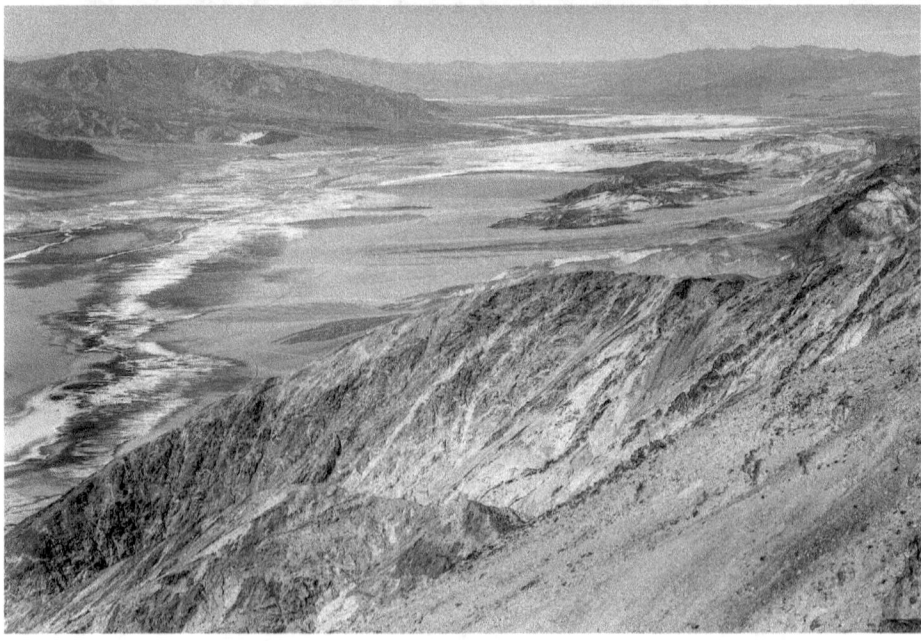
Long view of Death Valley

Chapter 20

The Nicholas Effect

We drove through rice fields on Highway 12, took a left on I-80, then a right on 37 above San Pablo Bay in dark skies and downpour. The rain stopped by Petaluma. Bodega Bay RV Park nested in hills above the bay. The friendly staff in the office wore golf shirts with the camp logo. If they would have let me chainsaw the Monterey cypress grove, we could have had a great view of the bay.

The next day, sunny, we hiked under arching cypress shade to Bodega Dunes. Since we were hiking, the ranger didn't charge us anything. The road to the beach snaked through shaggy dune scrub with flame patches of Hottentot Fig succulents. Like a military fortification, a two-story-high bank of dune palisaded the beach. The undulating high grass covering the dune reminded me of the back of my Chesapeake Bay retriever.

The grass, Ammophila arenaria, European beachgrass or marram grass, was the architect-in-chief of the steep-fronted dune wall. In the mid-1800s, well-intentioned citizen groups, reinforced with Boy Scouts and Girl Scouts, imported Ammophila to the U.S. west coast from Mediterranean beaches to stabilize the dunes. No one wanted migrating dunes letting themselves in the front door of their beach house like an aunt from Schenectady. People that built neighborhoods or parks in the wind shadow behind the grass-fortified dunes smiled at Ammophila. Everyone else, ecologists and snowy plovers and disgruntled arthropods, had nothing nice to say about Ammophila. They were Ammophilaphobes.

As with many imported species, the new boy kicked ass on the local competition. The wimpy native dune grass, Leymus mollis, preferred migrating dunes; it was not hardy enough to build a wind-resistant mound. Ammophila was like an ear-biting Mike Tyson to Leymus. The Vegas odds were laughable. Armed with tightly rolled, drought resistant leaves, superior nitrogen allocation and two-meter long rhizomes that made young girls blush, Ammophila displaced the native grasses. Many endemic species, bugs and birds, did not like the dense hummock. Snowy plovers would just as soon shit on a hummock as lay an egg there.

The shaggy sand wall spread, like a Chinese one, through Oregon, Washington and into British Columbia. With the rise of nativist philosophy and the search for endangered species, the bell tolled for Ammophila. The hummock monster became the John Barleycorn of beach grasses. Armies of saviors tried pulling him out by the roots or burning or poisoning or burning then poisoning the new shoots. Bulldozers scraped zones for the finicky snowy plover. Yet what victories gather may Pyrrhic be. Beach Boy heaven became a silicon Afghanistan.

Moro Buddy Bohn, a finger-style guitarist, toured with the Christy Minstrels, the original Minstrels, and once performed on the Andy Williams Show. The royalties from his hit tune, *Vermouth Rondo*, paid for his home and recording studio at Salmon Creek. Had I heaved a tangle of beach kelp over the foredune, I might have hit his house.

Buddy's studio is under attack by an evil sand dune. In the 1980s, a vessel beached in a winter storm. Bulldozers plowed a road through the dunes to bring in heavy rescue machinery. The naked breach grew into an angry, 40-foot wind-driven sand monster that wants to play the Ides of March in Buddy's studio. At its current rate, Bohn has only four or five years to record new hits. He is unhappy with the attitude of the state ecologist who is pleased that the dune is taking out another invasive species, Monterey cypress trees. Stay tuned.

On the beach, an elderly Hispanic man whipped his rigging (fishing) into the surf. He was old friends with this stretch of beach. Perch, he fished for perch. He showed us how to dig crablets out of the sand for bait. We hiked the arc of the shoreline and made our lunch under a beach ramp. The only music we heard was the hypnotic crashing surf.

The 1972 National Marine Sanctuaries Act authorized sanctuaries for protection of marine habitat and research. There are 13 national marine sanctuaries covering 170,000 square miles. NOAA, the National Oceanic and Atmospheric Administration, serves as the trustee of the sanctuaries. The Greater Farallones National Marine Sanctuary surrounds Bodega Bay. In 2015, the sanctuary tripled in size to 3,295 square miles.

The expansion of the Farallones, and the neighboring Cordell Bank Sanctuary, caused an embarrassing problem for the U.S. Coast Guard. No one is allowed to dump untreated sewage, known as poop, in sanctuary waters. The fish don't like it even though the algae love it. The borders of the expanded sanctuaries are forty miles out to sea. That's a long way to hold it. The Coast Guard has asked NOAA for a rule change to allow dumping beyond three nautical miles seaward.

A coalition of organizations, the Center for Biological Diversity, Earthjustice and Friends of the Earth opposed the rule change and called for an Environmental Impact Statement. The Coast Guard dismissed their suggestions to install shore pump stations or onboard sanitation. I'm against oceanic dumping and any other dumping. The Great Pacific Garbage Patch floats 80 metric tons of plastic. But maybe the Coast Guard should get a bathroom pass. Do you want a constipated rescue jumper trying to pull you out of the water after you swamped your fishing boat? We must wait and see how this comes out.

On the hike back we took an unintended turn into the campground. A gardener told us how to get out. In the corner of a small park stood a curious structure, a metal scaffold festooned with bells of various size. A metal plaque told the story. It was the Children's Bell Tower, a memorial to 7-year-old Nicholas Green of Bodega Bay.

On a beautiful September day in 1994, the Green family, parents Margaret and Reginald and children Nicholas and Eleanor, were enjoying a vacation in southern Italy, in Calabria. Driving between Salerno and Reggio, a car pulled alongside. The men shouted something in Italian. Reginald accelerated, but the car followed. The men fired guns at the rear of the Green's car. Reginald fled at high speed and the pursuers dropped off. Young Nicholas had been shot in the head. Police ferried Nicholas to a hospital in Messina where he was pronounced dead.

The shooters were thieves who had mistaken the Green's car for that of a local jeweler. This time point, Nicholas' death, was the end of a horrible, tragic story, but the beginning of a tale of amazing beauty and uplifting grace. The Greens donated Nicholas' organs to seven patients, all Italians. This act of charity reverberated throughout all of Italy. Before Nicholas' gift, Italy had the lowest organ donation rate in Europe. After, the rate tripled.

Italians poured out their hearts to Nicholas and the Greens, as they would have to a saint. President Oscar Scalfaro presented the Greens with the Medaglia d'Oro al Merito Civile, the nation's highest honor for civilians. They coined the term, l'Effeto Nicholas, the Nicholas Effect, referring to both organ donation and the concept that good can come from tragedy. Grateful town folk have named 124 streets, schools, parks and squares in Italy for Nicholas.

The Children's Bell Tower, sculpted by San Franciscan Bruce Hasson, is a place of pilgrimage. Bells arrived from towns all over Italy. Forged in the papal foundry at Marinelli, the large center bell was blessed by Pope John Paul II.

Organ donation advocates show an educational video, *The Nicholas Effect*, to encourage giving. Reginald Green wrote a book, *The Gift That Heals*, published by UNOS, the United Network for Organ Sharing. A ski race in Switzerland for children with transplants was named the Nicholas Cup. Standing under the Bell Tower, the circles of bells cut holes in the blue sky promising passage to a different place, a place of healing.

I thought I could drive the Photon Bus ninety miles up the Pacific Coast Highway to Mendocino. After five miles of constant turning on S-shaped curves, I was beat up. At Jenner, we turned off the beautiful-view dominatrix of the PCH and followed the Russian River to 101. At Hopland, we cut across over the Coastal Range toward Clear Lake. Any transverse route in California is the love child of a roller coaster and a washing machine. Highway 175 with its hairpin path through the mountain pass was a vomit lovers convention.

We camped in Redding. Most of our neighbors towed boats destined for Lake Shasta. The next night we camped at Grant's Pass, where years ago I had walked through town, my thumb ignored by the local rednecks. At home, our house was cleaner than the year before. Joshua and his friends made a sincere effort not to repeat their previous fiasco. Still, it took two days of labor to bring the house back to Barb's strict standard. I think it's the German side of her brain.

I had enjoyed ten weeks of sun in mountain and desert and canyon. The sun had set. It would be at least two months before any dry golf. Same dilemma, same solution. Write a book. Relive the trip. Harass friends to proofread each chapter. Wait for the sun.

Photographing the American West

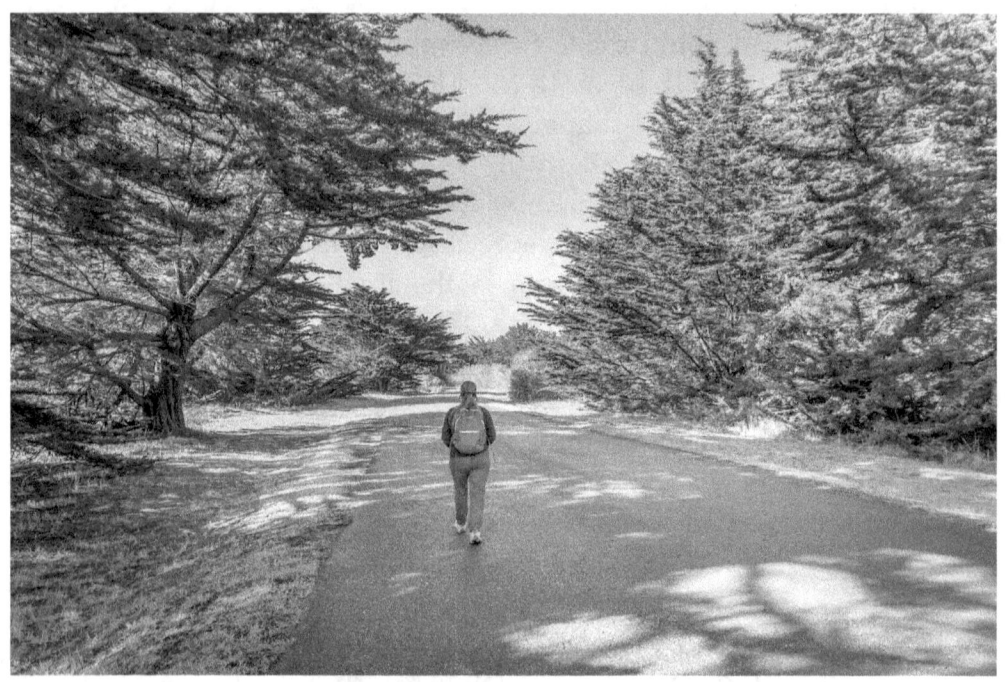

Monterey Cyprus

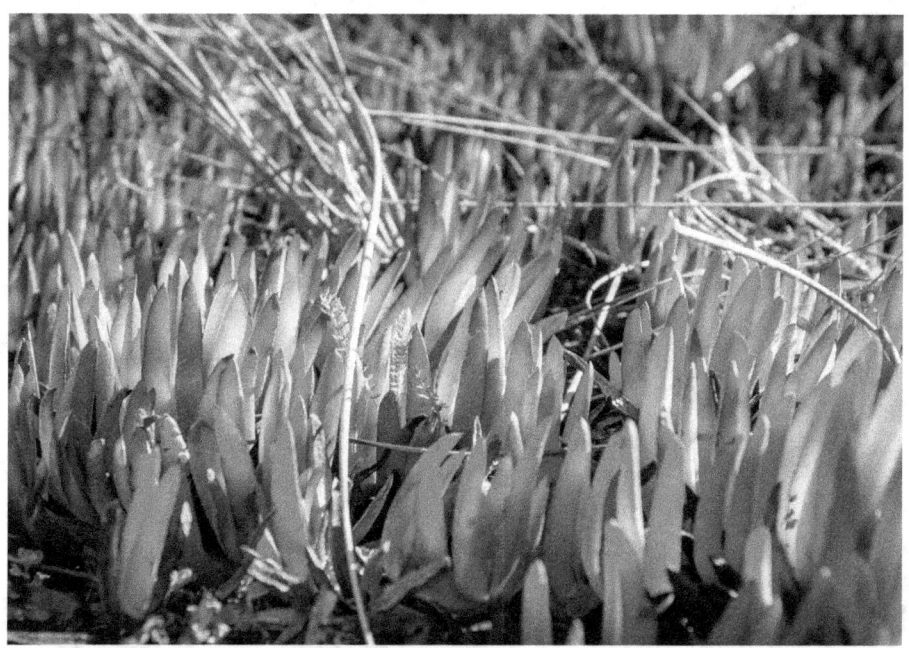
Hottentot Fig

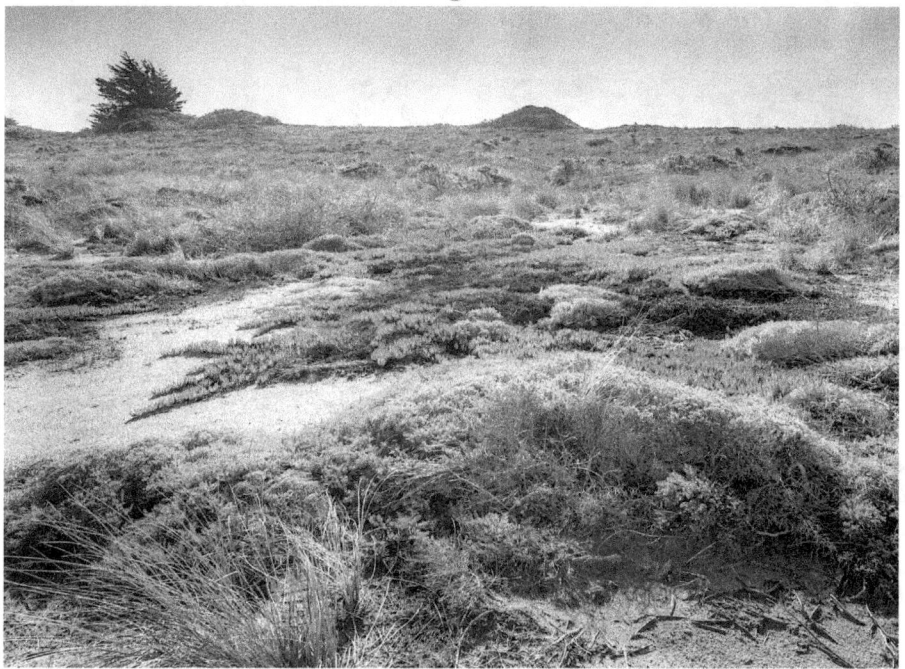
Dune scrub

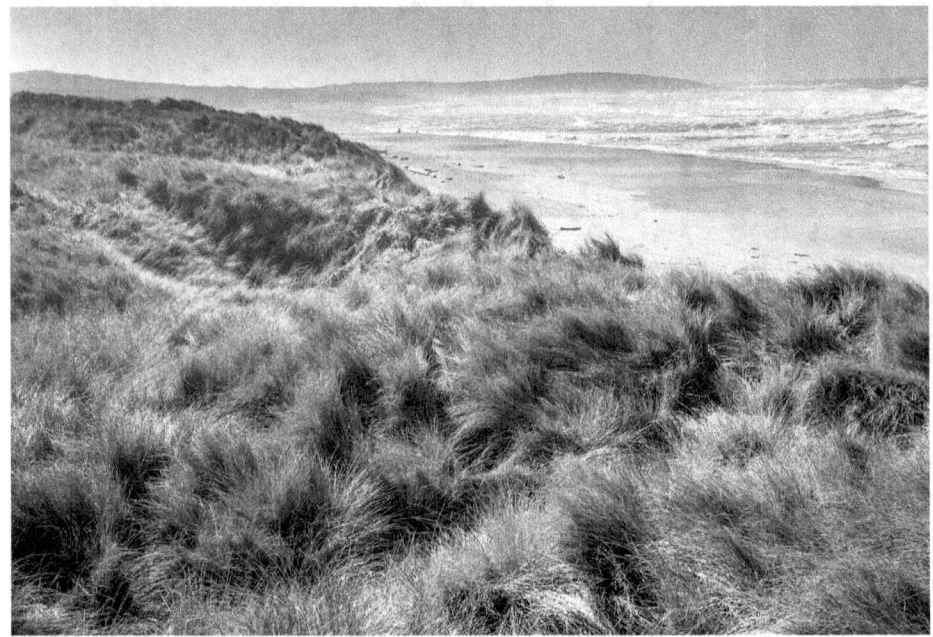

The wall of Ammophila

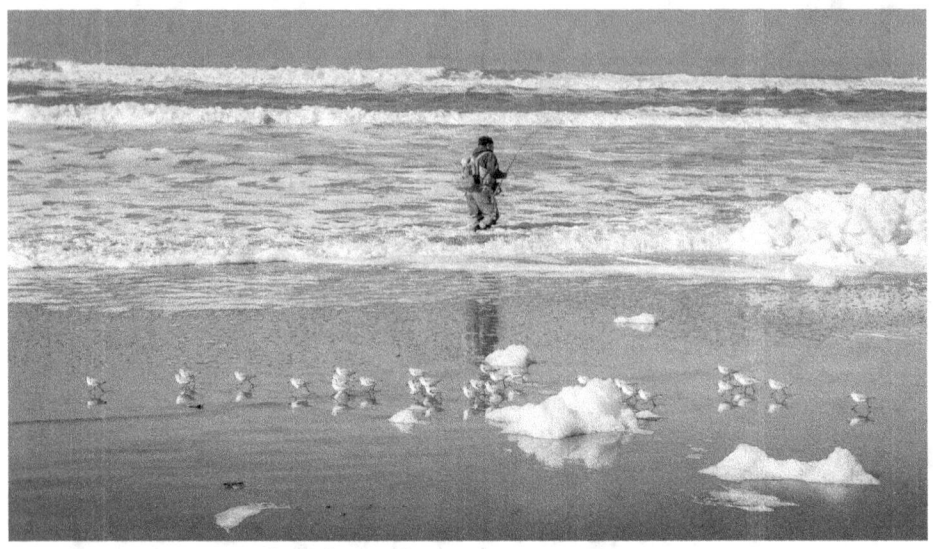

A fisher of perch

William J Wood Jr

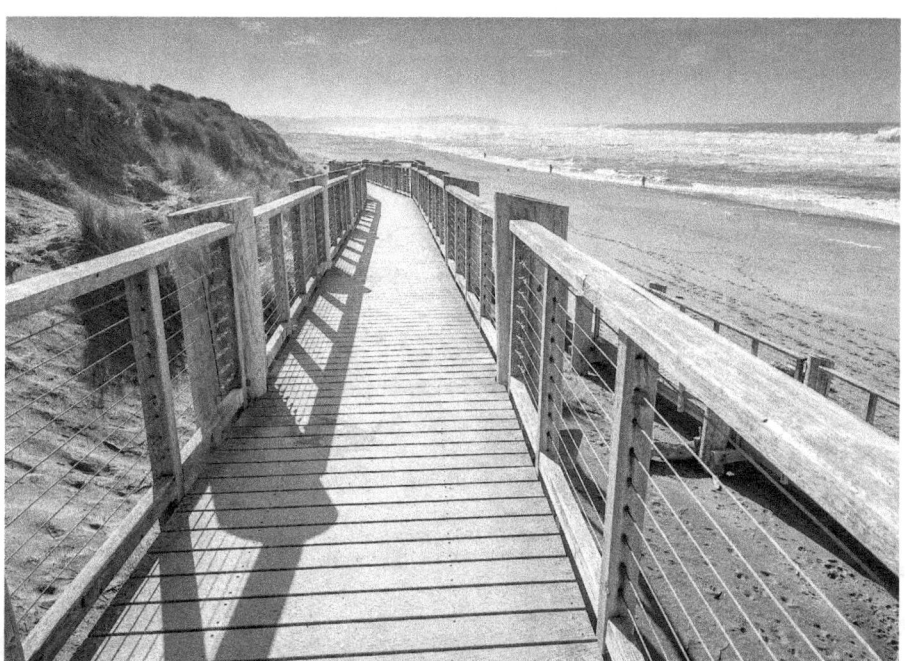

Beach lunch ramp

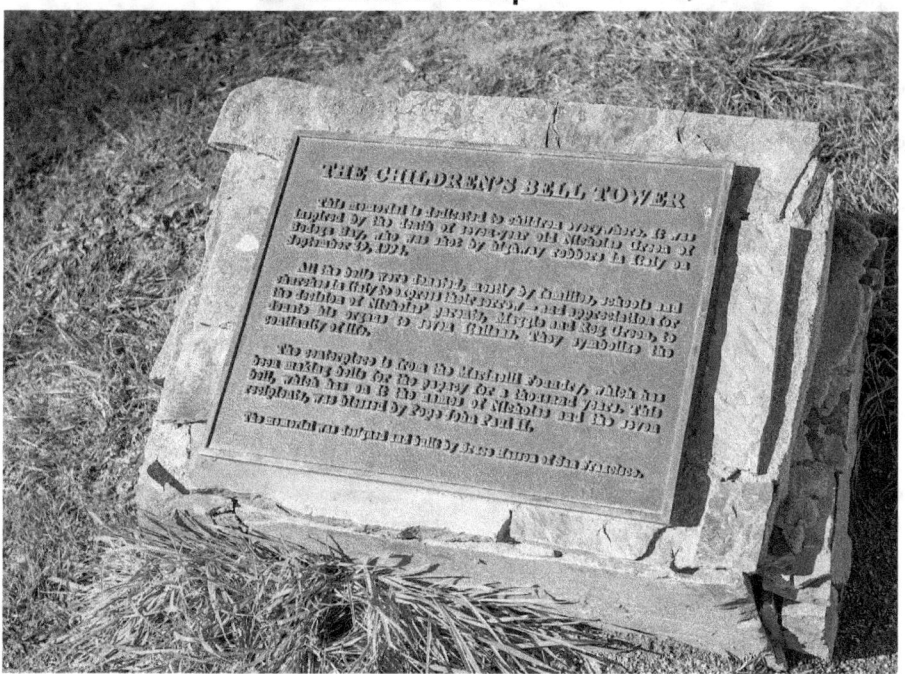

The Children's Bell Tower, Bodega Bay

Photographing the American West

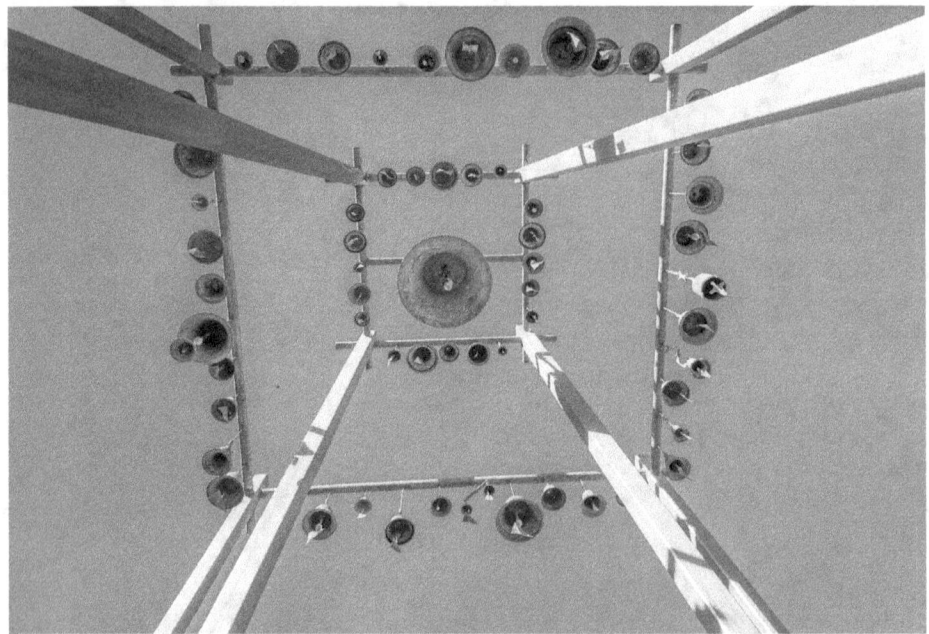

Cutting holes in the sky

About the Author

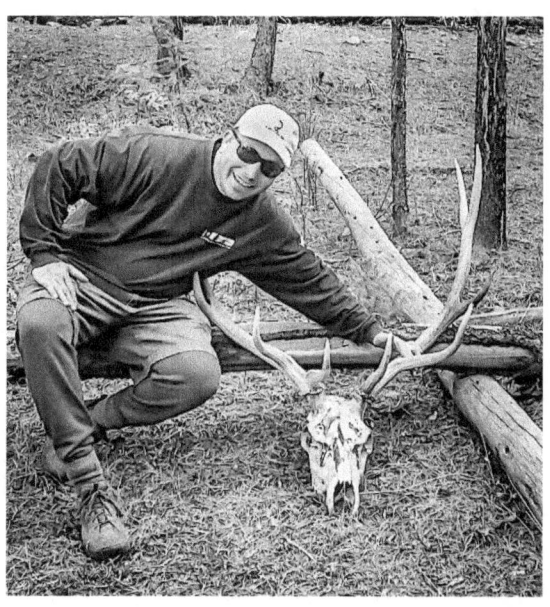

William J Wood Jr (Bill) lives in Clackamas, Oregon. His previous publications include *Harvesting Photons*, a photographic travel narrative, *Mothertime*, a medical thriller and *You No Buy You Make Me Sad, a Journal of Thailand and Cambodia* and *The Essays of William J Wood Jr*. Dr. Wood is a retired Surgical Oncologist and an avid photographer.

Harvestingphotons.com   William J Wood Jr – Autho#AE699

Amazon Author Link   www.amazon.com/William-Wo#AE693

Photographing the American West

OTHER BOOKS

BY WILLIAM J WOOD JR

Harvesting Photons, eBook and paperback, Kindle publishing
Harvesting Photons- A Pho#AE68E

Mothertime, Trafford publishing
Amazon.com- Mothertime Wi#AE690

You No Buy You Make Me Sad, Kindle Publishing
You No Buy, You Make Me S#AE691

The Essays of William J Wood Jr, Kindle publishing
Amazon.com- The Essays of#AE692